CATASTROPHE

OR

DEMOCRACY

Who Decides?

*For Peter
with hope!*

Thom Speidel

THOM SPEIDEL

509-429-5522

Catastrophe or Democracy
Who Decides?

Copyright © 2015 by Thom Speidel
All rights reserved. No portion of this book may be reproduced in any form—mechanically, electronically, or by any other means, including photocopying, recording, or by any information storage and retrieval system—without permission in writing from the author.

ISBN: 978-0-692-44898-4

Library of Congress Control Number: 2015907635

Go to www.catastropheordemocracy.com for one-click access to web sources.

Layout and formatting by Cris Wanzer at MANUSCRIPTS TO GO
spuntales@gmail.com

Printed and bound by Gorham Printing in Washington State

CATASTROPHE

OR

DEMOCRACY

Contents

Acknowledgements vii
Author's Notes... ix
Glossary xi

Introduction: Our Ecological Imperative xiii
1   Worldviews and Truth 1
2   Uncle Sam in Guatemala 13
3   Selling Wars.. 23
4   From World War to Cold War 35
5   Uncle Sam in Postwar Greece... 45
6   Corporations Then and Now 55
7   Wealth, Democracy, and the Earth 65
8   Cold War Maintenance 75
9   The Kennedy Reelection Promise... 95
10 A Final Peace Initiative: Vietnam 103
11 News, Propaganda, and US Foreign Policy 115
12 United States Mass Media 129
13 Who Decides?... 137
14 The New Military Complex 147
15 From Cold War to Terror War 153
16 Facing the Rascal 165
17 Launching a Movement 171
18 Sustaining a Movement.. 179
19 Democratic Strategic Initiatives... 183
Afterword: What I Believe 191

Appendix I: Current Ecological Trends... 193
Appendix II: The Cold War Worldview 203
Appendix III: Bay of Pigs 207
Appendix IV: Who Ran the Investigation?.. 213
Appendix V: Afghanistan Revisited 215
Appendix VI: The Land of Desire: From Citizens to Consumers 217
Endnotes 221
Index.. 275
About the Author... 305

Acknowledgements

For innumerable corrections and improvements, as well as the overall readability of the book, I am most indebted to my good friend Gerald W. Paulukonis. Jerry focused professional editing skills on the manuscript and became my confidant and partner in the project. I am grateful for the sharp technical eye, unsparing criticism, and helpful suggestions of this dear friend.

Heartfelt thanks to Will Downs, Dave Gamrath, and Sue Shidaker, who thoroughly reviewed an early manuscript and gave valuable constructive criticism and support.

Early encouragement to undertake the project came from dear friends Linda Nelson and Marie Blackburn. For someone who dreaded even a term paper in college, I needed this prodding, and appreciated their confidence.

Twelve of my hometown community members attended a potluck dinner discussion and offered valuable feedback on a 2014 draft of the book. My sincere thanks to these people for their criticisms, suggestions, and encouragement: L D Albin, Rick & Jeré Gillespie, Sam Howell, Hanna & David Kliegman, Virgil & Judy Palmer, Betsy Rainsford, Harvey Swanson, Rob Thompson, and Jill Trueblood.

Other friends and family reviewed early drafts of the manuscript and their comments and critiques helped move the work forward: Kristin & Bodhi Ackerman, Bill Alford, Jennifer Baerwald, Marie Blackburn, Joel Bleifuss, Patton Boyle, Kent Butterfield, Ann Clark, Merry Colony, Harris Dunkelberger, Randy Engle, Jody Grage, Jay Horstman, Dave Jette, Lauren Johnson, John Jones, Janet Jordan, Mary LaDuke, Juniper Mason, Ron McCabe, Jim Merkel, Laura O'Brady, Cindy Pederson, Ed Prophet, Mark Sinclair, Dave Sinclair, John Sisko, Michael Soulé, Christine & Jacob Speidel, Jeff Speidel, Russ Speidel, Jennifer Sullivan, Harry Sutton, Elaine Thomas, Janis Tipton-King, Treebeard & Raina, Sandy Vaughn, Jim Vernon, Dan Warner, Mary Zepernick, and Barrie Zwicker.

I am also indebted to Richard B. Komen, founder and long-time board chair of Restaurants Unlimited, for the appreciation of organizational Values I developed while associated with his company. Komen's nurturance of a corporate culture anchored in strong and progressive Values provided the guidance that made Restaurants Unlimited an industry leader and an outstanding employer.

The North Central Washington Regional Library, with its helpful staff and efficient website, has been a marvelous resource. And electronically, three cheers (and an annual donation) for the administrators and contributors at Wikipedia!

Author's Notes

A glossary of terms used with specific meanings appears on the following pages. The capitalization of these terms signals their specific meaning.

All the book's endnotes are numbered sequentially, regardless of the chapter or appendix in which they appear. Endnotes that are underlined (like this[xx]) provide additional information or comment. All other endnotes merely cite sources.

Information readily available by an Internet search has not been cited. Obscure or especially informative webpages are indicated.

For one-click access to web sources, go to the endnotes page at www.catastropheordemocracy.com

The appendices provide further detail and context regarding six topics, but this information is not necessary to the text's central themes.

Chapters 1 through 15 survey history and developments that have culminated in our democratic and ecological predicaments, and chapter 16 draws conclusions from these findings. If at any point a reader wants to jump to the discussion of *solutions*, skipping ahead to chapter 16 or 17 is an option.

Glossary

Balance A dynamic and sustainable equilibrium between Life and the Earth's natural resources, where Life exists in an ever-changing—but stable and vibrant—condition.

Creation Planet Earth and the entirety of its life forms.

Democracy Movement A mass effort of a People to prohibit Elite rule and establish or enhance democratic self-rule.

Ecological Imperative The obligation of current generations to restore and preserve Balance for future generations. (The word "ecological" is preferred over the word "environmental," which tends to portray humanity's existence as separate from the rest of Creation.)

Elite A tiny minority of humanity who exercise disproportionate political and economic power.

Life All the plant and animal inhabitants of the Earth's ecosystems.

Peace Peaceful and egalitarian human relations.

People Any group or society, from a region or nation to the citizenry of the Earth. (We the People refers specifically to the US citizenry.)

Rascal An assortment of untenable worldviews and problematic human behaviors now pushing Life toward a worldwide collapse.

SCAD (state crime against democracy) A covert government action that alters society or manipulates public opinion to facilitate Elite agendas of political/economic power and control.

Strategic Initiative An action or proposal capable of wide-ranging effects.

Terror War The US foreign policy stance that the George W. Bush administration launched in response to the events of September 11th.

Terror Worldview A post-9/11 worldview holding a worldwide terrorist network (and terrorism itself) as a perpetual enemy of the United States.

Tipping Point An historical moment when major social change becomes possible.

Values The enduring foundation of moral, ethical, and sometimes spiritual beliefs that anchor our decisions and priorities. Values are evident in social mores and customs, and are exercised in government budgeting priorities.

Worldview A deep-seated belief system about how the world works. Specific worldviews, such as the Cold War Worldview, are capitalized.

Introduction

Our Ecological Imperative

Our human destiny is integral with the destiny of the Earth.

Thomas Berry
The Dream of the Earth, 1988

This book aims to encourage a Democracy Movement: a peaceful revolution to put We the People in charge of our government and our future. Our democracy is not functioning today. When eligible voter turnout is under 40 percent and a single industry pledges $889 million to influence one election cycle, we have fallen into plutocracy—rule by the rich.

A comprehensive intervention is needed. This is not about defeating a pipeline, saving public education, or winning any particular skirmish. We need an overhaul that dismantles the power structure of the one percent and restores democratic governance for all.

Elite appropriation of political/governmental power is nothing new. But the backdrop to this situation is now a global emergency. The life-sustaining systems of the Earth are blinking red. Planetary ecosystems are being pushed beyond sustainable limits, toward a state of collapse that may be abrupt and irreversible. (Our ecological predicament is not just global warming or any singular trouble. Twelve factors that are contributing to this crisis are discussed in Appendix I, Current Ecological Trends.)

And there is a linkage here. The same force that is dismantling our democracy is also driving the ecological unraveling. The members of a tiny but ultra-rich minority have been advancing national policies to further boost their wealth, while discarding all ecological caution and plunging us headlong toward a worldwide catastrophe.

Our ecological problems slowly expanded with the Industrial Revolution, but began accelerating in the mid-20th century. Rachel Carson's *Silent Spring* (1963) boldly announced a major culprit: pesticides. But another momentous development of this era went largely unnoticed: the United States began establishing a global military empire, eventually spreading several hundred military installations around the world.

The US military empire is now continuously engaged in the resource wars and occupations required to sustain a fossil fuel-based energy system. Foreign policies of war are intertwined with energy policies anchored in fossil fuels, and the war and fossil fuel industries are reaping tremendous profits from this state of affairs. These profits are a major source of the money now dominating our political system and our government.

This whole system amounts to an enormous taxpayer subsidy to the war and fossil fuel industries. But our taxes can no longer shoulder this trillion-dollar-a-year endeavor, so the military-industrial proponents of this system are pushing austerity budgets. These budgets don't touch Elite wealth, but they squeeze the populace in order to continue funding the military operations that are enabling fossil fuel corporations' expansion into oil-rich nations.

We can change all this. United under a common vision of a vibrant society and a healthy planet, we can launch an unstoppable Democracy Movement. When our government is responsive to an engaged and well-informed electorate, we can design a healthy and sustainable world for ourselves and future generations. This is our Ecological Imperative. We need to launch a Democracy Movement and make this happen.

The Earth is in our hands.

CHAPTER ONE

Worldviews and Truth

All the efforts at restoration and healing will be piecemeal and, I think, ultimately futile if we can't bring ourselves to do the true peace work: the truth-telling. As long as the lies continue, nothing can be resolved.[1]

Kathleen Dean Moore
2001

Worldviews are deep-seated beliefs about how the world works. Our worldviews interpret the world around us; we use them to understand facts and evaluate new information. When confronted with information that contradicts our worldviews, our initial reaction is often one of disbelief—"I just can't *believe* that." It turns out this oft-uttered statement can be literally true: the new information contradicts a deep-seated worldview and bounces off. By causing us to reject or ignore verified facts, our worldviews can compromise our ability to discern truth from fiction.[2]

A significant change in worldview—known as a paradigm shift—does not happen easily or rapidly. Consequently, worldviews embraced early in life can govern our evaluation of information throughout our lives. So worldviews established during our school years can have enduring effects. This chapter examines some worldviews presented in our public education system, and then discusses ramifications of these worldviews.

University of Vermont sociology professor James Loewen analyzed twelve US history textbooks in common usage in our public high schools,[3] and found incomplete truths, outright falsehoods, and unsubstantiated myths in all twelve books. Part of Loewen's study examined the history textbooks' treatment of six events in US foreign policy.⁴ Below, the accounts Loewen found in the twelve textbooks are measured against various sources of documented history.

One

US assistance to the shah of Iran (Reza Shah Pahlavi) in deposing Iranian Prime Minister Mossadegh and returning the shah to the throne in 1953.

DOCUMENTED HISTORY

In March 1951, the Iranian parliament voted unanimously to nationalize their oil industry and eject the British-owned Anglo-Iranian Oil Company. Alarmed at these developments, the British obtained support from the Truman administration, and the shah of Iran was prompted to issue a royal decree dismissing Iran's recently elected Prime Minister, Mohammed Mossadegh. This action backfired when Mossadegh publicly aired the royal decree, forcing the shah into exile.

The US Central Intelligence Agency (CIA) then covertly deployed Operation Ajax, destabilizing Iran's social and political climate through bribery, targeted acts of aggression, and hired street demonstrators. Eventually, Tehran was consumed with chaos and violence as CIA-hired gangs staged battle with each other, exchanging gunfire. Some chanted "Long live Mossadegh and communism!" while others shouted allegiance to the shah.⁵

On August 19, 1953, CIA-operated radio broadcasts in Tehran announced the arrival of a new (CIA-selected) Prime Minister and the triumphant return of the shah, who would ensure western control of Iran's oil industry. Dissenters were tortured and thousands were summarily executed by US-trained and -supplied military forces.⁶

ANALYSIS

Eight of the textbooks Loewen surveyed make no mention of the 1953 Iranian overthrow. Two of the textbooks presented fairly accurate descriptions of the event, this paragraph from *Life and Liberty* being the more accurate of the two:

> The United States had been a long-time friend of the ruler of Iran, Shah Reza Pahlevi. In fact, the United States had helped him to his throne by overthrowing a democratically elected

government in 1953, which the United States felt was too leftist. America supplied the Shah with large numbers of arms, and also trained the Shah's army and police. Unfortunately, the Shah used the army and police to form a police state.

"Unfortunately" indeed. During this time, Amnesty International stated, "No country in the world has a worse record in human rights than Iran."[7] To its credit, *Life and Liberty* acknowledges the US overthrow of a democratically elected foreign government. *Land of Promise*, however, exemplifies the altogether inadequate accounts offered in two other textbooks:

> In 1953, a communist-backed political party seized control of the government and attempted to assert control over Iran's oil resources.

In this account, the democratic election of a Prime Minister enjoying widespread popular support is portrayed as having "seized control." Furthermore, Mossadegh neither requested nor received any Soviet support during his administration, and he had also led Iranian efforts to expel the Soviets from Iran following World War II. Despite these facts, this textbook describes Mossadegh's administration as "communist-backed."

Two

US overthrow of the democratically elected government of Guatemala in 1954.

DOCUMENTED HISTORY

As the following chapter examines in greater detail, the CIA covertly planned and orchestrated the overthrow of the democratically elected government of Guatemala in 1954, restoring the nation to dictatorship under the CIA's hand-picked President Carlos Castillo Armas.

ANALYSIS

Only one of the twelve textbooks Loewen surveyed, *The American Tradition*, mentioned this event in the history of United States foreign policy, stating:

In the 1950s the United States, concerned with stopping the spread of communism, directed its attention to Latin America once again. In 1954 the CIA helped to overthrow the leftist government of Jacobo Arbenz Guzman in Guatemala. In following years, in order to prevent communist takeovers, the United States continued to support unpopular conservative or military governments in Latin America.

As with *Life and Liberty*'s account of Iran above, this textbook accurately acknowledges US involvement in the overthrow of a foreign government, as well as US support of "unpopular conservative or military governments." The misrepresentations contained in this account, however, will become more apparent in the following chapter.

Three

US orchestration of the 1957 election in Lebanon, which fraudulently empowered the Christian Democratic Party and led to Muslim revolt and protracted civil war.

DOCUMENTED HISTORY

Lebanon was the United States' closest Middle Eastern ally in the mid-20th century, due largely to its pro-US president, Camille Chamoun. To increase Chamoun's sway over Lebanese affairs, the CIA funded the political campaigns of Chamoun-supporters for Lebanon's June 1957 parliamentary elections. A suspicious landslide favoring Chamoun's minority (the Christian Democratic Party) outraged the Lebanese Muslim majority.

When an anti-Chamoun newspaper editor was murdered the following May, armed rebellion broke out, including attacks on US assets in Beirut. President Eisenhower dispatched 15,000 US Marines with police supplies and tanks, in support of President Chamoun against the majority of his country's population.[8] In sum, the United States' interference during this time stifled Lebanese democratic processes and precipitated a civil war that persisted for decades.

ANALYSIS

None of the textbooks that Loewen examined mentioned the US orchestration of the 1957 election in Lebanon. Five of the textbooks mention the 1958 US-Lebanese intervention, but they all frame the event as an effort to defend the Chamoun government against a "leftist coup."

Four

US involvement in the assassination of Congo's Prime Minister Patrice Lumumba in 1961.

DOCUMENTED HISTORY

Elected Prime Minister following Congo's independence from Belgium on June 30, 1960, Patrice Lumumba immediately faced a secession movement of the province of Katanga, led by Moise Tshombe. Tshombe supported US corporate interests, whereas Lumumba was calling for Congo's economic and political independence from extractive foreign industries. A number of Eisenhower administration officials supported the Katangan secession movement, and United Nations Secretary-General Dag Hammarskjöld shared Washington's hostility toward Lumumba.[9]

Trapped by Washington's refusal of aid and a sabotaged United Nations' intervention, even Lumumba's appeal for Soviet military aid came too late. With the encouragement and support of the CIA, Congolese President Joseph Kasavubu summarily dismissed Prime Minister Lumumba on September 5, 1960. Despite Lumumba's immediate reaffirmation by both houses of Parliament, his tenure ended abruptly on September 14 when a US-backed military coup installed Joseph Mobutu as the new Congolese head of state. With CIA assistance, Lumumba was captured by Mobutu's troops and delivered to Moise Tshombe for assassination.[10]

ANALYSIS

The two textbooks that mention this event give none of the above context to Lumumba's tenure as Prime Minister, nor do they mention the US involvement in his ejection from office or his subsequent assassination. *Triumph of the American Nation* gives this account:

A new crisis developed in 1961 when Patrice Lumumba, leader of the pro-communist faction, was assassinated. . . . By the late 1960s, most scars of the civil war seemed healed. The Congo (Zaïre) became one of the most prosperous African nations.

Here again the documented history is ignored or distorted. A duly elected and widely popular head of state is portrayed simply as the leader of a faction, and the stated historical outcome of this event is incorrect. While it is true that the US-installed head of state, Mobutu, became one of the world's most prosperous *individuals*, his personal wealth was extracted from the Congolese people, who suffered abject poverty and brutal repression under his authoritarian dictatorship.[11]

Five

Repeated US attempts to assassinate Cuban Premier Fidel Castro.

HISTORY AND ANALYSIS

Despite abundant documentation of the CIA's plans and attempts to assassinate Fidel Castro, none of the textbooks Loewen examined make any mention of these operations.

Six

US overthrow and assassination of Chilean President Salvador Allende in 1973.

DOCUMENTED HISTORY

As a champion of Chile's economic and political independence, Salvador Allende's rising popularity drew CIA attention in the 1950s. Draining the US Treasury of some $3 million ($24 million in 2010 dollars), the CIA tipped Chile's 1964 presidential election toward its favored Christian Democratic Party candidate Eduardo Frei Montalva. But despite continued CIA opposition, Allende won the next presidential election of September 4, 1970; the Chilean Congress was to certify Allende's election on October 24. This situation elicited one of Henry Kissinger's most famous lines as President Nixon's National

Security Advisor when he stated, "I don't see why we need to stand by and watch a country go communist because of the irresponsibility of its own people."

President Nixon ordered the CIA to orchestrate a military coup to prevent Allende's presidential certification. When the Chilean Army's Commander in Chief, General René Schneider, proved to be incorrigibly dedicated to democratic processes, the CIA oversaw Schneider's assassination on October 22. This action backfired, however, eliciting outrage from the military establishment and inspiring even more enthusiastic support for Allende, who was swiftly certified as president by the Chilean Congress.

The Nixon administration, now resolved to remove Allende by whatever means necessary, covertly drew pliant Chilean military officials (including a certain Augusto Pinochet) into a CIA-orchestrated coup d'état. Foretelling the severe pressure that would come to bear, US Ambassador Edward Korry threatened the Chilean Minister of Defense, stating, "Not a nut or a bolt will be allowed to reach Chile under Allende. We shall do all within our power to condemn Chile and the Chilean people to utmost deprivation and poverty."[12]

Over the next three years, Washington turned Ambassador Korry's threat into reality. In a debilitating climate of disintegration and chaos including food shortages, power outages, and horrendous monetary inflation, Salvador Allende was captured and murdered on September 11, 1973, following a sustained aerial attack on the Presidential Palace in Santiago. Augusto Pinochet was placed in power and immediately initiated decades of terror in which thousands were executed and tens of thousands (including women and children) were imprisoned and tortured.[13]

ANALYSIS

The quality of the accounts that three of Loewen's textbooks give of this event is illustrated by these lines from *The American Adventure*:

> Some people, in the United States and abroad, said that the United States arranged the overthrow of Allende. Indeed, in 1974, Pres. Ford admitted that the United States CIA had given help to the opposition to Allende. However, he denied that the United States encouraged or knew of the revolutionary plan.

Students of this textbook might wonder how or why the CIA would be aiding Allende's enemies without even knowing of their revolutionary plan. But in any event, "some people" were right. The US did, in fact, "arrange" the overthrow of Allende. So while the true nature of this event is presented as mere speculation, President Ford's contradictory remarks conceal this truth and disguise the central role of the CIA in the assassination of the democratically elected president of Chile.

THE FOLLOWING TABLE SUMS UP THE HISTORY TEXTBOOKS' TREATMENT OF THESE SIX US FOREIGN POLICY EVENTS:

Event	Accurate	Somewhat accurate	Not accurate	No mention
Iran, 1953	0	2	2	8
Guatemala, 1954	0	0	1	11
Lebanon, 1957	0	0	0	12
Congo, 1964	0	0	2	10
Fidel Castro	0	0	0	12
Chile, 1973	0	0	3	9
TOTAL	0	2	8	62

Two themes are generally evident throughout the twelve textbooks, as well as Loewen's interviews with high school history teachers and classroom observations. First, there is a tendency to promote US nationalism (American Exceptionalism)—a belief in the moral supremacy and incontestable ascendancy of the United States. Second, a "Beneficent Uncle Sam" image of United States foreign policy is promoted, portraying US actions as enduringly devoted to the world's betterment.

Facts and information detracting from these two themes tend to be ignored. Indeed, *half* of the textbooks fail to mention *all six* of the US foreign policy events examined above. (Conversely, accounts of the Peace Corps and President Kennedy's Alliance for Progress[14] are included in the textbooks almost without fail.) Additionally, distortions in the textbooks' historical accounts almost always reflect favorably on the United States, by concealing or misrepresenting disreputable US actions.

Students who take US history at the university level often discover the true nature of US foreign policy history, when the false and inaccurate lessons taught in high school are exposed and corrected. Unfortunately, about 80 percent of US citizens never take a history course beyond high school.[15] Thus, a majority of US citizens may remain unaware of the existence and/or true nature of many US foreign policy events.

BEYOND SCHOOL YEARS

> *Our firmest convictions are apt to be the most suspect,*
> *they mark our limitations and our bounds.*[16]
>
> José Ortega y Gasset

A Beneficent Uncle Sam Worldview can obstruct our comprehension of information that contradicts it. For example, many United States citizens could not understand the bitter animosity of the Iranian People which culminated in the 1979 Iranian Hostage Crisis (an uprising by Iranian students that occupied the US Embassy in Tehran for 444 days). Unlike most US citizens, however, the Iranian People knew that the United States had deposed Prime Minister Mossadegh in 1953, and restored the shah's reign under which they had suffered grinding poverty, police terror, and torture. Unaware of this history, befuddled US citizens began asking the now-familiar question "Why do they hate us?"[17]

Beneficent Uncle Sam perspectives found in high school history lessons have been reinforced in the larger public arena. For example, during the CIA's Guatemalan overthrow, the John Foster Dulles (JF Dulles) State Department stated, "The Department has no evidence that indicates this is anything other than a revolt of Guatemalans against the government."[18] And President Eisenhower later stated, "The people of Guatemala, in a magnificent effort, have liberated themselves from the shackles of international communist direction, and reclaimed their right of self-determination."[19]

Eisenhower's account of Guatemalans reclaiming their "right of self-determination" was not what had occurred. As surveyed in the following chapter, his words came at a time when the Guatemalan people were ruled by a dictator whose rise to power had been overseen by State Secretary JF Dulles and his brother, CIA Director Allen Dulles. The mass media's failure to expose the true nature of events such as these will be explored in chapter 11. However, at this point, one might well ask, why do lies such as these *persist*?

One reason is that admission of the true nature of these events requires the United States to acknowledge the use of tactics that it condemns as state-sponsored terrorism when committed by *other* nations. The violent overthrow of democratically elected foreign governments is terrorism.

Another reason for the durability of these lies is that exposing the true nature of these events would also necessarily expose the cover-up operations that suppressed the truth in the first place. In other words, it is the official *lies* told by US government representatives during these events—possibly more than the government's *actions*—that have resisted correction in the face of evidence to the contrary. Misrepresentations such as Eisenhower's and Dulles' statements above have almost never been acknowledged in our history textbooks or mass media. They remain as components of a distorted version of our nation's history, providing moorage for the Beneficent Uncle Sam Worldview. (Additionally, there seems to be an intergenerational resistance to correcting historical distortions.[20])

The official history taught in our public school system has sometimes been reconstructed and mythologized in directions that promote US nationalism at the expense of the dignity of other nations. For example, author and environmental activist Rex Weyler writes, "Because the American (including Canadian and South American) people deny their history, they tend to project the taboo horror out on to the evildoers of the world. No holocaust happened in Canada or the United States. That was something Hitler did to the Jews."[21] In reality, the European assault on the Americas was the most expansive geographic invasion and demographic holocaust of all time.[22]

The United States is no better or worse than some other nations in promoting versions of history that foster nationalistic pride. But there can be an unfortunate consequence of this. As humanitarian journalist Chris Hedges has described, the sentiments produced by nationalistic reconstructions of history can predispose a nation's citizenry toward war.[23]

The US interventions surveyed in this chapter had profound effects on other nations' social, political, and economic destinies. The following chapter finds that powerful interests have sometimes driven such US foreign policy events—often without the consent or even the knowledge of the US electorate.

CHAPTER TWO

Uncle Sam in Guatemala

*When dictatorship is a fact,
revolution becomes a right.*

Victor Hugo
Time, June 3, 1957

The 1954 intervention in Guatemala is representative of many US foreign policy events of the early Cold War era. This chapter examines the forces that collaborated to carry out this event, and the affects the intervention had on the Guatemalan People and on the United States' reputation in the Latin American region.

COLONIAL GUATEMALA[24]

Colonial control of Guatemala began with the Spanish conquest of 1523. Following 4,000 years of Mayan civilization, the Spanish introduced European principles of land ownership, and 98 percent of the population became either servants of a small aristocracy or laborers for their enterprises.

In 1823, the Monroe Doctrine announced US opposition to European activity in the Caribbean and Latin American region, and in 1904, the Monroe Doctrine's (Theodore) Roosevelt Corollary asserted the United States' *exclusive* right to the entire region. Thus, at the turn of the 20th century, US industries began pouring into Latin American and Caribbean nations, usually escorted by the US military.[25]

US-based railroad, telephone, and electric power monopolies became established in Guatemala during the first half of the 20th century, each benefiting from a series of military dictatorships that provided business security and control of the indigenous labor force. Over time, one corporation became the focal point of US-Guatemala relations, United Fruit Company (UFCO). (UFCO actually arose from the Central American railroad ventures of US entrepreneur Minor Keith, who began acquiring banana companies to finance his railroad ambitions.)

When UFCO was incorporated in 1899, it was instantly the world's largest banana operation, with holdings in several Latin American countries, its Great White Fleet of steamships, and the lucrative railroad monopolies from which it had emerged. In 1929, UFCO merged with its major competitor in Honduras, Sam Zemurray's Cuyamel Fruit Company, netting Zemurray a personal fortune and (in 1933) operational control of the corporation.

Agents of both the US government and UFCO facilitated the rise of Guatemalan dictator Jorge Ubico in 1931, and Ubico began showering UFCO with benefits and government concessions. By 1936, Ubico had abolished government regulation of UFCO's operations, granted the company exemptions from virtually all taxes and duties, and established loopholes that enabled UFCO to declare fictitious overseas earnings in order to conceal its domestic profits. These measures enriched the corporation at the expense of both the Guatemalan nation and the US Treasury.

This was the sort of "order" Sam Zemurray strove to achieve in his business affairs. As a virtually unregulated enterprise, UFCO became the largest landowner in Guatemala, monopolizing the country's banana exports, railroads, and various other industries including Guatemala's only Caribbean sea port—hence UFCO's Guatemalan nickname *El Pulpo*, "The Octopus."

Guatemala's agricultural production was increasingly diverted to foreign markets during this period, rising to over 85 percent by 1950. Consequently, local food became scarce and Guatemalans' need to purchase imported food increased their dependency on paid employment. In this manner, Guatemalans became a labor force readily available to corporate enterprises.

While it is true that UFCO employed tens of thousands of Guatemalans over the years, the cyclic nature of agricultural operations offered only part-time employment, and the income from this intermittent employment could not provide enough income to keep food on the tables of Guatemalan families. The vast majority found themselves sliding into a desperate situation. They were caught between forces that limited their income and at the same time deprived them of the ability to grow subsistence crops (over three-fourths of the population was now landless).

Guatemala's national statistics indicated economic expansion during this period, but the aggregate numbers did not reflect what was really going on. Extreme wealth was flowing into the hands of the aristocracy, while the majority of the population was forced to live closer to the bone. Malnutrition became widespread, life expectancy was under 40 years, and Guatemalan infant mortality was the highest in the Americas, reaching 60 percent in some communities.

DEMOCRATIC REVOLUTION, 1944

Given these social and economic conditions, Guatemala was ripe for revolution. When increasing agitation resulted in massive street protests in the fall of 1944, military officers ousted Ubico's dictatorship and took control of the government. In the country's first free election, Guatemalans chose a visionary young professor, Juan José Arévalo as their president. The Guatemalan National Assembly soon ratified a constitution with over 60 provisions for strengthening democratic processes. Governmental authority was divided between executive, legislative, and judicial branches, and freedoms of speech, press, and public assembly were guaranteed. Social reforms were initiated and governmental agencies addressing the economy, cooperative development, and labor issues were established. In short, a democracy was born.

The vitally important agricultural sector was an immediate focus of the new government. Technical services were provided for farmers, soil and forest conservation was enacted, and programs in modern farming techniques were implemented. President Arévalo enacted Guatemala's first Labor Code in February 1947 and a Social Security system was inaugurated in 1948. As the Ministry of Public Health worked to reverse the country's dismal trends in infant mortality and life expectancy, the National Literacy Committee built schools, increased the pay and prestige of teachers, and conducted mobile cultural missions to teach health care and elementary education to adult citizens in rural communities.

Arévalo's six-year term as president established a framework for what was to become a comprehensive program of democratic reform.

Though very popular with the vast majority, the aristocratic minority had witnessed these developments with anxiety and disapproval. By the end of Arévalo's term, he had survived two dozen coup attempts. His successor, on whom the full expression of these well-laid plans depended, would not be so fortunate.

On March 15, 1951, in the country's first peaceful transition of state authority, the presidential sash was placed on Jacobo Arbenz—a 37-year-old army colonel who had participated in the overthrow of Ubico. In addition to his brilliant academic record, exceptional oratory powers, and handsome Latin profile, the new President was married to the beautiful proponent of democratic reform, Maria Cristina Vilanova. The Arbenz administration brought renewed vigor to the reform agenda, and the Guatemalan National Assembly passed their long-promulgated Agrarian Reform Law on June 17, 1952—only months before many of UFCO's oldest and best friends began settling into Washington with the new Eisenhower administration.

A Counterrevolution Takes Shape

Few corporations in the mid-20th century enjoyed government connections as deep and wide as United Fruit Company. Eisenhower's head of the National Security Council, General Robert Cutler, had formerly been UFCO's board chair. Assistant Secretary of State for Inter-American Affairs John Moors Cabot held substantial UFCO stock, and his brother Thomas Dudley Cabot (who had been UFCO's first president) was now the State Department's director of international security affairs. John McCloy, another former UFCO board member, was now the president of the International Bank for Reconstruction and Development. UFCO also had hired agents in Washington, including Thomas G. "Tommy the Cork" Corcoran and Truman's former Assistant Secretary of State for Latin America, Spruille Braden.[26] Sam Zemurray, UFCO's board chair and Chief Executive Officer during this era, had extensive personal contacts in both houses of Congress. His most valuable assets, however, were two veterans of UFCO's law firm, the Dulles brothers. John Foster Dulles had become Eisenhower's secretary of state, and Allen Dulles was now director of the CIA.

Zemurray, worried since the 1944 revolution, panicked with the election of President Arbenz in 1951. The new administration announced plans to construct a publicly owned power company and a new sea port and highway system, both of which would compete with existing UFCO monopolies.

But the greatest threat to UFCO's Guatemalan operations was the new Agrarian Reform Law. The National Assembly, determined to return the nation's natural resource wealth to the Guatemalan People, called for government seizure and redistribution of uncultivated land on large estates. At this time, over 85 percent of UFCO's 560,000 acres (875 square miles) of Guatemalan banana fields sat fallow.

The Guatemalan government seized 234,000 acres of uncultivated UFCO land in early 1953, offering the company's own declared tax value of $1,185,000 as compensation. UFCO representatives countered with a demand of $19 million, which the Arbenz administration ignored. The enactment of the Agrarian Reform Law enabled some 87,000 Guatemalan families to return to the land and begin growing desperately needed food crops.

Meanwhile, Zemurray's efforts to "restore order" in Guatemala were getting underway. Among Zemurray's numerous contacts was Edward Bernays, a nephew of Sigmund Freud who had become known as the father of the fledgling public relations (PR) industry. Bernays proposed a plan to convince the US citizenry that communists were seizing control of the Guatemalan government. Taking advantage of the wave of anti-communist McCarthyism then sweeping the nation, the US citizenry would be turned against the Guatemalan government. Zemurray liked the plan and gave Bernays the job.

Bernays met with *New York Times* publisher Arthur Hays Sulzberger, and a series of *Times*' articles then portrayed Guatemala as falling victim to the Reds.[27] Leading magazines echoed the *Times*' "communist takeover" thesis, and similar alarms were sounded in the House and Senate. House Majority Leader John McCormack of Massachusetts rose regularly to declare that Guatemala's leaders had become subservient to the Kremlin's design for world conquest and were turning their country into a Soviet beachhead.[28]

In fact, there *was* a Communist Party in Guatemala, but it was no larger or better represented in government than during Ubico's reign. There were no communists in the Arbenz Cabinet, and the Soviet Union had no economic, military, or even diplomatic relations with Guatemala. Nevertheless, a "communist threat" was the principal theme in Bernays' campaign to turn US citizens against the government of Guatemala. The US Ambassador to Guatemala, John Peurifoy, had his first and only meeting with President Arbenz on December 16, 1953. In a telling moment, Peurifoy then cabled Secretary of State Dulles, "If he is not a communist, he will certainly do until one comes along."[29]

The Dulles brothers were also laboring to restore order in Guatemala. Under the direction of Allen Dulles, the CIA launched its confidently-named Operation Success. The Guatemalan military was infiltrated and coup supporters were recruited. Following his military training at Fort Leavenworth, Kansas, former Guatemalan army officer Castillo Armas was recruited to be the next Guatemalan dictator. Guatemalan print and radio propaganda campaigns were conducted to turn Guatemalans against the Arbenz administration, and in an effort conceived by CIA agent Howard Hunt, the Roman Catholic clergy were drafted to the cause. Pastoral letters were read all across the country warning the faithful that a demonic force called communism was destroying their homeland.

Meanwhile, the US-friendly dictators of neighboring Honduras and Nicaragua provided a network of airstrips for the CIA's aerial operations, as well as base stations for the "Voice of Freedom" radio network. Overseen by CIA agent David Atlee Phillips, this network broadcasted from Operation Headquarters at the Opa-Locka Naval air base outside Miami.[30]

Operation Success was not without its glitches. An article appeared in the *New York Times* suggesting that Guatemalans were caught up *not* in communism but in fervent nationalism. And in Washington, Deputy Undersecretary of State Robert Murphy discovered Operation Success by accident, and delivered a stern memorandum of protest to JF Dulles. But problems like these were quietly resolved, often by the Dulles brothers. JF Dulles simply ignored dissenters as their objections drifted through the upper echelons of his State Department. The reporter responsible for the *Times'* fervent nationalism article was summarily recalled from Guatemala after Allen Dulles had dinner with *Times* business manager Julius Adler.[31]

Whereas the Bernays PR machine successfully vilified the Arbenz administration in the United States, public opinion in most Latin American countries remained supportive of the Guatemalan democracy. The governments of Ecuador, Argentina, Uruguay, and Chile officially condemned American intervention and aggression in Guatemala, and large public demonstrations against US involvement in Guatemala occurred in eleven countries during the early 1950s.[32]

The US mass media upheld the Bernays storyline in the face of these foreign condemnations and anti-US public demonstrations. The February 8, 1954 issue of *Time* magazine explained that the whole exposé had been masterminded in Moscow, and on July 5, 1954, *Newsweek* reported that Washington officials interpreted these demonstrations as an indication of the depth of Red penetration into the Americas.[33] For its part, the Dulles State Department announced that it was continuing its longstanding policy of non-interference in the internal affairs of other nations.

LAUNCHING THE COUP

On June 18, 1954, Castillo Armas, following CIA orders, used an old station wagon to lead a small convoy of vehicles six miles into Guatemalan territory, where they stopped, awaiting further orders.[34] Thus, the *reality* of the invasion consisted of a rag-tag group of ruffians at the side of a road somewhere. Yet, the *illusion* created for public consumption in Guatemala was something entirely different.

At David Atlee Phillips' direction, the Voice of Freedom began broadcasting hysterical accounts of the invading forces of Castillo Armas. Announcers stated that the rebels were gathering volunteers as they marched, that armed conflict was breaking out nationwide, and that the Guatemalan army was suffering major defeats.

CIA planes had been sprinkling propaganda leaflets around the country for weeks, preparing the citizenry for the Voice of Freedom's invasion illusion. Now, a more lethal force appeared in the sky. P-47 Thunderbolts, with insignia of the Armas rebellion, began dropping fragmentation bombs and strafing targets in and around Guatemala City. Military barracks and ammunition dumps exploded and the international airport was disabled. The Thunderbolts' assault went on for days, and as the destruction spread to other cities, most Guatemalans became convinced that the Voice of Liberation's invasion story was true.

President Arbenz recognized that the United States was behind the Armas rebellion, but he and his military commanders agreed that armed resistance would only bring massive bloodshed. Trapped in the CIA's illusion, Arbenz radio broadcasted an impassioned farewell address to the People before retreating into political asylum at the Mexican Embassy. The iron-fisted rule of President Armas officially began on July 5, 1954.[35] Guatemala's decade of democracy had ended.

DICTATORSHIP RESTORED

President Armas, taking full advantage of his US-backed powers, promptly repealed the 1945 constitution and issued a political statute that invested in him all legislative and executive functions. In short order, the progressive reforms of the democratic era were unraveled. Indigenous land rights and cooperatives were again abolished, and Guatemalans farming subsistence plots were evicted by the thousands under the Armas version of agrarian reform.

Armas branded all who opposed him as communists, and within days, over 2,000 were arrested as alleged subversives. Overflow from Armas' jails were shuttled into concentration camps.[36] July 12 was proclaimed Anti-Communist Day—a theme that was exploited at every opportunity. A National Committee for Defense Against Communism was vested with extraordinary powers and had its own special police force under the same chief (José Bernabe) that Jorge Ubico's dictatorship had employed. Eventually over 70,000 Guatemalans were consigned to Bernabe's list of suspects, for crimes such as signing a petition or accepting a homestead from the Arbenz government.[37]

Armas returned UFCO's expropriated lands to the company and abolished all taxes on profits of foreign business interests. The Guatemalan aristocracy, after their many failed attempts to overthrow the Arévalo and Arbenz administrations, could once again relax under renewed military control of the masses.

In summary, a democratically elected and widely popular government achieving improved health, social, and economic conditions was overthrown by agents of the US government and replaced with a military dictatorship that sacrificed these progressive trends to the priorities of United Fruit Company and other US corporations. This US government action was concealed by Bernays' PR campaign centered on the spurious notion of a communist takeover. Thus, the true nature of this event escaped the attention of the US citizenry almost entirely, while the Guatemalan people were returned to the poverty, hunger, and suffering they knew all too well.

Further Understanding

The American Tradition was the only textbook James Loewen examined that mentioned the Guatemalan coup d'état. *Tradition's* statement that the "CIA helped" in this event is, of course, a gross understatement of the agency's key role. And to portray the replacement of a thriving democratic government with a brutal military dictatorship as stopping the spread of communism is a fabrication that completely contradicts the documented history.

The number of Latin American governments that condemned the US intervention, as well as the anti-US public demonstrations that occurred in the region, indicate widespread knowledge of the true nature of this event. As with the Iranian Hostage Crisis cited earlier, these people understood US foreign policy better than most US citizens.

Guatemala's failed attempt at democracy was a common occurrence in mid-20th century Latin America, an era New York University professor Greg Grandin chronicled in *Empire's Workshop* (2006). Grandin's synopsis of this period is quoted here at length, for it concisely depicts the plight of the entire region during this era:

> Starting in 1944, reform swept the continent, revitalizing old democracies in Chile and Columbia, among other places, and creating new ones in countries such as Guatemala, Peru, Argentina, and Venezuela. Within two years, every Latin American country save Paraguay, El Salvador, Honduras, Nicaragua, and the Dominican Republic was operating under constitutional rule. Broad coalitions ranging from political liberals to communists toppled dictators throughout the continent, while new reform governments extended the franchise, legalized unions, expanded public education, provided health care, and implemented social security programs. The United States at first backed this process of democratization. But in 1947 [the Truman administration in] Washington began to send signals that its preference for democrats over autocrats was now contingent on political stability. Support for dictators . . . was now understood to be the centerpiece of U.S. policy toward Latin America. . . . By 1952, when Fulgencio Batista took power in a military coup in Cuba, nearly every democracy that had come into being in the postwar period was upended.[38]

And so it was that Guatemala's democracy and other progressive, left, and democratic movements in Latin America were sacrificed to (in Grandin's words) political stability, or (as Sam Zemurray would say) restoring order.

The electorate's opinions have been inconsequential in covert foreign policy events such as the Guatemalan overthrow, because most citizens have not been aware that the US was involved. But public opinion *has* been an important component of overt US military engagements—wars. The following chapter surveys efforts that have influenced public opinion at these critical junctures.

CHAPTER THREE

Selling Wars

War, like any other racket, pays high dividends to the very few....
The cost of operations is always transferred
to the people who do not profit.

US Marine Commander Smedley Butler
Forum Magazine, September, 1934

When I say I am opposed to all wars, I mean ruling-class wars,
for the ruling class is the only class that makes war.

Eugene V. Debs
Socialist Party Convention Address, 1918[32]

Historically, US citizens have been reluctant to support foreign military interventions. This chapter examines government efforts to gather public support for declarations of war at four pivotal junctures in our history. (Later chapters discuss post-WWII conflicts.)

1846: THE MEXICAN-AMERICAN WAR

> *To this day [I] regard the [Mexican-American] war as one of the most unjust ever waged by a stronger against a weaker nation.*[40]
>
> Ulysses S. Grant
> Personal Memoirs (1885)

President Thomas Jefferson's negotiation of the Louisiana Purchase doubled the size of the United States in 1803. But migrating US citizens not only moved west, into the new territory, but also south, crossing the US border into Mexico. For decades, various skirmishes and stand-offs took place (including the legendary Battle of the Alamo) as US citizens increasingly asserted themselves against the Mexican state. Bolstered by the new notion of Manifest Destiny[41] in the mid-1840s, the settlers began agitating for independence from the Mexicans, declaring themselves the Lone Star State.

President James Polk, with support from expansionist democrats, approached the Mexican government in November 1845, attempting to purchase what is now New Mexico and California. When the Mexicans refused to sell, Polk's next annual address began building a case for war against Mexico.

Both Congress and the US citizenry gave Polk's pitch a cool reception. In an effort to overcome this resistance, Polk sent General Zachary Taylor south to the Rio Grande in March 1846. Taylor's troops forcibly displaced Mexican inhabitants from the Rio Grande's north shore to the town of Matamoros on the south shore. Taylor then established a north-shore fort with artillery facing Matamoros. The Nueces River, about 150 miles north, had been recognized by both Mexico and the United States as the border between Texas and Mexico. Polk's deployment of troops to the Rio Grande was clearly a provocation.[42] And it worked.

Resentful of this armed military occupation, Mexicans attacked a patrol of Taylor's troops on April 25, 1846, killing 16. President Polk acted immediately to secure the unanimous support of his Cabinet. Polk then rallied Congress by asserting that Mexico had invaded the United States, and that duty, patriotism, and national interest required military action against such an aggressor. In reality, Polk had ordered US troops to invade a foreign country, and his claim that these soldiers had been killed on US soil was totally spurious, as was his claim that the US had made every effort to avoid war.[43]

Public opposition to war continued. Henry David Thoreau's refusal to pay his 1846 poll tax was anchored in pacifist sentiment. (He spent a July night in Concord Jail before friends paid the tax over his objection.) In a speech denouncing the war, theologian Theodore Parker called the war "treason against the People," and "a great sin not lightly to be spoken of."[44]

Opposition expanded as the war continued; in the end, a reported 9,207 soldiers had deserted the US Army. Former Presidents John Quincy Adams and Martin Van Buren denounced the war as violating American principles, and Polk's deception was eventually denounced on the floor of the House by a newly elected representative from Illinois, Abraham Lincoln.[45]

But the war's opposition was too little and too late. Polk's stage-managed incident at the Rio Grande initiated a stampede that overwhelmed anti-war voices and reversed the People's peaceful inclinations. Both houses of Congress passed a war resolution with supermajorities amid expanding public enthusiasm. An emerging US poet by the name of Walt Whitman declared, "Yes, Mexico must be thoroughly chastised!" The Illinois State Register asked, "Shall this garden of beauty be suffered to lie dormant in its wild and useless luxuriance?"[46] In the ensuing war, the United States absorbed half of the national territory of Mexico, at a cost of over 13,000 US and 25,000 Mexican citizens' lives. President Polk and the expansionists had won the day.

1898: The Spanish-American War

A splendid little war.[47]

Secretary of State John Hay

[Even] if a war be undertaken for the most righteous end, before the resources of peace have been tried and proved vain to secure it, that war has no defense, it is a national crime.[48]

Charles Eliot Norton
Address denouncing the
Spanish-American War, 1898

At the close of the 19th century (with the Monroe Doctrine in place and its Roosevelt Corollary in ascension), US corporations had heavy investments in Cuban agriculture, mining, and other sectors. Thus, President William McKinley and foreign policy circles in Washington held a keen interest in the Pennsylvania-sized island, only 90 miles from Key West.

In 1898, indigenous Cubans had been fighting for independence from Spain for three years. The majority of US citizens, especially labor, supported the Cubans' struggle for independence. President McKinley and the business community, however, saw the possibility of Cuban independence as a threat to US economic interests. They favored a US military intervention that would essentially allow the US to replace Spain as Cuba's overlord.[49]

The *USS Maine* was deployed to Cuban waters and situated in Havana harbor, where it sank, killing 268 men, following a mysterious explosion on February 15, 1898. Although the *Maine's* sinking was never conclusively investigated, some speculated that the ship's sinking was a covert action the US used to justify war against Spain.

But whatever the cause of the explosion, the *Maine's* sinking enabled one of our nation's most colorful episodes of yellow (sensationalist) journalism, arousing public animosity toward Spain. Joseph Pulitzer's and William Randolph Hearst's New York newspapers headlined (and exaggerated) Spanish atrocities, as Spain continued efforts to retain colonial control of the island. A (possibly apocryphal) story emerged that when Hearst's agent in Cuba, Frederic Remington, reported that there was no war and asked to return home, Hearst cabled back, "Please remain. You furnish the pictures. I'll furnish the war."[50] The Pulitzer and Hearst newspapers were instrumental in establishing the war cry, Remember the Maine, to Hell with Spain!

Two months of pro-war campaigning led to a declaration of war. US forces quickly swept the Spanish from power in Cuba, and Puerto Rico and the Philippines were also transferred from Spain into the US sphere. Although the 1898 Treaty of Paris gave Cuba its independence, Senator Orville Platt (R-CT) attached an amendment to a 1901 appropriations bill which effectively made Cuba a satellite of the United States. Provisions of this Platt Amendment were then forced into the Cuban constitution in 1902, establishing US dominance over the island's economic and governmental institutions and creating a US military base at Guantánamo Bay.

Labor and Socialist newspapers condemned the war, but there were official actions that supported it. For example, New York City authorities prohibited an anti-war parade on May Day 1898, but allowed a pro-war parade the same day. Predictions of wartime corruption and profiteering came tragically true when thousands of US soldiers died from food poisoning. The disease came from a Chicago meatpacker's 500,000-pound beef shipment that had been refused in Liverpool and was then sold to the US army.[51] But the war lasted only three months, and (in the US) was soon forgotten.

1917: World War I

He kept us out of war.

President Woodrow Wilson
Reelection campaign slogan, 1916

War means an ugly mob-madness, crucifying the truth-tellers, choking the artists, sidetracking reforms, revolutions, and the working of social forces.[52]

John Reed
Whose War?, 1917

For most, the national recession of 1913 brought hard times that lasted until the US entry into World War I in 1917. But during those years, US war industries escaped the worst of the downturn by selling $2 billion in war goods to the Allies (over $40 billion in 2010 dollars). Also, when President Wilson lifted a ban on overseas bank loans in 1915, US banker J. P. Morgan opened large lines of credit to the Allies. This boosted the US financial sector's interest in the war, and gave all these US business interests a stake in an Allied victory. While a majority of US citizens were opposed to US involvement in the evolving European conflict, industrialists and financiers stood to make fortunes on war sales and loans.[53]

The public's perspective of the war began shifting when the Germans sank the British luxury liner RMS *Lusitania* on May 7, 1915. The death of 124 US citizens in this event is often cited as the event that triggered the US entry into World War I. Although the *Lusitania*'s sinking did not produce an immediate declaration of war, the Wilson administration used the event to introduce a theme of "unacceptable German submarine warfare." This theme was amplified into a war cry that eventually enabled President Wilson to gather public support and prompt Congress to declare war.

A prolonged controversy over the circumstances surrounding the *Lusitania*'s sinking left many questioning the way the Wilson administration used the event to rally the nation to war.[54] But it appears more likely that the British—desperate for the US to enter the war—orchestrated this event to their advantage.

British Naval officials subsequently admitted that the *Lusitania* was deliberately routed through British waters where German submarines were present, and that no effort was made to protect the *Lusitania*.[55] Winston Churchill, who served in the British Admiralty's Office of the First Lord during the run-up to WWI, makes a revealing statement in his memoir of World War I when he asserts, "The maneuver which brings an ally into the field is as serviceable as that which wins a great battle."[56] The British Admiralty's maneuvers on May 7 were, in fact, instrumental in bringing their US ally "into the field."

But how did the push for war play out in the United States? From the beginning of European hostilities, talk of US entry into the war encountered widespread public resistance. President Wilson's proclamations about a war to end all wars and make the world safe for democracy failed to produce even 10 percent of the targeted number of armed forces volunteers.[57]

Undeterred by their constituents' anti-war sentiments, a congressional majority initiated conscription and enacted the 1917 Espionage Act, under which 2,000 citizens were eventually prosecuted for denouncing the war. Outspoken labor leader Eugene Debs received a ten-year prison sentence under the Act for delivering a speech that was deemed to be an obstruction of recruiting efforts. Skirting Bill of Rights protections, the Sedition Act of 1918 enabled the US Post Office to confiscate publications critical of the government's war efforts.

Mass arrests were employed nation-wide against anti-war demonstrations, and a pro-war campaign was launched by the Creel Committee on Public Information. The committee's recruits delivered a remarkable 750,000 speeches in 5,000 US cities. When President Wilson eventually parlayed Germany's continued submarine warfare into a congressional declaration of war, the *Akron Beacon-Journal* declared that the country had "never embarked upon a more unpopular war."[58]

1941: WORLD WAR II

> *Yesterday, December 7, 1941 . . . the United States of America was suddenly and deliberately attacked by naval and air forces of the Empire of Japan.*[59]
>
> President Franklin Delano Roosevelt

Those with vivid memories of the horrors of World War One greeted the 1930s' return of European hostilities with apprehension. By the end of that decade, however, key members of the Franklin Roosevelt administration had come to believe that the Axis powers posed a serious threat to the United States. So under somewhat different circumstances, the isolationist sentiments of the citizenry were once again at odds with a small group in Washington. This conflict between pro-war elements in Washington and a generally pacifist citizenry was acknowledged and addressed in a classified document discovered in 1995 by investigative author Robert Stinnett.[60]

In an October 1940 memorandum, Lieutenant Commander Arthur McCollum, head of the Far East Desk of Naval Intelligence in Washington, stated concern over the possibility of a German victory over the British. McCollum was further concerned that Germany, Italy, and Japan might then attack the United States. McCollum's analysis of the strategic danger posed by Japan concluded that prompt aggressive action against Japan was appropriate. But there was a problem: the US public was opposed to another war. McCollum suggested that "more ado" could reverse this public opinion.[61]

McCollum proposed an eight-step plan of action that included the deployment of heavy cruisers and submarines into Asiatic waters, the coordination of an international embargo against Japan (essentially severing the island nation's lifelines), and one action that would prove tragically pivotal to the pro-war effort: keeping the main strength of the Pacific Fleet in the vicinity of the Hawaiian Islands. McCollum concluded his proposed plan of action stating, "If by these means Japan could be led to commit an overt act of war, so much the better."

The pacifist sentiment of the US citizenry was not lost on Roosevelt. Then facing the popular isolationist candidate Wendell Willkie in his bid for an unprecedented third term in the White House, Roosevelt felt compelled to promise the electorate that there would be no foreign wars if he were to be reelected. While Roosevelt was issuing politically expedient promises of peace, however, he and key members of his administration were becoming increasingly concerned over Japan's swelling presence in the South Pacific. A State Department memorandum of 1940 voiced an *economic* concern as well, recognizing the potential loss of Asian markets as well as US access to vital natural resources in the Asian and Oceanic regions.[62]

Roosevelt's inner circle shared these economic and national security concerns, and greeted McCollum's agenda with enthusiasm. All eight of McCollum's action steps were implemented over the 14 months between his memorandum's tight circulation and the Japanese attack on Pearl Harbor. Roosevelt's fingerprints are found at every turn.

Roosevelt acted on a war footing, as evident in his aggressive deployment of US naval assets into Japanese waters. Nicknaming these actions "pop-up" cruises, Roosevelt told his Chief of Naval Operations, "I just want them to keep popping up here and there and keep the Japs guessing. I don't mind losing one or two cruisers, but do not take a chance on losing five or six."[63]

Roosevelt's determination to carry out McCollum's plan was also evident in his handling of Admiral James O. Richardson, Commander of the United States Fleet. Richardson, who understood the underlying strategy of the events taking place, voiced detailed and strenuous objections to the detainment of naval assets in Hawaiian waters.[64] Roosevelt fired Richardson in January 1941, replacing him with Admiral Husband Kimmel, on whose watch the Pearl Harbor tragedy would transpire.

The necessity of Japan committing the first strike—McCollum's "overt act of war"—became a crucial element of the plan. Secretary of War Henry Stimson's diaries state that in spite of the risk involved in letting the Japanese fire the first shot, he realized that this was the best strategy to secure the full support of the populace. That way, there would be no doubt in anyone's mind as to who the aggressor was.[65] In the weeks before the Pearl Harbor attack, a series of memoranda emanating from Washington predicted an imminent Japanese attack. By November 28th, Washington naval command instructed the Pacific Fleet to "undertake no offensive action until Japan has committed an overt act."[66]

During this critical period when Roosevelt's inner circle knew that an aggressive Japanese movement was eminent, a Vacant Sea order was issued from naval command in Washington. This astonishing order emptied the entire North Pacific Ocean of all US and allied vessels. Issued within an hour of the Japanese attack force's departure from Japan, this order cleared the route the Japanese would traverse to their attack position at the Prokofiev Seamount some 200 miles north of Oahu.[67]

Questioned about the Vacant Sea order during a 1944 US Navy Court of Inquiry, Rear Admiral Richmond K. Turner, a Navy War Plans officer in 1941, explained that the US Navy diverted Pacific shipping activity "so that the track of the Japanese task force would be clear of any traffic." This revealing statement—that is still on record—was ignored by Congress and the news media covering the 1945-46 Pearl Harbor investigation.[68]

A second event that escaped scrutiny by the official investigations involved a valiant effort of Admiral Husband Kimmel. In defiance of Washington's Vacant Sea order, Kimmel commanded the Pacific Fleet into naval exercises scouting the waters surrounding the Prokofiev Seamount. When Washington learned of Kimmel's location, directives were immediately issued, forcing Kimmel to order the Pacific Fleet back to its Pearl Harbor anchorages. Following the Japanese attack, Kimmel was accused of failing to conduct precisely this type of reconnaissance.[69] There has never been an official recognition of the fact that Washington's directives forced Kimmel to confine the Pacific Fleet in Pearl Harbor on December 7th. Charged with errors of judgment and dereliction of duty following the Japanese attack, Kimmel was demoted and relieved of his command.

Although they may have been surprised and remorseful by the extent of the carnage, Roosevelt's inner circle regarded the Pearl Harbor event as a necessary step toward achieving their desired outcome. The isolationist sentiments of the US citizenry were reversed into enthusiasm for war. Congress rallied, and Roosevelt signed a resolution of war against Japan the following afternoon. The losses at Pearl Harbor were "a pretty cheap price to pay for unifying the country," according to the memoir of Lieutenant Commander Joseph Rochefort, chief US Naval intelligence officer on Oahu (whose management of 1941 intelligence kept Admiral Kimmel in the dark).[70]

Following Pearl Harbor, Roosevelt encouraged Hollywood to promote a social climate conducive to the war. Lowell Mellett was appointed as coordinator of government film, and he later stated that in this position, he was asked to persuade the movie industry to insert morale-building and war-rallying themes in its films by all means possible.

Also during this time, Joseph Breen was head of the Production Code Administration that enforced censorship guidelines on all members of the Motion Picture Association of America. Breen once directed the Association's members to delete any footage that portrayed war as anything but "glamorous and noble." To support the war effort, Frank Capra produced a seven-part series of government-sponsored propaganda films between 1942 and 1945 entitled *Why We Fight*.[71]

The present survey is not meant to question Roosevelt's judgment regarding US entry into the war, nor to disparage those who responded to the war's calling. Rather, the emphasis here is on the *process* that left the US citizenry uninformed of important pre-war analyses, while Roosevelt's inner circle enacted a secret course of US foreign policy. We are left to imagine how all this may have transpired had Roosevelt chosen a different course.

For example, had a series of his popular Fireside Chats apprised the electorate of the administration's national security concerns, a majority may have agreed with Roosevelt and supported a war declaration without the Pearl Harbor event. But as it happened, the arguments advanced in the McCollum memorandum were not publicly aired. Instead, pro-war sentiment was manufactured by the emotionally dramatic losses incurred in an attack that was deliberately provoked and accurately anticipated—it was *not* a surprise.

Our nation's founding principles of representative democracy have at times been undermined by US government actions. Chapters 1 and 2 surveyed anti-democratic government actions that were undertaken without the electorate's awareness, and this chapter examined government efforts to overcome pacifist sentiment and manufacture enthusiasm for wars. The two chapters that follow examine the functioning of our democracy during the political and economic turmoil of the early Cold War era.

CHAPTER FOUR

From World War to Cold War

Through headlines and congressional "investigations" three simple ideas are being hammered into the American consciousness. One is that we will have to fight Russia. The second is that we must rebuild Germany. The third is that Roosevelt was no good.[72]

I. F. Stone
I. F. Stone's Weekly, 1947

Despite all hope, the Axis powers' surrender in 1945 did not bring world peace, but only another variety of war. In this conflict, our WWII ally, the Soviet Union, became our new enemy. This chapter examines the convergence of industrial and political forces that set forth this new paradigm of war, propelling the two superpowers into a 40-year arms race punctuated by various conflicts and skirmishes, often of crisis proportion and sometimes extensive duration.

POSTWAR: THE AIRCRAFT MAKERS' DILEMMA

> *So, the aircraft builders ... are near disaster. ...*
> *Right now the government is their only possible savior*
> *—with orders, subsidies, or loans.*[73]
>
> Business Week, January 31, 1948

World War Two brought economic prosperity to US industry, especially to the largest of the war industries. Overall, wartime industrial profits expanded by 70 percent, but the war was particularly profitable for the aircraft manufacturing industry. *Business Week* commented that "no other business came near the aircraft makers' wartime performance." Moreover, the US Treasury poured $3.4 billion ($42 billion in 2010 dollars) into the aircraft industry's expansion, and this taxpayer-subsidy became a windfall for these corporations following the war.[74]

As expected, aircraft procurement contracts dropped sharply at the end of the war. Additionally, the commercial airlines were falling far short of postwar passenger and airfreight forecasts. These conditions suggested a reduction of manufacturing capacity, and Air Force Secretary Stuart Symington stated that paring down to 6 or 8 aircraft companies (from 13) would be sufficient to meet the nation's postwar needs.[75]

But the entire financial and industrial community had a stake in the health and survival of all the aircraft manufacturers. The January 1949 issue of *Automotive Industries* identified 12 corporations (including even General Mills) as co-beneficiaries of a current Boeing B-50 program. Huge commercial loans had been extended to the aircraft industry; Lockheed's Constellation venture alone was financed by $35 million in bank loans. Also, various corporations had become major stockholders in aircraft corporations. One of these investors was General Motors, whose executive, Harold Boyer, was encouraging permanent alliances between the Air Force and various industries.[76] Big Business was well aware that a round of aircraft company bankruptcies could destabilize the entire financial-industrial system.

There were proposals to nationalize the hemorrhaging aircraft industry—a solution successfully enacted in postwar France. The Progressive Party's presidential candidate, Henry Wallace, campaigned for this solution in the 1948 election, asserting that the best way to protect the peace was to place military aircraft manufacturing under government management. Industry leaders, however, were wary of nationalization. Navy Secretary James Forrestal referred to the nationalization option as a Marxist takeover, a move toward socialism and eventually communism. Wary of both free market forces and nationalization, Pentagon officials and aircraft industry executives advanced a third possibility: government subsidy.[77]

THE TRUMAN REELECTION CAMPAIGN

Very little of the industrial bonanza of WWII trickled down to the nation's workforce; discontent was seemingly everywhere. Exceeding any other period in US history, 14,000 labor strikes took place during the war, involving over six million workers in various industries. The Republican party's sweep of the 1946 midterm elections was widely attributed to frustration over President Truman's handling of postwar labor relations and food shortages. These deficiencies and other perceived bungling gave credence to the Republican campaign slogan, "To err is Truman."[78] Having made huge sacrifices during the war, the citizenry now demanded curbs on government spending, control of inflation, and a foreign policy free of off-shore entanglements.

Given these domestic issues, the US electorate was not enthusiastic about the European Recovery Plan, which proposed donating billions of dollars to European war recovery efforts. Dubbed the Marshall Plan, after its foremost advocate, Secretary of State George Marshall,[79] the program was portrayed as a humanitarian relief effort.

The Marshall Plan's primary purpose, however, was to ensure US industries' access to European markets and expand US political and military influence abroad. Marshall stated as much in an early 1948 State Department memorandum, and when Dean Acheson succeeded Marshall as secretary of state, he admitted that the Marshall Plan was promoted "chiefly as a matter of national self-interest."

Indeed, of the $50 billion disbursed through the Marshall Plan over the decade of its existence, $45 billion was poured into foreign military aid; only $5 billion was spent on nonmilitary programs.[80] So in effect, Marshall's European Recovery Plan was a multi-billion-dollar boost to US armaments industries. For both economic and political reasons, the Marshall Plan became a top priority of the Truman administration.

By the beginning of the 1948 election year, the electorate's faith in Truman's leadership was approaching its nadir. Polls showed that

Truman's *dis*approval rating had risen to 50 percent.[81] For all the woes facing the Truman reelection campaign, the President's chief political advisor, Clark Clifford, had a solution.

In a November 1947 memorandum, Clifford advised Truman that a crisis in US-Soviet relations could be used to his political advantage. Clifford also suggested that Truman could be politically vulnerable to Republican claims that he should have assertively opposed Soviet expansion in Europe. In light of these concerns, Clifford suggested that the US electorate could be rallied behind the Commander in Chief during a foreign relations crisis.

Unfortunately for Clifford's political agenda, a crisis appeared nowhere on the horizon. Nearly all analysts were forecasting an era of peace and the near impossibility of hostilities emanating from Washington's chief suspect, the Soviet Union. General Eisenhower derided fears of Soviet aggression on the front page of the *New York Times*.[82] James Forrestal (now secretary of defense) privately expressed his belief that a balance with the Soviet Union was entirely possible, and President Truman, as will be evident below, shared this perspective.[83] Nevertheless, the crisis needed for Clifford's political agenda soon appeared.

DRUMMING UP TROUBLE

In February 1948, US Army intelligence director, Lieutenant General Stephen Chamberlin, met in Berlin with General Lucius Clay, the US military governor in Germany. Chamberlin advised Clay that congressional apathy was obstructing the Pentagon's efforts to rejuvenate and expand US forces worldwide.[84] Back at the Pentagon on March 5, Chamberlin received a cable from Clay in which Clay stated that he had recently changed his long-standing opinion and now "felt a subtle change in Soviet attitude" which gave him a "feeling that [war] may come with dramatic suddenness." This vague report of an emerging Soviet threat continued, "I am unable to submit any official report in the absence of supporting data but my feeling is real."[85]

Clay's biographer Jean Edward Smith uncovered the primary purpose of the Clay cable: it was to assist the Pentagon in congressional testimonies advocating increased military budgets. For her biography, Smith questioned Clay regarding contradictions between his message to Chamberlin and other correspondence Clay wrote the same day. Clay replied that, in fact, Chamberlin had requested just such a cable from him, and that if he had known that the cable would be revealed outside of congressional committee sessions, he would not have sent it.[86] In short, the Clay cable was a hoax.

No intelligence desk of the State Department, Navy, or Air Force supported the contentions contained in Clay's cable to Chamberlin. Nevertheless, Chamberlin embellished the Clay cable into a long and incendiary memorandum to US Army Chief of Staff General Omar Bradley on March 14, 1948, in which he asserted that the Soviets had been actively pursuing a policy aimed at securing world domination. Chamberlin's document described all manner of Soviet threats including the ability to quickly overrun great expanses of the European continent. Bradley, in turn, (sounding very much like the original Clay cable to Chamberlin) testified before the Senate Armed Services Committee on April 21, 1948, stating, "So many things have happened and you cannot put your finger on any one of them, but it seems to be a difference in attitude on the part of the Russians."[87]

Through the efforts of Chamberlin and Defense Secretary Forrestal, Clay's spurious report of impending war reverberated throughout Washington's foreign policy establishment. The effort paid off; "a real war scare ensued," as the State Department's George Kennan later recalled.[88] Anti-Soviet sentiment was aroused in Congress, where Pentagon appropriations were allocated to ensure military preparedness. While the Clay cable was parlayed into the activation of Washington, an unrelated event was utilized to rally the US electorate.

Marshall's Reign of Terror

Czechoslovakia was a low priority on the Truman administration's agenda. In the developing East-West contest of the Cold War, the administration had all but conceded the Czech government to the Russian camp. Marshall himself stated that a seizure of power by the Communist Party in Czechoslovakia would not materially alter the situation there.[89]

The widely forecasted transition quietly transpired. As Cold War author David Yergin described it, "The communists took power by pushing hard against a door that was already half open."[90] Whereas this takeover was quietly received by the Truman administration as a *fait accompli*, another event two weeks later provided an opportunity to create the air of international crisis needed to activate Clifford's political strategy.

On Wednesday March 10, 1948, Czechoslovakian foreign minister Jan Masaryk died following a nighttime plunge out a third floor bathroom window of his Prague residence. Amid unresolved speculations of murder and suicide,[91] Marshall summoned the press. The world situation had suddenly become "very, very serious," announced Marshall, describing the state of affairs in Czechoslovakia as a Reign of Terror. A front-page *New York Times* headline the following day proclaimed REIGN OF TERROR SEEN BY MARSHALL with the byline, "Masaryk Case Shows 'Plainly What Is Going On.'" A Truman press conference and another Marshall address the next day both coupled the "great crisis" facing the world with the necessity of advancing the Marshall Plan.[92]

The crisis was amplified on Monday, March 15, by a White House announcement that the President would address a joint session of Congress that Wednesday—news that immediately achieved front-page *New York Times* headlines. In his congressional address, Truman stated,

> . . . the Soviet Union and its agents have destroyed the independence and democratic character of a whole series of nations in Eastern and Central Europe. It is this ruthless course of action, and the clear design to extend it to the remaining free nations of Europe, that have brought about the critical situation in Europe today. The tragic death of the Republic of Czechoslovakia has sent a shock-wave through the civilized world...

Adopting the Commander in Chief stature Clark Clifford had recommended, Truman told the nation, "There are times in world history when it is far wiser to act than to hesitate."[93]

In the ensuing atmosphere of world crisis, Truman and Marshall won congressional approval of the Marshall Plan, increased Pentagon budgets, and the restoration of conscription. A $3 billion defense supplement was soon raised to $3.46 billion, and Defense Secretary Forrestal managed to pry $2 billion from the fiscal 1949 budget for immediate airframe procurements. *Business Week* announced that the aircraft manufacturing industry was finally beginning to recover from its postwar slump, and that this upturn was the result of large Pentagon procurement programs.[94]

In light of the intelligence and analysis available to Truman prior to his congressional remarks, his fiery oratory appears unjustified. The day prior to his speech, Truman received a memorandum stating that the intelligence desks of the Department of State, Army, Navy, and Air Force all concurred that a Soviet military threat was not imminent.[95] Events in the following weeks further indicted Truman's credibility.[96] But nevertheless, as Clifford had predicted, Truman's decisive Commander in Chief image facilitated his November reelection. The Czech foreign minister's death plunge had been used to great political and military-industrial advantage.

SUSTAINING PENTAGON BUDGETS

The Truman/Marshall war scare had boosted Pentagon budgets in 1948, but gathering support for military budgets was an ongoing endeavor. In 1950, President Truman commissioned a study of Soviet military capabilities that resulted in a National Security Council report designated NSC-68, which became known as the Blueprint of the Cold War. The document stated that the Soviet Union was "animated by a new fanatic faith," and sought to "impose its absolute authority over the rest of the world."[97] NSC-68 asserted that coexistence with the Soviet Union was impossible, and that defeating the Soviets would require tripling defense spending from its current $15 billion level into the $50 billion range.[98]

The obstacle to implementing the proposed military expansion was public and congressional malaise. But Assistant Secretary of State for Public Affairs Edward Barrett suggested that this resistance could be overcome by "emphasizing the menace of expansionist communism."[99] In May 1950, Secretary of State Dean Acheson obliged, sounding the alarm in a major address to the American Society of Newspaper Editors.[100] ACHESON DECLARES U.S. IS IN DANGER AS KREMLIN TARGET announced the front-page of the *New York Times* the following day. Then on June 25, 1950, North Korean troops suddenly stormed across their southern border, lending new strength to NSC-68's call for military escalation.

Decades of Japanese occupation of the Korean peninsula had ended with Japan's surrender following WWII. Then, in a scenario prefiguring events in Vietnam four years later, Korea was bisected at the 38th parallel. The North was governed by a North Korean socialist dictatorship in the Soviet sphere. In the South, the United States installed a right-wing military dictatorship under Syngman Rhee. The cancellation of nationwide elections in 1948 deepened North-South divisions, and cross-border skirmishes and raids gradually escalated into the North's major incursion across the 38th parallel.

Truman declared the North's actions to be the rule of force, and announced that the United States would respond by upholding the rule of law. General Douglas MacArthur then pushed the North Korean invasion back *not* to the 38th parallel, but all the way to China, which escalated the conflict by provoking the Chinese to enter the war.

Truman's press assistant described the Chinese entry into the war as "the barbarous aggression of the Chinese hoards."[101] Such rhetoric helped mobilize public support of the President and create the national unity needed to support interventions abroad and military spending at home; NSC-68's $50 billion defense budget was achieved. There were 35,000 US and 3,000,000 Korean fatalities during three years of bombing, shelling, and Napalm deliveries—all justified by the Cold War ethos and Truman's rule of law.

COMMUNISTS LURKING *EVERYWHERE*

During the early years of the Cold War, various government campaigns promoted anti-communist sentiment and Red hysteria. A Truman Executive Order established the Federal Employee Loyalty Program in 1947. With intentions similar to the 1917 Espionage Act and the 1918 Sedition Act (chapter 3), the Loyalty Program resulted in the investigation of millions of US citizens, with secret evidence and neither judge nor jury. No case of espionage was ever uncovered in Loyalty Program proceedings. Nevertheless, hundreds of citizens were summarily fired from their jobs for "questionable loyalty" to the United States, creating an atmosphere of fear and suspicion.[102]

During this same time, Attorney General Tom Clark composed the Attorney General's List of Subversive Organizations, which was an intrusion into civil liberties that gave legal force to rumor and innuendo.

Truman's Loyalty Program and Clark's List helped to legitimize the more far-reaching attacks on civil liberties that followed.[103]

Clark initiated a series of anti-communist prosecutions, the most famous of which was against Julius and Ethel Rosenberg in 1953. There was evidence to support the conviction of Julius, even though the intelligence he provided to the Soviets was essentially worthless. Most historians, however, believe that although Ethel was aware of Julius' spy activities, she was not a participant in any way. (Ethel's own brother, David Greenglass, later recanted his trial testimony that the prosecution used to establish her guilt.[104]) For many, Ethel's gruesome electrocution remains a dark stain on our nation's reputation for justice and civility. Albert Einstein, Jean-Paul Sartre, and Pablo Picasso were among those who participated in a worldwide protest against her execution.

On February 9, 1950, Senator Joseph McCarthy dramatically claimed the anti-communist crusade as his own, waving a document at a West Virginia audience which purportedly listed 205 communist spies employed in the US State Department. The nation's mass media did not question McCarthy's unrevealed sources or self-contradictory claims (his "facts" varied from one speech to another).

Independent journalist George Seldes *did* investigate McCarthy's statements. The April 17, 1950 headline of Seldes' weekly newsletter *In Fact* announced, MCCARTHY'S DATA ON STATE DEPT "REDS" LIFTED VERBATIM FROM ANTI-SEMITE'S SMEAR PAMPHLET.[105] Rather than follow Seldes' lead and scrutinize McCarthy's unsubstantiated claims, the mass media launched a character assassination of Seldes.[106] Seldes provided an early warning to his limited audience, but the vast majority of US citizens saw only sensational and uncritical mass media coverage which legitimized McCarthy's pronouncements and exacerbated "communist infiltration" hysteria.

In this frightful public atmosphere, *In Fact* subscribers abandoned their subscriptions in droves, forcing the publication's closure in October 1950, after ten years of revelations often found nowhere else in the US media. It was not until December 1954 that the Senate voted 67 to 22 to condemn McCarthy's duplicitous campaign.

McCarthy's Senate investigations shared headlines with the House's Committee on Un-American Activities (HUAC). With rarely explicit and never verifiable accusations of communist sympathies, HUAC hearings investigated suspected subversion and anti-government propaganda. (One HUAC offshoot was the creation of the Hollywood Blacklist that forced scores of entertainment industry employees from their jobs.[107]) The momentum of the HUAC hearings resulted in the perjury conviction of suspected spy Alger Hiss, whose guilt has never been confirmed. As McCarthy fell from favor, the HUAC began to suffer a tarnished image as well. In 1959, former President Truman called the HUAC "the most un-American thing in the country today."[108]

President Truman's political fortunes became intertwined with US interventions in Italy and Greece. (The Italian intervention is surveyed in Appendix II, The Cold War Worldview.) As will be seen in the following chapter, the US intervention in Greece provides another example of a foreign populace understanding US foreign policy better than many US citizens.

CHAPTER FIVE

Uncle Sam in Postwar Greece

*From Stettin in the Baltic to Trieste in the Adriatic
an iron curtain has descended across the Continent.
Behind that line ... Athens alone—Greece with its immortal glories—is
free to decide its future at an election under
British, American and French observation. ...
The communist parties ... have been raised to pre-eminence
and power far beyond their numbers and are seeking
everywhere to obtain totalitarian control.*[109]

Winston Churchill
Iron Curtain Speech
Fulton, Missouri, March 5, 1946

*Our postwar relations with the capitalist countries were damaged
severely by that arsonist and militarist Churchill.
His famous [Iron Curtain] speech urging the imperialist forces
of the world to mobilize against the Soviet Union
served as a signal for the start of the Cold War.*[110]

Nikita Khrushchev

BRITISH RULE

Despite a formal declaration of independence in 1922, Greece continued to be a British protectorate, as it had been since the 1880s. When Nazi troops invaded in 1941, the Greek People's Liberation Army (ELAS) coalesced and marshaled strong resistance—Winston Churchill applauded the ELAS as "gallant guerillas."[111] Following their expulsion of the Nazis, the ELAS aspired to democratic self-rule. But when the war ended, two divisions of British troops returned with the intention of restoring Britain's overlord status.[112]

The ELAS resisted the return of British domination, and in December 1944, conflict escalated to bloodshed in the streets of Athens. British-sponsored Greek forces fired into a crowd of pro-ELAS demonstrators, who then attacked police headquarters in reprisal. ELAS fighters and a growing number of sympathizers headed for the mountains to organize guerilla warfare, this time not against the Nazis, but against the British-sponsored Greek Police. Suddenly, Churchill's "gallant guerrillas" became the "miserable banditti."[113]

In the ensuing civil war, the Greek aristocracy, the monarchy, and the British found themselves isolated in Athens, while broad areas of the mountainous countryside were occupied by the ELAS. The British orchestrated a rigged election in 1946 that brought a faction of right-wing Greek Royalists to power and restored the monarchy.

Backed by the British government, the Greek Royalists' rule was brutal. A succession of corrupt puppet governments terrorized, tortured, and otherwise suppressed any attempt at Greek independence. CBS chief European correspondent Howard K. Smith remarked, "There are few modern parallels for government as bad as this."[114] Another report stated, "An American investigating team found huge supplies of food aid rotting in warehouses at a time [in 1947] when an estimated 75 percent of Greek children were suffering from malnutrition."[115]

The ELAS comprised 20 percent of the Greek population and included prominent clergymen and some 800 former officers of the Greek National Army. The Greek Communist Party constituted only 20 percent of the ELAS movement and had no affiliation with the Soviet Union. Nevertheless, Cold Warriors in Washington became preoccupied with this small group of Greek communists.

The Greek government's failings and excesses were known to the Truman administration. A 1946 cable from Paul Porter, then in Athens as head of the Office of Price Administration, informed President Truman, "You are aware of the complete reactionary nature of the present government.... Their principal asset is the wide fear in Greece of communist excesses, yet this was offset by their own policies of violence and exploitation." In 1947, Howard K. Smith publicly denounced the Athens government, and Churchill, troubled by the Greek Royalists' brutality, stated, "... it seems to me very unwise for the present Greek government to carry out mass executions of this character . . ."[116]

Nevertheless, under a mantra of anti-communism, Washington's foreign policy leaders were eager to intervene on behalf of the Greek Royalists. They were soon invited to do so. Overextended and approaching bankruptcy, the British announced they were pulling out of Greece.

Empire Change

The Truman administration was already busy rallying support for a US intervention in Greece. At an Oval Office meeting for congressional leaders in February 1947, Undersecretary of State Dean Acheson stated,

> Like apples in a barrel infected by one rotten one, the corruption of Greece would infect Iran and all to the east. It would also carry infection to Africa through Asia Minor and Egypt, and to Europe through Italy and France, . . .[117]

(Acheson's "rotten apple" depiction would later become the "domino theory" in Southeast Asia.)

To strengthen the case for US intervention, the State Department asked the Greek Ambassador in Washington to produce a written request for US assistance.[118] This letter was then cited by President Truman in his famous Truman Doctrine speech to a joint session of Congress on March 12, 1947. Truman declared,

> The United States has received from the Greek Government an urgent appeal for financial and economic assistance. . . . The very existence of the Greek state is today threatened by the terrorist activities of several thousand armed men, led by communists, who defy the government's authority . . .[119]

Although Truman allowed that the Greek government was "not perfect" and had "made mistakes," nothing he said explained that the driving force of the conflict was the Greek government's brutal repression.

Truman's campaign succeeded; the $400 million Greek-Turkish Aid Act passed both houses of Congress by supermajorities. The US soon established a Greek "intelligence" agency patterned after the CIA and began overseeing Greek domestic and foreign affairs.[120] By the 1950s, Washington exercised almost dictatorial control over Greek affairs, requiring that the signature of the chief of the US Economic Mission appear alongside that of the Greek Minister of Co-ordination on any important documents.[121]

Thus, allegedly fending off a communist takeover, the United States assisted an aristocratic minority and their titular royalty in the brutal repression of the Greek population's democratic aspirations. "In spite of ample warnings," investigative author and foreign news correspondent Kati Marton later observed,

> the Truman administration failed to use economic and political leverage to pressure Greek politicians to moderate their policies. It chose the quicker and more expedient route of massively backing a regime its own people found repellent, supposedly in the interest of "world peace."[122]

The situation in Greece came to bear on President Truman's political fortunes. Clark Clifford advised the President that the Truman Doctrine of communist containment was on trial in Greece. Any communist success there would be seen as Truman's failure. The stakes were high; public opinion of events in Greece would be a vital White House commodity.

GREECE: ILLUSION VS. REALITY

While the Truman administration was blaming communists for all the trouble and backing the Greek Royalists, the December 1947 issue of *Harper's* magazine carried a strong indictment of the Greek government and its relationship with Washington. The article's author, George Polk, was a CBS European correspondent and protégé of Edward R. Murrow. The *Harper's* article named names and gave details:

> Right-wing Napoleon Zervas, . . . Minister of Public Order in a recent Royalist Cabinet . . . directed a ruthless campaign against the opponents of the government, no matter what their political convictions. A secret official American document has referred to

> Zervas's "dictatorial and fascist tendencies" as being "at variance with the ideals of American democracy." ...
>
> Thirty-five families dominate the country financially... exerting control or influence through interlocking directorates.... These thirty-five families are the ruling clique of the two percent of the Greek people...
>
> What before the war was a system designed to make the wealthy wealthier, now has become a system designed to squeeze from the country every penny possible as quickly as possible...[123]
>
> Today, large stocks of UNRRA [United Nations Relief and Rehabilitation Administration] supplies are still lying unused in Greek Warehouses.... Only after months of battle did CARE [the humanitarian relief organization Cooperative for American Relief in Europe] succeed in getting release of six thousand gift packages of clothing, food, and vitamins. Greek government officials used every excuse to prevent distribution of the packages...[124]

CBS President Frank Stanton soon received a brusque letter from the Greek government. While admitting that a few unscrupulous individuals succeeded in evading governmental controls and that some may have arranged to send capital abroad, the letter otherwise held that Polk's report was grossly exaggerated and constituted a complete distortion of the truth.[125] Stanton stood foursquare; Polk remained on assignment in Greece.

In late April 1948, Polk learned that one of the "few unscrupulous individuals" evading governmental controls was Constantine Tsaldaris, the head of the Greek Royalist party. The Greeks had made foreign bank deposits illegal in an effort to resolve their currency crisis. Polk confronted Tsaldaris with evidence of a $25,000 ($220,000 in 2010 dollars) deposit to his account in a New York bank. Six days after this meeting, Polk was reported missing from his hotel in Salonika (now Thessalonica). His corpse later surfaced in the waters of Salonika Bay, with hands and feet bound execution-style and a bullet through the head.

Under the direction of the Salonika Chief of Security, Major Nicholas Mouscoundis (who would head the Greek government's murder investigation), the government began to dispense a "communist conspiracy" narrative of the crime. Kati Marton observed, "Like an incantation, the police began to repeat this point over and over. George Polk's was a 'communist-style murder.'" Mouscoundis issued a report stating, "Police believe that the plot was organized by the Communist Party, not by a Greek mind. The police cannot prove this, but fully believe that they are on the right track and know what they are looking for."[126]

The government's narrative of the crime was eventually supplied with the necessary characters. A hapless newspaperman, Gregory Staktopoulos, was apprehended on August 14, 1948 at his regular workday bus stop, taken to Salonika security headquarters, stripped, and isolated in a basement cell. Two days following Staktopoulos' capture, Major Mouscoundis ordered the arrest of Anna Staktopoulos, the reporter's sixty-eight-year-old widowed mother, and his two unmarried sisters were hauled in later that week. No charges were pressed against any of them.

After six weeks of increasingly draconian torture, Staktopoulos was regaining consciousness following a brutal interrogation session when Anna Staktopoulos was brought into his cell. The sight of his gaunt and dispirited mother, and Mouscoundis' recent threats to assassinate her, were finally enough to extract a "confession" from Staktopoulos.[127]

The Greek's sham investigation was followed by a kangaroo court that began in April of 1949. Staktopoulos and his mother were tried as "accomplices," and two communists—the "real murderers"—were accused in absentia. Summarizing Staktopoulos' case, his court-appointed defense attorney called his client "guilty," and applauded the prosecution's handling of the case.[128] Staktopoulos was sentenced to life in prison, his mother was acquitted, and the two communists were convicted in absentia.

WASHINGTON'S INFORMATION PRIORITIES

State Secretary George Marshall oversaw the US citizenry's understanding of the Polk affair. In this effort, the chargé d'affaires of the US Embassy in Athens, Karl Rankin, provided invaluable assistance. In the spring of 1948, mass arrests of suspected leftists and executions of

Greek communists were taking place under conditions of martial law. Nevertheless, Rankin complained that US journalists were being too critical of the Greek government, and feared that adverse publicity would unduly restrain Greek government actions. During this time, Rankin summoned Pulitzer Prize-winning *New York Herald Tribune* reporter Homer Bigart to the Embassy, and scolded him for reporting news that might jeopardize US aid to Greece.[129]

Many US journalists were distraught over Polk's murder. Political commentator Walter Lippmann assembled a committee to investigate the event, and hired General Bill Donovan as counsel and chief investigator. Donovan was a poor choice. Founder of the wartime Office of Strategic Services, Donovan remained closely connected to that organization's descendant, the CIA. But his top assistant for the investigation, Air Force Lieutenant Colonel James G. L. Kellis, was the world's best chance to learn the truth of the Polk murder.

Kellis wasted no time discovering that the Greek investigation was a sham. Confronting Mouscoundis, the Security Chief lamely responded, "Colonel, don't press me.... I have my orders. I have only a few years of my career left, I don't want to lose my pension."[130] In July, Kellis uncovered the Tsaldaris scandal of the $25,000 bank deposit, and in a grave strategic error, shared this and other information with Rankin at the US Embassy. Rankin telexed Marshall, and Kellis was immediately recalled to the Pentagon.

Kellis' blind spot was his undying loyalty to Donovan and his failure to recognize Donovan's true agenda in Greece. Even as he was being yanked from the investigation, Kellis informed Donovan of a list of several suspects he had identified during his brief assignment, all but one of which were Greek Royalist officials. The stand-out was a newspaperman that Kellis knew to have met with Polk in Salonika. Donovan ignored all the Greek Royalists on Kellis' list and instructed Mouscoundis to concentrate on the newspaperman—a certain Gregory Staktopoulos.

Following Kellis' return to Washington, his informant inside the British gendarmerie hit pay dirt: Polk's assassin was a member of the Royalist Party.[131] By this time, however, Kellis finally understood that Washington was not interested in such intelligence.

Aftermath

The handling of the Polk affair was not Walter Lippmann's finest hour. Through Donovan and otherwise, Lippmann was aware of at least some of Kellis' discoveries, and had other important information as well—none of which he ever shared with the US citizenry. For example, Lippmann sent a copy of Staktopoulos' confession at trial to Harvard criminal law professor E. M. Morgan. Morgan's written report to Lippmann declared flatly that Staktopoulos' statement was *not* a confession, and that the story of the murder itself was "fantastic" and "beyond comprehension."[132]

Lippmann buried Morgan's credentialed opinion in his files and concluded the whole affair by assembling his committee in the elegant private dining room of a Washington hotel on September 15, 1949. At this event, he presented Donovan with an inscribed bowl, stating, "We have learned that your sense of justice is the equal of your courage." With astounding hypocrisy, Lippmann also proclaimed, ". . . we can at least say that one of the guilty men has been caught and that no innocent man has been made the scapegoat for a crime of which he is innocent."[133]

Ghost-written by an attorney on his staff, Donovan eventually produced a final report of the Greek affair in 1952. In a five-part exposé entitled Polk Murder Case Whitewash, I. F. Stone identified the Donovan report as "a feeble bit of whitewash," and astutely concluded that the Truman Administration and the Greek government had equally large stakes in the outcome of the Polk Affair.[134] George Seldes had also been exposing his *In Fact* subscribers to reports from Greece that were unavailable in the mass media. On March 22, 1948, *In Fact* carried a report by Homer Bigart (that his *Herald Tribune* editor had blocked), which stated that the Greek government's executions of its detractors were the result of the Greek government's interpretation of the Truman Doctrine.[135]

Although Stone's and Seldes' publications informed a minority of the US citizenry of the Greek Royalists' brutal repression, the vast majority heard only the communist storyline disseminated by the Truman administration. By the fall of 1948, with George Polk dead, Homer Bigart transferred to Washington, and other courageous correspondents reassigned to other beats, the Truman administration became the unquestioned voice of authority on the Greek situation.

James Kellis—a man of uncompromising integrity—eventually wrote a summary analysis of his investigation, an abbreviated version of which appeared in the *New York Times* on September 17, 1977. The article contained evidence that US, British, and Greek authorities were determined to hide the truth in 1948. Furthermore, Kellis stated, "Mr. Rankin, Major Mouscoundis and others tried to impress on me the need to pin this murder on the communists," and that this communist storyline was essential in maintaining the flow of US aid to Greece.

≈

A multifaceted synergy developed in US domestic and foreign policy arenas as the Cold War Worldview became established. In what was represented as a struggle against international communism, Truman was portrayed as a decisive head of state, and the necessities of military preparedness triggered renewed military spending that cascaded through industrial and financial sectors. Thus, a peacetime contraction of war-inflated industries was avoided, and Truman's anti-communist vigilance won his reelection. Pacifist sentiments were stifled by communist witch-hunts, blacklists, and prosecutions later recognized as extremist injustice.

And internationally, the Cold War Worldview provided ideological justification for covert and military interventions that facilitated the expansion of transnational corporations.[136] Indeed, during this era, communist insurgencies were repeatedly discovered in nations possessing resources coveted by US corporations. These powerful interests are the subject of the following chapter.

Chapter Six

Corporations Then and Now

The mischief springs from . . . the multitude of corporations with exclusive privileges which they have succeeded in obtaining . . . and unless you become more watchful in your States and check this spirit of monopoly and thirst for exclusive privileges you will in the end find that the most important powers of Government have been given or bartered away, and the control of your dearest interests have been passed into the hands of these corporations.[137]

President Andrew Jackson
Farewell Address, 1837

This is a government of the people, by the people, and for the people no longer. It is a government of corporations, by corporations, and for corporations.[138]

President Rutherford B. Hayes, 1876

Note: As used here, "corporation" refers to outsized business enterprises owned by absentee stockholders. While these corporations may have thousands of stockholders, a small group of majority stockholders usually control the board of directors. Boards, in turn, set corporate policy and choose the corporate officers who manage the business. The subject of this chapter is *not* the hundreds of thousands of relatively small, closely held corporations whose owners are directly involved in the operation of their business.

CORPORATE PERSONHOOD

Early European corporations were chartered at the discretion of European monarchs. The East India Company and the Massachusetts Bay Company were chartered by Queen Elizabeth I and King Charles I, for example. American revolutionaries eventually fought for independence not only from the Crown, but from the economic exploitation of these royally-chartered corporate entities. One of the most famous protests against the East India Company's monopoly on Eastern trade was the Boston Tea Party.

Through visible actions such as the Navigation Acts, the invisible power behind these corporations became evident. Beginning in 1651, the Navigation Acts were established by the British Parliament.[139] This legislation required that American raw materials be shipped to England for manufacture. The finished products were then returned to the North American colonies for sale by British corporations, often in a monopoly environment.

The British corporate class used governmental connections to thrust the British Navy into mastery of the world's sea-lanes, which then provided safe passage for their corporate shipping enterprises. Thus, a *nation's* resources were employed in the establishment and protection of *private* enterprises. These European investors were the invisible power structure behind the great battles that were waged under the flags of England, France, and Spain during this time, as they vied for colonial possessions and supremacy of the high seas.

By the early 19th century, corporations were forming in North America, chartered and regulated by individual states, with the US Supreme Court replacing the Crown as the final regulatory authority. The state charters of early US corporations were issued with specific expiration dates, and narrowly restricted their business activity. There was no such thing as a conglomerate. A corporation couldn't own another corporation, and stockholders were liable for the corporation's actions. Following the enormous growth that the Civil War brought to corporations, their attorneys began efforts to remove the constraints originally placed on corporate entities.[140]

The Fourteenth Amendment was adopted after the Civil War to prevent states from depriving African Americans of life, liberty, or property. Corporate attorneys went to work, and the 1886 US Supreme Court case *Santa Clara County v. Southern Pacific Railroad* was used to create an opening that established the legal personhood of corporations.¹⁴¹ This maneuver extended the meaning of the Fourteenth Amendment beyond the boundaries of race relations into the realm of Big Business. Despite the fact that the United States Constitution makes no mention of corporations, Bill of Rights protections intended for individual citizens were thus granted to corporate persons, while continuing corporations' exemptions from most responsibilities and liabilities of citizenship. Regarding the ramifications of *Santa Clara*, economist and former Harvard professor David Korten states:

> The subsequent claim by corporations that they have the same right as any individual to influence the government in their own interest pits the individual citizen against the vast financial and communications resources of the corporation and mocks the constitutional intent that all citizens have an equal voice in the political debates surrounding important issues.¹⁴²

The US Supreme Court's *Citizens United v. Federal Election Commission* ruling of January 2010 was a landmark decision that enhanced the political clout of corporations. This ruling struck down lower court opinions that attempted to curb corporations' political campaign contributions. With four Justices dissenting, the Court's majority claimed that corporations belong to a class of disadvantaged persons entitled to free speech rights. This placed corporations in a legal realm that government regulation cannot easily enter.¹⁴³

The *personality* of corporate persons was influenced by the 1919 Michigan Supreme Court case *Dodge v. Ford Motor Company*. In this case, the court ruled that a "business corporation is organized and carried on primarily for the profit of the stockholders. The powers of the directors are to be employed for that end." In effect, *Dodge* tied the hands of corporate directors and executives, setting forth a legal requirement that they maximize financial profit over all other concerns, including workers' rights and environmental protections.¹⁴⁴

The consequences of *Dodge* were evident in the West Virginia coal mine disaster of April 2010, where Massey Energy executives found it more profitable to pay nearly $400,000 for repeated and serious safety violations than to incur the expense of resolving those hazards. Thus, profits trumped worker safety at Massey's Upper Branch Mine, costing 29 lives.¹⁴⁵ The dictates of *Dodge* were also evident in the 2010 explosion of BP's Deepwater Horizon drilling rig in the Gulf of Mexico.

During the ensuing oil spill, *Mother Jones'* editors Clara Jeffery and Monika Bauerlein observed,

> There is no reason for [BP] to put the public interest above those of their shareholders and executives; to do so would be a violation of a CEO's fiduciary duty. No matter any amount of rhetoric to the contrary, BP is organized to serve one thing first and foremost: BP.[146]

Corporations have long pressed for legislation that safeguards and enhances their profitability. In 1989, for example, news of negative health consequences of a chemical used in fruit orchards triggered nationwide lobbying for food disparagement laws by agribusiness corporations. (This event was known as the Alar scare.[147]) These laws enhance food producers' ability to sue their critics for libel, and tilt the legal system against citizens in favor of industry. (The Alar case also illustrates the chemical industry's disregard of public safety.[148])

Probably the most famous food disparagement case is the multi-million dollar lawsuit brought against television hostess Oprah Winfrey and her guest Howard Lyman by members of the cattle industry. The suit was brought after Lyman told Winfrey's audience how agribusiness feedlot practices dangerously increased the public risk of Bovine spongiform encephalopathy, commonly known as Mad Cow Disease. A US Court of Appeals ruled in favor of Winfrey and Lyman, stating, "Stripped to its essentials, the cattlemen's complaint is that [Winfrey's] 'Dangerous Food' show did not present the Mad Cow issue in the light most favorable to United States beef. This argument cannot prevail."[149]

As persons, many modern corporations have been found to exhibit all of the characteristics that define the personality disorder known as psychopathy, including: reckless disregard for the safety of others; deceitfulness (repeated lying and conning others for profit); and failure to conform to social norms with respect to lawful behaviors.[150] Whereas these corporate behaviors were not as evident in centuries past, continued legal and lobbying efforts have transformed the corporate form into an entirely different entity.

Court rulings like *Santa Clara, Dodge,* and *Citizens United* have been milestones in the evolution of the corporate form, but these efforts continue. The US Chamber of Commerce's Institute for Legal Reform strives to maintain a legal environment conducive to corporate profitability. The Institute's annual lobbying expenditures have been between $20 and $31 million in recent years.[151]

DEREGULATION AT HOME, RE-REGULATION ABROAD

Initially, government regulation of corporations was intended to ensure their positive contribution to society. In the 1970s, however, corporations began promoting *de*regulation as an economic cure-all. The commercial airlines were the first target (during the Carter administration), and the fundamental problems resulting from that deregulation continue to plague the airlines and their workers.[152]

In his 1981 inaugural address, President Reagan stated that government was not the solution but the problem itself.[153] The Reagan administration then removed the financial industry safeguards, leading to the 1980s Savings & Loan Crisis and $160 billion public bailout. More recently, the Enron and WorldCom scandals and the 2008 global financial crisis have all resulted from dismantling or blocking regulations on finance and industry.[154] (In less than two minutes, Senator Elizabeth Warren explained to Jon Stewart's *Daily Show* how deregulation has perpetually disrupted the US economy.[155])

In 1944, the World Bank, the International Monetary Fund (IMF), and the General Agreement on Tariffs and Trade (GATT) were all created at a United Nations Conference held in Bretton Woods, New Hampshire. Following the deregulatory actions that improved the *domestic* business climate during the Reagan era, these Bretton Woods institutions were then utilized to shape and strengthen a *global* economic system designed to facilitate the profitability and hegemony of transnational corporations. Under a free trade mantra, corporate lawyers targeted a worldwide variety of policies, laws, and cultural Values, calling them barriers to free trade. When the Uruguay Round of GATT negotiations spawned the World Trade Organization in 1995, the WTO began dismantling these barriers in a process advocates call harmonization.

Free trade has been portrayed as the dismantling of unwieldy trade regulations. Nothing could be further from the truth. Whereas a global free trade agreement could be written on a single sheet of paper (Cut tariffs, eliminate quotas, . . .), the WTO has some 800 pages of regulations under 12 separate agreements, all drafted by attorneys of transnational corporations. So it becomes clear that the free trade slogan is a sham. This is a plan for managed trade—corporate-managed trade.

Powerful enforcement mechanisms of the WTO were designed to overrule national and regional laws and agreements in favor of the WTO's corporate-biased regulations. These legislative and judicial powers are particularly troublesome to any sense of democracy. The WTO's combination of expansive rules and strong enforcement mechanisms has spawned a slow-motion coup d'état against democratic, accountable governments. With prescient recognition of the sea-change then taking place, David Korten wrote in 1995:

> The WTO is, in effect, a global parliament composed of unelected bureaucrats with the power to amend its own charter without referral to national legislative bodies. Under the WTO, a group of unelected trade representatives will become the world's highest court and most powerful legislative body, to which the judgments and authority of all other courts and legislatures will be subordinated.[156]

Unfortunately, Korten's predictions have come to pass. WTO tribunals have challenged numerous laws and standards, particularly environmental protections. The WTO's very first ruling was against the United States' Clean Air Act, which found that the Act's high standards against polluting gasoline failed to comply with WTO trade rules and had to be softened.[157] Similarly, in 2011, the WTO struck down dolphin-safe tuna and country-of-origin meat labeling as violations of trade obligations.[158]

GLOBAL CORPORATE SYNERGISM

Whereas a dog-eat-dog image of the corporate business world has some basis in reality, it is also true that an integrated corporate class network exists, both nationally and globally. This cohesion arises, in part, from board interlocks, whereby individuals sit on the boards of two or more corporations. For example, in recent years, there have been around 30 board interlocks between the New York Times Company and other major corporations, including Carlyle Group, Chase Manhattan, Ford, Metropolitan Life, PepsiCo, Sears, and Texaco.[159]

In addition to board interlocks within national business communities, economic globalization has resulted in global (transnational) interlocks. A wave of cross-border corporate acquisitions in the late 1990s brought a corresponding increase in the number of different nationalities represented on the boards of these combines.[160] Thus, there has become an increasingly global network of directors and executives, with a common interest in policies and institutions that promote corporate prosperity.

International strategic alliances are another aspect of global corporate integration. Under these alliances, multinational corporations enter into pragmatic partnerships with competitors or actively explore cooperative alliances. Companies might share certain commercial assets, pool capital and research capabilities, or trade technological knowledge. There are now thousands of these alliances throughout the corporate world.[161] So not only has corporate merger activity resulted in ever-larger corporations and conglomerates, strategic alliances between these giants can exert a more powerful market force than any one of them individually.

THE CORPORATE-GOVERNMENT REVOLVING DOOR

Whereas board interlocks and strategic alliances facilitate connectivity within the corporate community, the infamous revolving door provides continuity between corporate industries and government sectors. Dick Cheney's career offers an illustration of this corporate-government synergism.

Cheney's political ascendancy included service as Chief of Staff to President Ford, five terms in the US House of Representatives (R-WY), and secretary of defense to President George H.W. Bush (GHW Bush). Following these government posts, Cheney moved to the corporate sector as CEO of the petroleum services conglomerate Halliburton. Then, Cheney became vice president for two terms during the George W. Bush (GW Bush) administration.[162]

While defense secretary in 1992, Cheney awarded a $9 million contract to Halliburton subsidiary Kellogg, Brown, & Root to study possibilities for private sector involvement in ancillary and even military Defense Department functions. Unsurprisingly, the KBR study found that the privatization of Defense Department functions was a great idea. Cheney then left the Pentagon and was CEO at Halliburton when the corporation and its subsidiaries received several hundred government contracts. During this time, Cheney's net worth went from about one million dollars to over 60 million dollars.[163] So when Cheney returned to government office as vice president in 2001, he was a wealthy government contractor.[164]

Donald Rumsfeld spun through the revolving door as well, becoming CEO and eventually board chair of the pharmaceutical giant G. D. Searle & Company between his two stints as secretary of defense in the Ford and GW Bush administrations. Although not widely publicized, the advent of the artificial sweetener aspartame was the foremost public interest story of Rumsfeld's tenure at Searle. Rumsfeld became extraordinarily wealthy by fighting unscrupulously for the public release of this toxic chemical.[165]

Beyond the high-profile careers of Cheney and Rumsfeld, the revolving doors are open in all branches, agencies, and levels of US government. For example, here are four of Monsanto Corporation's numerous government connections:[166]

> Michael (Mickey) Kantor promoted the creation of the WTO and the North American Free Trade Agreement during his tenure as President Clinton's US Trade Representative (1993-1997). Then, joining Monsanto's board of directors in 1997, Kantor assisted US government efforts to pressure the European Union regarding their resistance to Monsanto's genetically engineered crops.

> US Supreme Court Justice Clarence Thomas was formerly a Monsanto attorney. Thomas wrote a Court majority opinion in 2001 that opened the door for biotechnology corporations' lawsuits against farmers for saving seed for their next year's crop. This ruling has economically devastated farmers whose crops have been unwittingly contaminated by airborne pollen from other farms' Monsanto-engineered crops.[167]

> Linda J. Fisher practiced law at a firm known for fighting tougher regulatory standards on behalf of corporate clients. After an interlude as vice president of government affairs at Monsanto, Fisher spent eight years at the Environmental Protection Agency, where she held deputy director posts and

was Chief of Staff to the Administrator. Fisher then moved from the EPA to a corporation regulated by the EPA, becoming vice president for safety, health, and environment for chemical giant DuPont.[168]

Michael R. Taylor's career began at the Food and Drug Administration (1976 to 1981). He then became the food and drug specialist at a law firm representing Monsanto. Taylor was back at FDA as its Deputy Commissioner for Policy from 1991 to 1994, and then administered the Food Safety and Inspection Service at the Department of Agriculture before returning to Monsanto's service as vice president for public policy. In July 2009, Taylor made a fourth trip through the revolving door to become a senior advisor at the FDA, where he became its Deputy Commissioner of Foods in January 2010.

The revolving door has increased corporations' influence with government entities—often resulting in the corporate "capture" of government agencies. These agencies were created to represent the public interest and the common good. However, as with Rumsfeld's finagling of aspartame's FDA approval, regulatory capture can cause the public interest to be sacrificed to corporate interests.

Many revolving door moves are between regulatory agency posts and the industries regulated by those same agencies. For example, in GW Bush's first term, more than one hundred former lobbyists were appointed to agencies that regulate industries they had recently worked for. And in 2010, 148 former federal regulators from entities like the Securities and Exchange Commission and the Federal Reserve became registered Washington lobbyists.[169]

Industry-to-government career moves are now turbocharged by corporate cash injections. Many corporations give departing executives bonuses and other incentive pay *if* they take government jobs. Citigroup, for example, awards additional retirement pay to take a "full time high level position with the US government or regulatory body."[170] Bank of America's Stefan Selig received a $9 million bonus as he left the bank to become the Undersecretary for International Trade at the Department of Commerce, and Michael Froman, the current US Trade Representative, received over $4 million as part of multiple exit payments when he left Citigroup to join the Obama administration.[171]

The political and economic power of the modern transnational corporation could scarcely have been imagined at the founding of our nation. Following centuries of corporate expansion and the gradual erosion of constraints and public safeguards, many corporations now exceed the majority of sovereign governments in size and power. Indeed, 53 of the top 100 economies in the world are now corporations.[172]

Transnational corporations are increasingly stateless entities, moving factories and operations around the world in search of the lowest taxes, weakest labor protections, and least restrictive environmental standards, in what is referred to as a race to the bottom.[173] As discussed in the following chapter, corporations' economic dominance and *Dodge*-mandated creed of profit *über alles* now pose a threat to our democracy and the ecological integrity of the Earth.

CHAPTER SEVEN

Wealth, Democracy, and the Earth

Concentration of economic power in all-embracing corporations [is] a kind of private government which is a power unto itself— a regimentation of other people's money and other people's lives.[174]

Franklin D. Roosevelt
1936

We can have democracy in this country or we can have concentrated wealth in the hands of a few, but we cannot have both.[175]

Supreme Court Justice Louis Brandeis
1941

Economic disparity in the United States is the highest of any first-world nation (but similar to monarchies, dictatorships, and autocracies). Global averages, too, evidence disparity; the top one percent of the planet's population owns roughly 40 percent of all financial wealth. This top one percent group owns twice as much wealth as the bottom 80 percent of humanity.

Corporate class apologists claim these national and global disparities are unintended byproducts of market forces and invisible hands. In truth, however, this situation is the intentional result of an economic system designed with one over-riding purpose: the concentration of financial wealth at the top of an economic pyramid.[176]

US Economic disparity has increased during recent decades, primarily due to the financial gains of a tiny, ultra-rich minority, the top one hundredth of one percent income group (one in 10,000 households). Resembling the robber baron era that preceded the Great Depression, these roughly 14,000 households have annual incomes averaging over $30 million.[177] So wealth has indeed been concentrated into the hands of a few. What, then, of Justice Brandeis' observation?

LEVERAGING CAPITAL: CAMPAIGN FINANCING

The commercial media give little, if any, meaningful coverage of electoral campaigns.[178] The vast majority of presidential campaign stories are about the latest polls or the tactics of a campaign, with little attention to what the candidates stand for or how their proposals might affect the populace.[179] The disappearance of meaningful campaign coverage has coincided with a rise in paid political advertising—the majority of which is now attack advertising. Examining a week in August 2012, a study found that 99 percent of broadcast political advertising was negative.[180]

The 2012 US election spending set a new record: $6.2 billion. The Romney and Obama campaigns alone spent over $2.6 billion. The finance-insurance-real estate sector contributed $60 million to the Romney campaign *and* $21 million to the Obama campaign. Campaigns in the House and Senate spent an average of $1.5 and $11.5 million, respectively, and a record $50 million was poured into the McMahon Senate campaign in Connecticut.[181]

These cash infusions have crippled our electoral processes and warped the political landscape. The flow of campaign contributions from corporations, special interest groups, and wealthy individuals has made fund-raising an obsession for most politicians, and it serves as the main prerequisite for success. But 96 percent of the electorate never give a campaign contribution; most politicians are beholden to a tiny minority for their political survival.[182] For example, the Swift Boat Veterans for Truth ads (deceitfully attacking John Kerry's military service record in the 2004 presidential campaign) were financed primarily from individual donors putting up anywhere from $10,000 to $500,000.[183] Texas oilman T. Boone Pickens contributed $500,000, while Sam Fox contributed $50,000 (and was later named US Ambassador to Belgium in a GW Bush recess appointment).

Over 90 percent of US citizens think too much is spent on political campaigns, and 70 percent want campaign finance reform.[184] The predominant media corporations, however, do not want election reform; one reason is that campaigns bring substantial sums of money into their coffers. Going into the 2008 election year, CBS Chief Executive Leslie Moonves stated, "We're seeing a very robust amount of money. . . We do not want election reform."[185] (Moonves' 2008 compensation of $33 million jumped to $69 million in 2011.) Indeed, television advertising revenues for the 2012 election cycle topped $3 billion. Clearly, vast sums of money are sloshing around in our electoral system. What about the machinery of legislation and governance?

LEVERAGING CAPITAL: CONGRESSIONAL LOBBYING

There are roughly 12,000 lobbyists in our nation's capital, outnumbering our elected representatives 22 to one. Annual expenditures for the lobbying of Congress and federal agencies now total around $3 billion. The top spenders are almost exclusively large corporations and conglomerates. Blue Cross/Blue Shield and General Electric spent $16 and $15 million respectively in 2012, and the top spender that year was the US Chamber of Commerce at $95 million.[186] What is the *purpose* of these huge expenditures?

In light of the *Dodge* ruling that requires corporations to maximize profits, these lobbying expenses are revealed as investments that are expected to have a favorable return. So the truth becomes obvious: lobbying expenditures continue because they get results. For example, the Business Roundtable is a lobbying group of large corporation's CEOs. Congress has not passed an environmental law without the Business Roundtable's approval since 1975.[187]

In the United States today, we have a legislative and regulatory system that is responsive to cash. In this system, the majority favoring campaign finance reform is up against not only the personal fortunes of corporate class individuals, but also the communications resources and deep pockets of multi-billion dollar corporate persons.

Perhaps this is exactly the situation Justice Brandeis foresaw. A tiny, ultra-rich minority now exercises extremely disproportionate influence. Their financial wealth is leveraged into legislative actions and regulatory captures that enhance the profitability of the corporations from which their wealth is derived. Thus, our democracy has been largely superseded by a plutocracy—governance by a wealthy Elite. There is perhaps no better example of this trend than the American Legislative Exchange Council (ALEC).

ALEC AND GOVERNMENT PRIVATIZATION

The American Legislative Exchange Council was created in 1973 by Moral Majority founder Paul Weyrich. It has billed itself as a *non-partisan*, individual *public-private* membership *association of state legislators*. This self-description distorts reality. Is ALEC non-partisan? All of ALEC's directors and board members are Republicans, and the Democrats on ALEC's roster of 2000 state legislators can be counted on one hand.[188] Is ALEC a public-private association? The $50 annual membership fees of (public) state legislators total around $100,000; however, ALEC's annual operating budget of over $6 million is supplied by its 300 (private) corporate members. So to say that ALEC is an association of state legislators is misleading; the organization is sustained by its corporate members' cash. Charles and David Koch have given ALEC at least $1 million, not counting a $500,000 loan they granted during an ALEC budget crunch.[189]

And exactly what does ALEC do? In a nutshell, ALEC brings corporate representatives together with state legislators to produce model legislation (boilerplate bills).[190] Participating legislators then introduce these bills in statehouses across the nation, usually without disclosing the corporate sponsorship of the bills.[191] Long-suspected details of ALEC's operations were confirmed in 2011 by leaked ALEC documents showing that behind closed doors, ALEC's corporate representatives hand state legislators the legislation that corporations desire.[192]

One refrain appears throughout ALEC's statements of its goals and priorities: privatization. Claiming an unfair government monopoly on public goods and services, ALEC advocates the transfer of a wide range of governmental functions into corporate hands.[193] The scope of this privatization agenda is evident in the sectors targeted by ALEC's nine task forces, the bodies from which its model legislation emanates. The task forces are:

- Public Safety and Elections
- Civil Justice
- Education
- Energy Environment and Agriculture
- Health and Human Services
- Commerce, Insurance and Economic Development
- Tax and Fiscal Policy
- International Relations
- Telecommunications and Information Technology

CORPORATE-MANAGED BALLOT BOXES

In 2013, ALEC renamed its Public Safety and Elections task force. But regarding the privatization of elections, corporate persons were already largely in charge of our nation's ballot box by that time. Volumes have now been written documenting electoral fraud involving these corporations' computerized (often paperless and unverifiable) voting systems. These corporations' claims of proprietary technology have prevented any independent oversight of the programming of computers now counting our votes.[194]

The 1996 Senate race in Nebraska remains a disturbing example of the ramifications of these developments. American Information Systems (AIS, later ES&S) was under contract to provide the computerized voting machinery for 80 percent of Nebraska's precincts in the 1990s. Republican Chuck Hagel (who later became Obama's secretary of defense) was AIS's board chair in July 1992, and also became its CEO in November 1993. Hagel resigned these posts just two weeks prior to a March 1995 announcement of his (first ever political) candidacy for a Nebraska seat in the US Senate. In other words, Hagel was running AIS while the company was building and programming machines that would later count his votes.

Hagel achieved a stunning upset, winning even African American precincts that had *never* voted Republican. Looking into candidacy filing information, election sleuth Bev Harris found that on Hagel's required personal disclosure documents, he never mentioned his salary from or stock holdings in ES&S. Then in October 2002—the year Hagel handily won reelection—he *still* had undisclosed ownership of ES&S through its parent company, the McCarthy Group—a firm then run by Hagel's campaign finance director.[195]

MEDDLING IN STATE ELECTIONS

The corporate cash that funds ALEC also directly sponsors political candidates. Over the decade ending 2010, ALEC's corporate leaders poured more than $370 million into state elections. These funds, and additional millions from other ALEC-aligned businesses, helped elect thousands of state senators and representatives willing to champion ALEC bills in their state capitols.[196] Additionally, millions of dollars have been injected into campaigns for and against state ballot issues affecting corporate interests. These efforts have contributed to a major shift in state governments. Anti-government, anti-tax zealots have taken power in statehouses across the country, driving home familiar themes: no taxes; government is in the way; public programs are wasteful and unnecessary; private enterprise can do a better job.[197] And as with their campaign and lobbying expenditures, the corporate Elite invest millions of dollars in ALEC because it gets results. In 2009, for example, 115 pieces of ALEC-generated legislation were passed into state laws.[198]

While ALEC strives to improve the national operating environment for corporations, other specifically targeted campaigns are periodically employed to suppress initiatives promoting the public interest. The campaign against the Obama administration's efforts toward healthcare reform provides an example.

CITIZEN HEALTH VS. INSURANCE INDUSTRY PROFIT

The United States has the highest per capita healthcare expenditures on the planet, and yet our 2012 ranking for life expectancy is 42nd and our infant mortality ranking is 55th.[199] (The US is also the only industrialized nation without universal healthcare.) The primary reason our costs are so high and our health so relatively poor is this: On one side of our healthcare equation we have the citizenry; on the other side of the equation we have healthcare practitioners, hospitals, and so forth; *in between*, we have the health insurance industry.

The primary objective of health insurance corporations is not the health of the populace; it is the generation of profit. Stripped to basics, the profit formula for a health insurance corporation is: Member Premiums minus Claim Payouts and Corporate Overhead equals Profit. In 2010, the five largest US health insurance corporations netted a combined $12.2 billion in profit.[200] *This* is why the US ranks first in per capita healthcare costs.

Following over 400 mergers around the turn of the century, a handful of health insurance giants now exercise monopolistic or oligopolistic control over wide geographic markets. As a result, competition in the health insurance industry is disappearing—a situation generating huge profits.[201] These profits were threatened by the Obama administration's 2009 agenda for healthcare reform. A 20-year veteran of the insurance industry's executive ranks has recently provided insight into the health insurance industry's response to these threats.

Wendell Potter was head of communications at Humana insurance corporation when health care reform was attempted during the Clinton administration. Potter witnessed the creation and execution of a campaign that industry front groups waged against that reform initiative. The Health Insurance Association of America, for example, funded the famous Harry and Louise television commercials that portrayed a fictional middle-aged couple fretting over government-controlled health plans. The industry-backed Healthcare Leadership Council sponsored a radio campaign warning that the Clinton plan could have Washington bureaucrats rationing health care.

The insurance industry's campaign frightened voters away from a universal healthcare option with cries of government bureaucrats coming between them and their doctors. But as Potter explains, US citizens instead got private insurance companies doing exactly the same thing.[202] The industry's campaign sustained its lucrative position between the populace and healthcare providers—the very situation that has driven US healthcare costs off global charts.

In 2007, while vice president of communications at health insurance giant CIGNA, Potter happened on a Health Care Expedition in Tennessee. At this event, Potter witnessed hundreds of people lined up in the rain to receive healthcare services from a traveling clinic whose examination rooms were the animal stalls at a fairground. The experience precipitated a personal epiphany. Subsequently, over lunch served on gold-plated china aboard a CIGNA corporate jet, Potter decided to resign at CIGNA and become an advocate for insurance industry reform. Potter believes that breaking the health insurance industry's monopoly is essential to effective healthcare reform. If healthcare reform does not include a public insurance option to compete with private insurers, Potter says it might as well be called the Health Insurance Industry Profit Protection and Enhancement Act.[203]

Sabotaging Healthcare Reform

When Congress adjourned for the 2009 summer recess, legislators scattered to their states and districts to hold Town Hall meetings addressing the healthcare reform issue. Potter was a guest of US Representative Bill Pascrell at a Town Hall meeting held in Montclair,

New Jersey. The event included testimony from a citizen who had heard that people working behind the scenes on the reform legislation had close ties to communists, and another who had heard that all the pizzeria owners in the area would be put out of business if health care reform legislation passed. Potter suspected that the insurance industry had played a role in what seemed to be a well-orchestrated fear-mongering campaign.[204] He was right.

Tea Party organizers had recruited thousands of protesters to the Town Hall meetings on healthcare reform and staged anti-reform rallies in front of over 100 congressional district offices.[205] On August 11, 2009, television commentator Rachel Maddow reported that two organizations, FreedomWorks and the Tea Party Patriots, were involved in this effort. Maddow pointed to strategy memos that gave specific instructions to protesters, encouraging them to disrupt the Town Hall meetings on healthcare reform.[206]

Despite a mass media portrayal as a grassroots phenomenon, the Tea Party's national organizers are highly networked and ideologically wedded to arch-conservative Republicans and corporate sponsors. FreedomWorks, for example, is one of the Tea Party's chief supporters, and is a champion of radical right ideology.[207] FreedomWorks' support of Tea Party efforts to disrupt public debate at the Town Hall meetings was part of a comprehensive campaign to sabotage healthcare reform in order to safeguard insurance industry profits.

The Tea Party is big business. Sal Russo, head of the Tea Party Express, made over $800,000 for his 2010 Tea Party efforts.[208] FreedomWorks principal Dick Armey reported $500,000 in Tea Party-affiliated income for 2010.[209] FreedomWorks has refused to disclose the sources of its funding ($4.3 million in 2008[210]), but one funding source has come to light. From 2001 to 2006, FreedomWorks engaged in an undisclosed agreement with health insurance brokers whereby those who purchased policies automatically became dues-paying members of FreedomWorks. In this manner, 16,000 people "donated" $638,040 to FreedomWorks.[211]

CEO Compensation and Planetary Ecosystems

The nation's healthcare system is certainly not the only casualty of corporate profit priorities. Sometimes, the multi-million-dollar salaries of corporate CEOs encourage them to put profits above the health of the Earth's ecosystems.

Beginning in 2003, a phenomenon known as colony collapse disorder (CCD) began devastating honeybee hives in Europe and North America. CCD was occurring worldwide by 2006, with annual losses averaging approximately one-third of total colonies.[212] CCD studies by the European Food Safety Authority and the Harvard School of Public Health have focused on a group of neonicotinoids (neonics)—systemic pesticides applied to plant seeds which then permeate all fibers of the adult plant, including pollen. These studies have concluded that neonics are fatally toxic to honey bees and are the suspected cause of CCD.[213] But neonics are also big business; Bayer alone reported over $1 billion in neonic sales in 2010.

Leaked Environmental Protection Agency reports indicate that the agency's scientists are aware of neonics' toxicity and implication in CCD. In a classic case of corporate capture, however, EPA officials have ignored the agency's scientists and continued to endorse neonic pesticides, citing the chemical industry's own studies that claim neonics are safe.[214] Perhaps these EPA officials have encountered CropLife America.

CropLife America is a lobbying group funded by the Big Six chemical industry giants, Monsanto, DuPont, Bayer, Dow, BASF, and Syngenta.[215] Despite the conclusions of peer reviewed research, CropLife America maintains that there is no linkage between CCD and neonics, stating, "Scientific literature examining the potential causes of CCD is incredibly varied and will need additional research."[216] The CEOs of the Big Six authorize funding for CropLife America's lobbying efforts, including the promotion of neonics. Why are these CEOs promoting the sale of chemicals that are poisoning planetary ecosystems?

The average annual earnings of the Big Six's CEOs is roughly $10 million, ranging from $5 million to $21 million.[217] (The after-tax take-home equivalent of a $10 million income is about $115,000 a week.) As per *Dodge*, these people are paid to sustain their company's profits, and this apparently involves the promotion of a class of pesticides that are devastating the primary pollinators of one-third of the food we eat. (This behavior is reminiscent of tobacco industry executives' decades of insistence that tobacco products were harmless—false assertions that a federal judge has recently ordered them to correct through advertisements and package warnings.²¹⁸) As will be discussed in chapter 16, personal wealth in these sums can become an addictive agent, eliciting behaviors that can be destructive to the individual, to society, and to the Earth.

Legal and legislative efforts were significantly increasing corporate power during the mid-20th century. At this same time, US interventions facilitating the global expansion of corporate industries were enabled by Cold War pronouncements of communist takeovers. The following chapter surveys events that brought Presidents Eisenhower and Kennedy into conflict with the forces involved in this Cold War corporate-military expansion.

Chapter Eight

Cold War Maintenance

*Why the sudden pretense . . .
that CIA operatives only spend their time translating Pravda?*[219]

I. F. Stone
1961

When created by the National Security Act of 1947, the CIA was assigned the collection, coordination, and dissemination of national intelligence. But in July of the following year, a top-secret National Security Council directive greatly expanded the nature of the CIA's mission. This directive, known as NSC-10/2, authorized the CIA to engage in propaganda, economic warfare, and sabotage, and included provisions for subversive actions in foreign nations.[220] NSC-10/2 was initially proposed by State Department advisor George Kennan, who later said it was the greatest mistake he ever made.[221]

By the mid-1950s, the CIA had grown larger than the State Department, and two-thirds of the agency's budget and personnel were committed to the covert activities authorized by NSC-10/2. As the CIA expanded into global operations, it acquired soldiers, bases, ships, and planes, but even so, the agency's overflowing aspirations needed support from the armed forces.[222] Thus it was that in 1955, Air Force Colonel Fletcher Prouty was commissioned to set up an office in the Pentagon that would coordinate US military support of the CIA's clandestine operations. But Prouty's commission didn't stop there.

CIA Director Allen Dulles got Prouty to create a secret network that began in the armed services and was then extended into Cabinet Departments, the FBI, the FAA, and other agencies. Thus, an extensive network of covert CIA agents was established in strategic positions throughout the US government. The network was composed of individuals whose primary allegiance was *not* to the department or agency where they were officially employed, but rather to the upper ranks of the CIA.[223]

In an effort codenamed Operation Mockingbird, the CIA's secret network was extended into national and worldwide media operations in order to influence public opinion through the news. Estimates of the number of reporters involved in Operation Mockingbird range into the hundreds.[224]

CBS President William Paley and CBS News President Sig Mickelson were both in the Mockingbird network, as were Henry Luce of *Time* and *Life* magazines and *New York Times* publisher Arthur Hays Sulzberger.[225] Through its Mockingbird connections, the CIA was able to suppress news of its covert operations and mold public opinion through PR efforts like the Guatemalan communist takeover story (chapter 2).

Within a few years of its inception, the CIA's operations were characterized by invisibility, widespread connections, and independence from presidential, congressional, or any other oversight. At times, even its own director could not control the agency. When President Kennedy appointed California businessman John McCone to replace CIA Director Dulles, the upper echelon of the agency coalesced around Dulles' deputy, Richard Helms. McCone was excluded from the camaraderie of the Dulles era. Attorney General Robert Kennedy knew more about some of the CIA's activities (such as Mafia plots against Castro) than McCone did.[226]

The CIA pushed to have foreign policy events classified as clandestine, which caused these operations to be added to its expanding list of assignments.[227] This assertive meddling frequently resulted in turf battles between the Pentagon and the CIA, and sometimes caused the agency to supply and support the declared *enemies* of other arms of the US government:

> In 1955, while the State Department facilitated the sale of fighter planes to Costa Rica's President José Figueres, the CIA was flying sorties for the rebel forces Figueres was defending himself against.
>
> During the 1960 secession movement of the Katangan province in Congo (chapter 1), the US Air Force was transporting and aiding Congolese troops against the Katangese rebels. At the

same time, the CIA assembled an air armada and mercenary units to aid the Katangese rebels.

In 1970, while the US military was assisting the Burmese air force strikes against Burmese rebels, the CIA was assisting the rebels from its bases in Laos.

During the 1960s and 1970s, the CIA funded Angolan revolutionaries attempting to overthrow their government while the US government was providing the Angolan government with arms to suppress the revolution.[228]

Most US citizens were unaware that their taxes were being funneled into armaments corporations supplying both sides of these conflicts. In fact, for thirteen years following its creation, most people remained largely unaware of the CIA's very existence. Its covert life was first exposed during the 1960 U-2 Affair, and again during the Bay of Pigs event the following year. The agency's image was further tarnished in 1975, when the Senate's Church Committee publicly revealed the agency's foreign assassination operations as well as unlawful surveillance of US citizens and mail tampering.[229] But with its black budgets beyond the scrutiny of Congress and its operations concealed behind an impenetrable barrier of national security classifications, the US citizenry has never had a clear idea what all the agency has been up to.

The remainder of this chapter surveys the CIA's orchestration of the U-2 and Bay of Pigs events, and the effect these events had on relations between the superpowers and the Cold War itself.

WAGING PEACE AND THE U-2 AFFAIR

*We had been assured categorically by the director of CIA, Allen Dulles, that no man would ever be taken alive.
... Allen Dulles lied to Dad.*[230]

John S. D. Eisenhower

Following a brilliant military career and a three-year presidency of Columbia University, Dwight D. Eisenhower was drafted as the Republican Party's presidential nominee in 1952.[231] Eisenhower's embrace of the Cold War Worldview influenced his approach to US foreign policy throughout his two-term presidency. He supported the "communist threat" framing of the CIA's overthrows in Iran and Guatemala during his first two years in office, and directed interference in the governmental affairs of other nations including Costa Rica, Syria, Jordan, Egypt, and Indonesia.[232] Eisenhower's memoir, *Waging Peace*, does not mention the CIA's election tampering in Lebanon that precipitated their civil war (chapter 1), but does state his "deep-seated conviction that the communists were principally responsible for the trouble."

Cold War or not, however, Eisenhower openly resisted the forces promoting a continuous stream of new weapons programs and Pentagon pork that had become entrenched in Washington during the Truman era. Ever the "Old General," his knowledge of the military afforded him an uncommon understanding of the Pentagon's ways and provided ballast for his resistance to military and congressional demands.

When the newly elected Eisenhower moved to cut $5 billion from Air Force appropriations in 1953, militarists countered with strident warnings that the US was falling behind the Soviet's air power—the so-called Bomber Gap. Similarly, Eisenhower's move to rein in the Nike-Hercules and Nike-Zeus missile projects elicited cries that a Missile Gap would leave the nation vulnerable to superior Soviet capabilities. In truth, both the Gaps were non-existent. A Bomber Gap *did* exist—in the United States' *favor*. And in 1961, Defense Secretary Robert McNamara conclusively dismissed the Missile Gap as an illusion.[233] Following the Truman era's persistent inflation of military budgets, only Eisenhower's firm and seasoned resistance prevented further peacetime expansion of the war industries.

Waging Peace

Given Eisenhower's extensive military background and demonstrated commitment to Cold War principles, it is somewhat paradoxical that his ultimate aspiration as president became the promotion of world peace—specifically striving for a level of Soviet détente capable of yielding a nuclear test ban treaty. Eisenhower joined Soviet Premier Nikita Khrushchev at a Geneva conference in 1955 and the two met again at Camp David in September 1959. Khrushchev's memoirs relate a conversation that took place during an informal walk around the grounds of the presidential retreat:

> "Tell me, Mr. Khrushchev, how do you decide the question of funds for military expenses?" Then, before I had a chance to say anything, he said, "Perhaps first I should tell you how it is with us.... It's like this. My military leaders come to me and say, 'Mr. President, we need such and such a sum for such and such a program.' I say, 'Sorry, we don't have the funds.' They say, 'We have reliable information that the Soviet Union has already allocated funds for their own such program. Therefore if we don't get the funds we need, we'll fall behind the Soviet Union.' So I give in. That's how they wring money out of me. They keep grabbing for more and I keep giving it to them. Now tell me, how is it with you?"

> "It's just the same. Some people from our military department come and say, 'Comrade Khrushchev, look at this! The Americans are developing such and such a system. We could develop the same system, but it would cost such and such'... and I end up giving them the money they ask for."

> "Yes," he said, "that's what I thought. You know, we really should come to some sort of an agreement in order to stop this fruitless, really wasteful rivalry."

"I'd like to do that. Part of my reason for coming here was to see if some sort of an agreement would come out of these meetings and conversations."[234]

It appears that an understanding was evolving between the two leaders. Although a nuclear test ban treaty remained elusive at Camp David, Khrushchev's visit did yield a plan for a Paris Peace Summit slated to begin on May 16, 1960. Khrushchev also invited Eisenhower to visit Moscow after the Paris Summit, in appreciative recognition of the President's Camp David hospitality. The Peace Summit collapsed and the presidential invitation to Moscow was withdrawn, however, following the crash of (Francis) Gary Powers' U-2 spy plane deep inside the Soviet Union on May 1, 1960.

COLD WAR RECONNAISSANCE

The CIA's aerial surveillance operations began with camera-toting balloons riding high altitude winds over the Soviet Union in the early 1950s. The CIA then developed a single-engine, solo-piloted aircraft capable of flight altitudes exceeding the reach of Soviet air defenses. Débuted in 1955, the Utility-2, or U-2, as it came to be known, was essentially a powered glider with cameras.

From the inception of U-2 operations, Eisenhower was wary of Soviet overflight maneuvers. He insisted that any Air Force involvement was to be concealed, and that knowledge of the program be confined to a tight circle.[235] But there were other concerns: Two monitoring groups were advising Eisenhower of CIA Director Allen Dulles' poor administrative abilities and weak governance of the CIA.[236] Given these concerns, Eisenhower began directly supervising the U-2 program himself, and authorized the first Soviet overflights in July 1956.

Initial flights returned impressively detailed photographs of Soviet industrial regions, but they also earned angry Soviet protests. Uneasy about the Soviet reaction, Eisenhower indefinitely suspended overflight operations, despite CIA requests for more flights.[237]

In August 1957, the Soviets tested the first intercontinental ballistic missile (ICBM), and put the first man-made satellite, *Sputnik*, into orbit. In Washington, these achievements elicited another round of Missile Gap pronouncements. With militarists clamoring for funding and sounding alarms over Soviet military developments, Eisenhower sent the U-2 soaring back into Soviet airspace. New photographs confirmed his suspicion that the Missile Gap claims were counterfeit, but the ultra-secret nature of this intelligence prevented him from publicly dismissing the alarmists. Armed with this knowledge and the strength of his legendary military acumen, however, the Old General simply refused demands for further escalation of US missile capacity.

Richard Bissell, a CIA deputy director to whom Dulles had delegated the U-2 program, requested permission for more Soviet overflights late in 1957. Eisenhower refused, even as further appeals came from State Secretary JF Dulles and Joint Chiefs of Staff Chair General Nathan Twining in January 1958.

A violation of Soviet airspace that Eisenhower had not authorized resulted in protests from the Soviet Embassy on March 6, 1958. Perturbed, the President nevertheless acceded to more overflights that spring, earning another Soviet protest on April 21.[238] And so it went, with Eisenhower continually balancing the value of the overflights' intelligence with their risk of diplomatic turbulence.

The approach of the Paris Peace Summit prompted an extended curtailment of U-2 operations during 1959. Despite the President's focus on the Peace Summit during this period, the CIA and the Pentagon repeatedly requested more U-2 missions. Under continued pressure, especially from Dulles and Twining, Eisenhower finally issued an authorization that resulted in an overflight on April 9, 1960.

Khrushchev and the Central Committee of the Soviet Communist Party were highly agitated over the April 9 overflight. But since all prior objections had come to no avail, the Kremlin declined to issue yet another diplomatic protest. In the silence, Allen Dulles urgently appealed for another mission, citing Soviet ICBM activities he deemed to be in a critical window of observability. Thus, Dulles used the CIA's own analysis of Soviet missile developments to override all other concerns—including the imminent Paris Peace Summit.[239]

Eisenhower relented; however, he set April 25 as a deadline. But CIA reports of bad weather conditions then resulted in repeated delays, causing the President to set Sunday, May 1 as the absolute last day an overflight was authorized. Unprecedented revisions in flight protocol would make this last overflight unlike any of the 23 Soviet missions undertaken since the U-2 program's inception.

THE LAST SOVIET MISSION

Stationed at Incirlik Air Base in Turkey, the hub of soviet overflight operations, Gary Powers was assigned to pilot the next flight. As his flight was repeatedly postponed by CIA weather reports, Powers took comfort in the fact that he would be flying the best U-2 in service at that time. A departure from established routine, however, resulted in the grounding of that plane.[240]

To Powers' consternation, U-2 Number 360 arrived as a substitute. Each U-2 was a custom-made aircraft, and Powers described 360 as a "dog," known to exhibit one malfunction after another. Its most recent problem was that one of its fuel tanks would sometimes fail to dispense its contents.[241]

Powers had good reason to be concerned about 360's unreliability: For the first time in four years of overflight operations, Powers' flight plan called for a transcontinental, 3,800 mile tour, winding all the way across the Soviet Union to a final destination near Bodø, Norway.

True to its reputation, 360 developed a new problem on Powers' flight: its auto-pilot failed. This was no minor complication.[242] Had the auto-pilot given out earlier in his mission, Powers later said he would have turned back. However, calculating that he was already 1,300 miles inside the Soviet Union, Powers held course.

Despite the CIA's weather forecast, a persistent cloud cover complicated Powers' navigation. With an uneasy eye on potential fuel tank problems and the extra effort necessary for navigation, flying without the auto-pilot meant that Powers' attention was now completely occupied with all the details of piloting the aircraft. Soaring into airspace over the industrial area of Sverdlovsk (now Yekaterinburg), the tragic moment arrived:

> ...suddenly, there was a dull "thump," the aircraft jerked forward, and a tremendous orange flash lit the cockpit and sky... Knocked back in the seat, I said, "My God, I've had it now!" ... Now the nose, very slowly, started to go down. ... I knew then I had no control of the aircraft.[243]

Powers' plane sustained critical damage from the near-miss explosion of a Soviet surface-to-air missile.[244] (Soviet MiG fighter jets were in the Sverdlovsk airspace as Powers approached, but could not reach the U-2 cruising three miles above their 55,000-foot service ceiling.) The spy plane broke up, becoming a wingless fuselage plunging tail-first to Earth. The g-force pinned Powers to the cockpit control panel. Unable to deploy the plane's self-destruct charge, Powers broke free of the wreckage and parachuted to safety.

Managing the Aftermath

As Eisenhower described in *Waging Peace*, on the morning following Powers' crash, Staff Secretary General Goodpaster entered the Oval Office and announced,

> Mr. President, I have received word from the CIA that the U-2 reconnaissance plane I mentioned yesterday is still missing. The pilot reported an engine flameout [engine stall] at a position about 1,300 miles inside Russia and has not been heard from since. With the amount of fuel he had on board, there is not a chance of his still being aloft.[245]

The CIA information was both dishonest and deceptive.

Soviet radar installations had been tracking Powers throughout his flight, and in Washington, the National Security Agency was following Powers' flight by, in effect, watching the Soviet's radar screens.[246] NSA operators saw missiles in the airspace near Powers' plane over Sverdlovsk, just before the U-2 suddenly disappeared from Soviet radar screens. And for this particular flight, Bissell had requested that the NSA's Soviet radar intelligence be sent directly to him at the CIA.[247]

So the CIA knew that Powers had crashed at Sverdlovsk on Sunday, yet this critical intelligence was not conveyed to the President on Monday morning; he received only the vague statement that there was not a chance that Powers was still airborne.

Furthermore, the engine flameout story itself is a CIA fabrication. Contrary to what Eisenhower was told, there has never been any evidence that Powers attempted radio communication during the mishap. Dulles himself was disseminating these fictions. Later, in testimony to the Senate Foreign Relations Committee, Dulles stated Powers had reported engine trouble and that this trouble was the cause of his mishap.[248]

Immediately following Powers' crash, there was no Soviet statement regarding the missing U-2. In the silence, a cover story, pre-approved and on file for just such an emergency, was released on Monday, May 2.[249] The publication of this fictitious cover story would prove to be a devastating and irreversible error.

KHRUSHCHEV RESPONDS

Matters became more complicated on Thursday, May 5, when Khrushchev announced to the 1,300 delegates of the Supreme Soviet (parliament) that a spy plane had been shot down. On the strength of Allen Dulles' assurance that a U-2 pilot would never survive a crash, Eisenhower and his advisors assumed that at worst, the Soviets were in possession of some plane wreckage and a dead pilot; the original cover story was maintained.[250]

On Saturday, May 7, the U-2 incident became an international conflagration when Khrushchev announced to the Supreme Soviet, "... we have the remains of the plane—and we also have the pilot, who is quite alive and kicking!" Furthermore, Khrushchev contended that Soviet ground radar recordings provided incontestable evidence of spying.[251] Suddenly, the Eisenhower administration's cover story was glaringly exposed as a deliberate fabrication.

The President, who had only days earlier been steering his administration toward a climactic Peace Summit as the crowning achievement of his presidency, soon found himself fending off a congressional investigation into the most damaging foreign policy event of his entire career. Visions of détente evaporated as the Paris Summit collapsed and the presidential invitation to Moscow was retracted.

As the debacle continued to unfold, the specific nature of Eisenhower's role in the U-2 program came under intense scrutiny. When the Senate Foreign Relations Committee convened behind closed, guarded doors on May 27, the administration's worst fears were realized when Cabinet members were drilled with specific questions regarding Eisenhower's personal role in the overflight program—a secret that was not to be disclosed. To a man, the Cabinet stood foursquare.[252] State Secretary Herter, for one, carefully chose statements during his six-hour testimony that absolved the President of direct responsibility.

EISENHOWER FLYING BLIND

The CIA had promoted a misunderstanding that the U-2's self-destruct charge would ensure that no incriminating evidence would ever survive a crash. The explosive charge was, in fact, not powerful enough to destroy even the cameras it was attached to, let alone render the entire plane unrecognizable as a US intelligence asset.[253]

Far surpassing the plane's identity, however, the most incriminating evidence in the event of a crash would be a live pilot. The CIA had steadfastly maintained that a U-2 pilot would never survive a mishap— Dulles had repeatedly stated that this was the case.[254]

Confusion over the self-destruct and live pilot issues extended all the way to the Oval Office. In a conversation with CIA Director John McCone four years later, Eisenhower stated that both Bissell and Dulles had assured him that there was no chance a U-2 pilot would survive a hostile mishap.[255] While these issues complicated the President's analysis and management of the U-2 Affair, he had also been deprived of CIA intelligence that could have avoided the Affair entirely.

In August 1959, a top-secret CIA report detailed the U-2's vulnerability to recent advances in Soviet surface-to-air missile (SAM) technology.[256] This report chronicled the Soviets' development of the SA-2 Guideline, an upgraded SAM that could reach up to 70,000 feet— the ceiling of the U-2's operating range. Debuted in 1957, these SA-2s were protecting military and industrial areas throughout the Soviet Union by 1960—including the missile battery in Sverdlovsk that the CIA's flight plan guided Powers over on May 1.

Eisenhower never saw the CIA's SA-2 report. Instead, he was continuously reassured of the U-2's high-altitude impunity. In *Waging Peace*, Eisenhower discusses his perennial concern over the U-2's vulnerability to Soviet defensive missiles, stating,

> ...each time a new series of flights was proposed, we held a closed meeting to determine whether or not new information on developing technology might indicate the unwisdom of proceeding as before.[257]

Eisenhower was excluded from the intelligence epicenter of the U-2 program, where Soviet SAM developments and the critical details of Powers' mishap were known. Specific actions and inactions of the Dulles CIA maneuvered Eisenhower into a trap that destroyed his expanding rapport with Premier Khrushchev and eliminated the possibility of peace between the superpowers at that time. Within a year, the new President Kennedy would have a similar experience.

THE CIA ENCOUNTERS JFK

President Kennedy, as the enormity of the Bay of Pigs disaster came home to him, said to one of the highest officials of his Administration that he wanted "to splinter the CIA in a thousand pieces and scatter it to the winds."

New York Times
April 25, 1966

THE CUBAN REVOLUTION

Following the Spanish-American War (chapter 3), US foreign policy supported generations of strong-arm rulers in Cuba, the last of which was Fulgencio Batista, who seized power in a 1952 military coup.[258] Facilitation of the Mafia's control of Havana's racetracks, casinos, and brothels brought Batista a personal fortune through kickbacks, rake-offs, and unscrupulous profiteering.[259] Batista deployed his US-supplied military power against outbreaks of discontent such as worker strikes and student protests, and political opponents were hounded off the island or executed. This violent repression left the island ripe for revolution, and one came to life.

Fidel Castro's revolutionaries had occupied the Sierra Maestra Mountains at the eastern end of the island since 1957. Determined to oust the Batista government, they began a 600-mile march to Havana in August 1958. With the Cuban military and a majority of the populace opposing Batista's regime, the advancing revolutionary forces encountered little resistance. Batista fled the island on New Year's Day, 1959, as Castro arrived triumphant in Havana.

Residing in Mexico in the 1950s, Castro had observed the CIA's overthrow of President Arbenz and the termination of Guatemala's democracy. Castro's fellow revolutionary, the Argentine physician Ernesto "Che" Guevara, was living in Guatemala at that time, and had witnessed the Arbenz overthrow in person. Thus, Castro and his inner circle regarded the United States with an apprehension that was anchored in a history of oppressive and anti-democratic US foreign policy in the region.[260]

Castro and Guevara felt compelled to resort to extreme measures to avoid Guatemala's fate. Their efforts included the brutal repression of any semblance of the old Batista regime. Hundreds of Batista's officials and soldiers were rounded up, tried by revolutionary tribunals, and either executed or imprisoned under long sentences. The Washington establishment took a dim view of these developments. State Department advisor William Wieland once lamented, "I know Batista is considered by many as a son of a bitch . . . but American interests come first . . . at least he was *our* son of a bitch."[261]

CUBAN UNIFICATION BEHIND CASTRO

During Castro's first years as premier, US-attributed acts of terrorism on Cuban soil enflamed anti-US sentiment, which was already running high on horrific memories of the Batista era. On October 21, 1959, a US-backed gunship raid on Havana killed two and wounded dozens. A general strike was called and thousands attended anti-US demonstrations at the US Embassy in Havana. US Ambassador Philip Bonsal issued a statement of sympathy for the victims and their families and a promise to "investigate fully any possible infraction of the United States laws in connection with such flights."[262] But the Ambassador's apologies and other attempts to maintain Washington's innocence soon became transparently deceitful.

A US plane fire-bombing Cuban sugar mills exploded over the island in February 1960—an event that closely followed several other aerial raids.[263] Even with two dead USAF pilots on the ground, a blather of regrets and promises to investigate continued to emanate from Washington and Ambassador Bonsal.

While offloading Belgian armaments in Havana on March 4, 1960, unexplained explosions aboard the French freighter *La Coubre* killed scores and wounded hundreds. Castro denounced what he believed to be another act of US terrorism. Despite enduring questions regarding the actual cause of the explosions, the incident fit the pattern of other recent events. So particularly for Cubans, the United States was the primary suspect. All of these events increased anti-US animosity and united Cubans behind the Castro government. Cubans felt they needed protection from Washington's aggressions.

Anticipating further United States' hostilities, Castro pursued an alliance with the only nation capable of countering US aggression: the

Soviet Union. In turn, Washington's Cold War paranoia was confirmed as Cuba drifted into the Soviet sphere. In a spiral of intensifying conflict, Washington sounded the "communist takeover" alarm and imposed a complete embargo. This, in turn, forced Castro into further reliance on the Soviet Union.

Then in January 1961, Castro's demand for an abrupt and drastic reduction in personnel at the US Embassy in Havana resulted in Washington's immediate severance of diplomatic ties. Thus, on the eve of John F. Kennedy's presidential inauguration, a consensus had developed within Washington's foreign policy establishment that Castro had to go.

COUNTER-REVOLUTION

As early as March 10, 1959, removing Castro from power was on the National Security Council's agenda. That fall, President Eisenhower gave general approval for a covert CIA program to support Cuban dissidents opposing Castro, including raids launched from US territory.[264] Allen Dulles had rewarded Richard Bissell's command of the U-2 program with a promotion to the CIA's number two position, deputy director of plans (a euphemism for chief of covert operations). Bissell was given overall responsibility for the planning and execution of the Cuban operation.

What began as a $4 million covert infiltration project was eventually transformed into a $46 million endeavor involving operations in several Latin American countries and requiring significant military assistance from the Pentagon. The original concept of guerrilla infiltration was expanded into an amphibious invasion by a Brigade of Cuban exiles who were to secure a beachhead on the island's south shore. There, they would announce the formation of a counter-revolutionary government. The Brigade would rally a Cuban uprising against Castro and then appeal to the United States for support. The end result, in other words, would be a US military invasion of the island justified by an appeal from the exiles' provisional government. During the Eisenhower-Kennedy interregnum, the CIA's new Cuban plan grew to encompass thousands of people in operations scattered from New York to Central America.

(There was an additional aspect of the overall Cuban plan, but under much deeper cover. In December 1959, the agency's highest ranks began discussing Castro's assassination, and covert operations toward this objective began in August 1960.[265])

Keeping Secrets, Stifling Dissent

A CIA report prepared on November 15, 1960 for Bissell's briefing of the president-elect stated that the plan "to secure a beach with airstrip is now seen to be unachievable, except as joint Agency/DOD [Department of Defense] action." A CIA document made public in 2005 indicates that Bissell never informed Kennedy of this analysis. As Kennedy later suspected, Dulles and Bissell assumed that the new President could be panicked into deploying Pentagon forces to rescue the operation during the eleventh hour.[266]

Soon after Kennedy's inauguration, Dulles told him that the exiles' invasion would trigger a great uprising and Castro would quickly tumble.[267] At a March 29 Cabinet meeting, Dulles and Bissell stated that the anti-Castro element on the island had some 20,000 sympathizers and that one fourth of the population would likely rise against the Castro government once the Brigade was settled in.[268] Dulles, especially, had to know this was a lie.

In January 1961, the CIA's own intelligence division had sent Dulles a pessimistic forecast regarding a Cuban uprising, warning that Castro's popularity was strong and rising. British intelligence had also informed the CIA that an uprising was unlikely.[269] The CIA Inspector General's report on the Cuban invasion later stated, "We can confidently assert that the Agency had no intelligence evidence that the Cubans in significant numbers could or would join the invaders . . ."[270] Nevertheless, Dulles and Bissell endeavored to suppress criticism and promote the uprising concept at every turn.

The Plausible Deniability Dilemma

Both Eisenhower and Kennedy were adamant that the hand of the US government never be revealed in the Cuban operation. US involvement was, in Washington jargon, to be plausibly deniable. But despite all efforts, the operation became impossible to conceal in the months leading up to the invasion. Even by the fall of 1960, word had gotten out that the CIA had a heavily guarded base in Guatemala, where it was training Cuban exiles for a Cuban invasion.[271] On October 7, Cuban

Foreign Minister Raúl Roa rose at the United Nations to denounce—with remarkable accuracy—US plans for a Cuban invasion.

Miami was a hotbed of CIA and exile activity. Local newspapers ran photographs of Cubans lined up at CIA recruiting stations, and Floridians flocked to the Opa-Locka air base outside Miami to watch blacked-out planes leaving for Guatemala. Reading one newspaper report, President Kennedy exclaimed to Press Secretary Pierre Salinger, "Castro doesn't need spies in the United States; all he has to do is read the newspapers!"[272]

US government involvement in the Cuban operation became even more evident due to an event that immediately preceded the invasion. Pentagon advisors had continually stressed the necessity of knocking out Castro's air force in advance of the exile Brigade's invasion. Toward this end, Bissell scheduled three separate air strikes originating in Nicaragua, the first of which was to be at dawn, two days before D-day (D-2). Many Cuban planes sustained damage in the D-2 strike, but at least one of the next two strikes would be necessary to disable the rest of Castro's planes.

But due to another D-2 event, the US government's involvement in Cuban affairs was glaringly exposed. Suddenly, plausible denial was a pathetic illusion. This is what happened:

In an effort to dissociate the United States from the D-2 air strikes, Cuban pilot Mario Zuñiga departed from Nicaragua and flew not to Cuba, but to Miami International Airport. Upon landing, Zuñiga announced that he had just defected from Cuba during a widespread insurrection on the island. Reciting lines provided by his CIA handlers, Zuñiga stated that his plane had suffered damage during his attack runs on Cuban military assets and that he was now seeking asylum in the United States. The deception collapsed almost immediately.[273] As Fidel Castro commented, "Even Hollywood would not try to film such a story."

All Kennedy's Fault?

Kennedy cancelled the remaining air strikes, acting on his initial and continuing resolve to conceal Washington's involvement and maintain plausible deniability. This presidential decision became widely, but incorrectly, regarded as the single most critical factor in the overall failure of the invasion—as evident in the title of CIA agent Grayston

Lynch's memoir, *Decision for Disaster*.[274] (The complexity and tragedy of the Cuban exile brigade's failed invasion is recounted in Appendix III, Bay of Pigs.)

The CIA Inspector General's postmortem of the event, however, told a different story. But this report was tightly circulated before CIA officials classified and buried it in their files as a national security concern. Released to the National Security Archive 36 years later, (February 1998), the report stated:

> In evaluating the [CIA's] performance it is essential to avoid grasping immediately, as many persons have done, at the explanation that the President's order canceling the D-Day air strikes was the chief cause of failure. . . . Furthermore, it is essential to keep in mind the possibility that the invasion was doomed in advance, that an initially successful landing by 1,500 men would eventually have been crushed by Castro's combined military resources strengthened by Soviet Bloc-supplied military matériel.[275]

So what *was* the chief cause of failure? The report noted that "there was failure at high levels to concentrate informed, unwavering scrutiny on the project and to apply experienced, unbiased judgment to the menacing situations that developed." As cited above, this was precisely the scrutiny that Dulles and Bissell perennially denigrated or ignored.

It was not National Security that kept the Inspector General's report hidden for decades, but the *CIA's* security. Agent Jack Hawkins (who witnessed the entire Bay of Pigs debacle) wrote in 1998 that the CIA's upper ranks regarded the report as a threat to the agency's very existence. When the Inspector General's report was originally released, an internal CIA memorandum by Deputy Director Charles Cabell stated, "In unfriendly hands, [the report] could become a weapon [used] to attack the entire mission, organization, and functioning of the Agency."[276]

The CIA's secrets and deceptions led Eisenhower and Kennedy into the U-2 and Bay of Pigs calamities. Why? Because the *result* of these events was actually their *purpose*, as intended by the

Dulles CIA.

Following WWII, the Truman administration's establishment of the Cold War Worldview prevented a major contraction of the war-inflated military industries (chapter 4). The perception of an irreconcilable East-West conflict was an essential component of this worldview. The CIA's management of the U-2 and Bay of Pigs events perpetuated the East-West divide by destroying Eisenhower's world peace initiative and setting the new Kennedy presidency on a collision course with the Soviet Union. The Cold War Worldview was sustained by the CIA's efforts; expansion of the war industries continued.

Eisenhower grappled with the CIA's U-2 deceptions for years. It appears that he never learned of the CIA's Soviet SAM intelligence, or the deep deception contained in the CIA's vague Monday morning statement that there was "not a chance of [Powers] still being aloft."

Kennedy was more skeptical. Ninety days in office, even before the Cuban exiles' invasion had collapsed, he recognized the CIA as a threat to his presidential authority, stating, "It's a hell of a way to learn things, but I have learned one thing from this business—that is, that we will have to deal with [the] CIA ... no one has dealt with [the] CIA."[277]

The two chapters that follow chronicle Kennedy's struggle with not only the CIA, but also with the larger military-industrial establishment of which Eisenhower had so articulately warned on his way out of the Oval Office.

CHAPTER NINE

The Kennedy Reelection Promise

*What is needed is ... depth, humanity and a
certain totality of self-forgetfulness and compassion,
not just for individuals but for man as a whole:
a deeper kind of dedication. Maybe Kennedy will break through
into that someday by miracle. But such people are before long marked
out for assassination.*[278]

Thomas Merton
1962

Following the Bay of Pigs debacle, the Joint Chiefs of Staff and the Allen Dulles CIA continued to campaign for pre-emptive action against Cuba and the Soviet Union. Three months after the Bay of Pigs event, for example, Dulles and the Joint Chiefs presented a plan for a series of actions that would escalate international conflict and justify a pre-emptive nuclear attack on the Soviet Union. Appalled, Kennedy walked out of the meeting and ignored the proposal.[279] But Kennedy's commitments to peace and justice continued to conflict with the priorities of Pentagon, CIA, and industrial forces that became aligned against him.

LAOTIAN INDEPENDENCE

Pursuing a communist containment policy, Eisenhower had sent several thousand troops and CIA agents into Laos in the late 1950s. The CIA had installed their hand-picked ruler, Phoumi Nosavan, and the neutralist and nationalistic priorities of the Laotian royal family had landed them in Nosavan's jail. President Kennedy decided to support Laotian neutrality. Eight weeks in office, he countermanded the

Eisenhower policy, calling for an end to Laotian hostilities and announcing a US goal of Laotian independence.[280] Kennedy reached an agreement with Premier Khrushchev and a Laotian Neutrality Declaration was eventually signed in Geneva on July 23, 1962. But this foreign policy success damaged Kennedy's relationship with the CIA and Pentagon establishment, who regarded such diplomacy as surrender to the communists.[281]

Curbing the CIA

Kennedy began reining in the CIA following the Bay of Pigs debacle. Allen Dulles and Richard Bissell were asked to resign, and Kennedy reduced the agency's budget for both 1962 and 1963.[282] More shocking to the entire military-intelligence establishment was Kennedy's National Security Action Memorandum #55 (NSAM 55) of June 28, 1961.[283] Since its inception, the CIA had assumed responsibility for peacetime intelligence and analysis. NSAM 55 abruptly shifted that responsibility to the Joint Chiefs; henceforth, the Pentagon would be the president's principal military advisers in peacetime as well as wartime. Kennedy was enacting his post-Bay of Pigs resolve to "splinter the CIA in a thousand pieces and scatter it to the winds."[284]

The Peace Race Challenge

In a September 1961 United Nations speech, Kennedy further frustrated the military establishment by inviting the Soviet Union to drop the arms race and join the United States in a peace race. Shortly after issuing this challenge, Kennedy received a deeply personal, 26-page letter from Khrushchev, secretly delivered via Press Secretary Pierre Salinger. With this letter, Khrushchev opened a back-channel dialogue that spawned the two world leaders' alliance toward peace. The Superpowers' heads of state were breaking free of the Cold War Worldview. (Khrushchev optimistically regarded Kennedy as a much better statesman than Eisenhower and was especially glad to be rid of JF Dulles.[285])

THE BERLIN CRISIS

At the close of Khrushchev's 1959 visit to Camp David (chapter 8), he and Eisenhower had issued a joint statement agreeing that US-Soviet disagreements, including the problem in Berlin, should be settled through peaceful negotiations, not by the application of force.[286] Unfortunately, these sentiments became a casualty of the U-2 debacle the following May, when further Berlin negotiations collapsed along with the Paris Peace Summit. Tensions in Berlin escalated in June 1961, when the Soviets threatened to end Western access to East Berlin, and President Kennedy responded with an increase in US troop levels. The march toward a standoff continued when East German President Walter Ulbricht began constructing the Berlin Wall on August 13, 1961. Unknown to Kennedy, the Berlin situation was further aggravated by US military mischief the following month.[287]

Pierre Salinger secretly met with a Khrushchev emissary during this time, and was told that the Soviet Premier was feeling intense pressure from the communist bloc to keep pushing Kennedy in Berlin. Khrushchev was in a compromised position; his attempt at peace with Eisenhower had ended in the U-2 Affair, damaging his credibility with Soviet military brass. Nevertheless, Khrushchev was now reaching out to Kennedy, hoping their cooperation could avert a military confrontation.[288] In a scenario prefiguring the Cuban Missile Crisis, back-channel communications enabled Kennedy and Khrushchev to circumvent the hardline components of their respective governments and resolve the crisis.[289] Again, Kennedy's peaceful diplomacy had disappointed those who believed that the proper solution to all such matters was military intervention.

CONFRONTATION WITH BIG STEEL

During the spring of 1962, Kennedy confronted the industrial side of the military-industrial complex. In an effort to counteract inflationary economic pressure, Kennedy personally intervened to broker an agreement between the United Steelworkers and United States Steel Corporation. This agreement traded modest labor benefits for controls on steel prices.

Four days later, labor's concessions in hand, US Steel announced the very price increase they had pledged to postpone, and the other major steel corporations immediately followed suit. The President was livid, stating to his Council of Economic Advisors, "My father always told me that all businessmen were sons-of-bitches, but I never believed it 'til now." (This remark found its way onto the *New York Times*' front-page ten days later.[290])

Kennedy brought the full force of his administration to bear. Within hours, the Defense Department was shifting lucrative steel contracts to minor steel companies that were holding the line on prices, and the Departments of Labor, Justice, and Commerce launched aggressive investigations of major steel corporations. The press was summoned to hear Kennedy speak with what the *New York Times* referred to as cold fury, calling the price increase "an unjustifiable and irresponsible defiance of the public interest."[291] United States Steel rolled back prices within days, but the damage was done. Many believed that the business community would never forgive Kennedy's reprimand of Big Steel.[292]

THE CUBAN MISSILE CRISIS

Khrushchev's memoirs state that the Kremlin was quite certain that the Bay of Pigs invasion was only the beginning, and that "the Americans would not let Cuba alone... unless we did something." Thus, during the summer of 1962, the Kremlin began installing missiles with nuclear warheads in Cuba.[293] This Soviet effort to defend Cuba against US aggression brought Khrushchev and Kennedy into another conflict with the militarists in their respective administrations.

Exposed by U-2 reconnaissance and trans-Atlantic shipping analysis, the Soviet missile deliveries resulted in Pentagon demands for pre-emptive attacks on Cuba. A tape recording of Kennedy's meeting with the Joint Chiefs on October 19, 1962, contains a tirade by Air Force Chief of Staff Curtis LeMay that concluded, "I just don't see any other solution except direct military intervention *right now*."[294] The Navy, Army, and Marine Corps Chiefs all joined LeMay's argument for an attack on Cuba. Kennedy, unyielding, thanked the Chiefs for their opinions. He then ordered a comprehensive Cuban quarantine, and publicly called for the prompt dismantling and withdrawal of nuclear weapons in Cuba.[295]

Despite Kennedy's restraint, the Pentagon ignored the President's authority and initiated belligerent actions against the Soviet Union, launching an intercontinental ballistic missile and sending USAF bombers into Soviet airspace.[296] Furthermore, despite US intelligence indicating that SA-2 missiles were fully operational in Cuba at this time, the CIA continued to send U-2s on Cuban overflight missions—with deadly results.[297] On Saturday, October 27, a U-2 was shot down in Cuban airspace, killing USAF pilot Major Rudolf Anderson.

The downing of Anderson's U-2 brought civilization to the brink of nuclear war. The President was suddenly confronted with a prior National Security Council resolution that any such action required immediate military retaliation.[298] But again, Kennedy refused to be stampeded into war. He turned urgently to the back-channel, dispatching his brother Robert to meet with Soviet Ambassador Anatoly Dobrynin, who relayed the President's desperation to Khrushchev. In his memoir, Khrushchev recalls Robert's message:

> The President is in a grave situation and he does not know how to get out of it. We are under severe stress. . . . Even though the President himself is very much against starting a war over Cuba, an irreversible chain of events could occur against his will. . . . We're spending all day and night at the White House; I don't know how much longer we can hold out against our generals.[299]

Khrushchev, too, was being pressured by Kremlin hardliners, and understood Kennedy's urgency: "I slept on a couch in my office . . . I was ready for alarming news to come any moment."[300] On the back-channel, Kennedy assured Khrushchev that the US would not invade Cuba if the Soviets would remove the Cuban missiles. Their peaceful cooperation expanding, Khrushchev pledged not to invade Turkey in exchange for the removal of the United States' Jupiter missiles from that region.

The White House soon received a report from Atlantic surveillance. Soviet vessels had stopped dead in the water; some had reversed course and were steaming east. The crisis had passed. Kennedy's refusal to activate a military response, combined with Khrushchev's cooperation and retreat, probably saved the lives of millions of people and the nuclear poisoning of the entire planet. Any appreciation of this feat, however, was utterly lost to the military hardliners within the Kennedy administration.[301]

Improving Cuban Relations

In their efforts to free the 1,201 Cuban exiles that Castro imprisoned following the failed Bay of Pigs operation, the Kennedy brothers enlisted New York lawyer James Donovan (who had negotiated the February 1962 release of Gary Powers following the U-2 incident). Over the course of the Cuban negotiations, Castro and Donovan became friends, and their rapport enabled the President to begin seeing Castro in a new light. Whereas both John and Robert Kennedy had been avidly anti-Castro, the President's expanding relationship with Khrushchev enabled him to see a rapprochement opportunity with the Cuban Premier as well.

At the same time Kennedy was considering peaceful coexistence with Castro, however, the CIA's U-2s were crisscrossing the island at twelve-hour intervals and a Cuban exile group known as Alpha 66 was raiding Soviet ships in Cuban ports.[302] Following raids on March 19 and 27, 1963, the President ordered a crackdown. Within a week, Robert Kennedy's Justice Department had seized several Alpha 66 vessels and arrested their paramilitary commandos.[303]

The President's shift toward co-existence with Castro brought him into conflict with the financial sponsor of Alpha 66, the CIA. The curb on the Cuban raids also elicited renewed animosity from the Cuban exile community. The head of the Cuban Revolutionary Council reacted explosively.[304] Thus, in the spring of 1963, Alpha 66, the Cuban Revolutionary Council, and various exile groups in Miami became aligned behind the CIA in opposition to the President.

Blocking Operation Northwoods

Following the CIA's failure to oust or assassinate Castro, the Joint Chiefs proposed their own plan for Cuba. Code-named Operation Northwoods, the Chiefs' plan offered several strategies for what investigative author James Bamford concluded was "a secret and bloody war of terrorism against their own country in order to trick the American public into supporting an ill-conceived war they intended to launch against Cuba."[305]

Among the creative possibilities suggested in the Chiefs' plans were: blowing up a US ship in Guantanamo Bay ("casualty lists in US newspapers would cause a helpful wave of national indignation"); exploding bombs on US soil and using forged documents to substantiate Cuban involvement; attempts to hijack commercial planes or ships that could be attributed to Castro; and a plan to make it appear that communist Cuban MiGs had attacked and destroyed a USAF aircraft over international waters.[306]

The Operation Northwoods plan carried the written approval of every member of the Joint Chiefs of Staff. The JCS chair, Lyman Lemnitzer, presented the plan to both Defense Secretary Robert McNamara and Kennedy's military advisor General Maxwell Taylor. Subsequently, on March 16, 1962, Kennedy informed Lemnitzer that he did not foresee any circumstances that would justify overt military action in Cuba.[307] Nevertheless, Lemnitzer continued pressuring McNamara for approval of a US military intervention in Cuba.[308] Kennedy removed Lemnitzer as JCS chair in September 1962, but the remaining Chiefs continued recommending contrived incidents to justify a US invasion of the island.

THE NUCLEAR TEST BAN TREATY

The deeply personal confrontation with nuclear war that Kennedy and Khrushchev endured through the Cuban Missile Crisis fortified their mutual interest in détente. Kennedy became resolved to terminate nuclear testing worldwide, knowing that Khrushchev would be his ally in this effort. "It seems to me, Mr. President," Khrushchev had written Kennedy the prior December, "that time has come now to put an end once and for all to nuclear tests, to draw a line through such tests."[309]

Kennedy launched a drive to win public and congressional support for a broad peace initiative that included nuclear testing limitations. In a 1963 commencement address at American University, Kennedy asserted that world peace was the most important topic on earth. The speech challenged all prior notions of arms control, advocating a general and complete disarmament and the construction of new institutions of peace which would take the place of arms. Kennedy specifically spoke of a need for a nuclear test ban treaty and announced that joint British-US-Soviet talks would soon address that objective.[310] Khrushchev was ecstatic, pronouncing the American University address "the greatest speech by any American President since Roosevelt."³¹¹ The Kremlin immediately began preparations to host the tripartite talks.

Despite its favorable worldwide reception, Kennedy's test ban initiative faced strong opposition on the home front. The JCS, the CIA, and the Atomic Energy Commission were adamantly opposed. New York governor Nelson Rockefeller denounced the whole idea, and prominent senators suggested that gathering a two-thirds Senate majority to ratify the treaty would be impossible.

Undeterred, Kennedy dispatched (former Ambassador to the Soviet Union) Averell Harriman to Moscow, where a Limited Test Ban Treaty was signed on July 25, 1963. Now focused on Senate ratification, the President took the initiative directly to the People, telling State Secretary Dean Rusk, "That's the only thing that makes any impression to these god-damned senators. . . . They'll move as the country moves."³¹² In a televised address to the nation the next evening, Kennedy announced the test ban treaty as "an important first step; a step toward peace; a step toward reason; a step away from war."

Kennedy told aides that he was determined to win the battle for ratification, even if it cost him the 1964 election. But, sweeping western states on a speaking tour in September 1963, Kennedy discovered that any mention of the test ban treaty elicited not resistance but enthusiasm. Even a crowd at the Mormon Tabernacle—a reported bastion of conservatism—gave Kennedy's ratification pitch a five-minute standing ovation.³¹³

Kennedy's earlier forecast that the country would move the Senate came to pass. With the electorate polling at 80 percent approval, the Senate ratified the Limited Test Ban Treaty on September 24, 1963, exceeding the two-thirds majority requirement by 14 votes.³¹⁴

In the fall of 1963, Kennedy's domestic policies and peace initiatives were gathering widespread support and he seemed assured of a second term in office. But he had been a disappointment to Big Business and militarist hardliners. The following chapter examines Kennedy's final confrontation with the military-industrial complex: the simmering conflict in Southeast Asia.

CHAPTER TEN

A Final Peace Initiative: Vietnam

*Any intelligent fool can make things bigger,
more complex, and more violent. It takes a touch of genius—
and a lot of courage—to move in the opposite direction.*[315]

E.F. Schumacher
1973

THE FRENCH OCCUPATION

The French had been overlords of Vietnam since the 1880s, but were displaced by the Germans in WWII. Following the war, the French returned and re-established themselves in Saigon, but by then, a Vietnamese independence movement was underway, led by Hồ Chi Minh in Hanoi. In an effort to regain colonial control, the French initiated a war against the Vietnamese independence movement.

The United States was a signatory of the 1941 Atlantic Charter, which announced the right of all peoples to independence and self-determination. Knowing this, Hồ was optimistic that the United States would support the Vietnamese independence movement against the French. Hồ sent eight letters to President Truman over the five months following the French reinvasion, informing him that the situation was dire. Two million Vietnamese had died of starvation while the French seized and guarded stockpiles of rice. Truman never even acknowledged Hồ's letters.[316] Why not?

Despite Hồ Chi Minh's close cooperation with the US Office of Strategic Services, his allegiance to the US during WWII, and non-existent relations with the Soviet Union, the Truman administration branded him a tool of international communism.[317] Dean Acheson's 1947 rotten apple argument now became the domino theory, framing events in Vietnam as crucial to the fate of the entire region. But perhaps communism was not the real or only issue.

A congressional study during this time concluded that Indochina's rice, rubber, coal, and iron ore resources made it a strategic key to the rest of Southeast Asia.[318] So in Vietnam, international communism was once again discovered in the company of valuable natural resources. And in Washington's foreign policy circles, the Atlantic Charter's guarantee of national self-determination nearly always took a back seat to US corporations' access to global natural resources.

In a quiet renunciation of Atlantic Charter principles, the Truman administration began unsparing support of the French. By April 1954, the US was bearing 78 percent of the cost of France's war against Vietnam's independence movement. The *New York Times* reported that French troops in Vietnam as well as the Cambodian and Laotian national armies were being supplied with US weapons.[319] Evidently, Southeast Asia was becoming a cash cow for US armaments industries. The cow was in danger of drying up, however, because peace in Indochina was on the agenda of an upcoming Geneva conference.

The 1954 Geneva conference's final declaration (the Geneva Accords) supported Vietnam's independence from France and called for a nationwide, Vietnamese election. The United States was the only nation refusing to sign the Geneva Accords.[320] Moreover, State Secretary JF Dulles and other militarist voices began advocating direct military intervention in the event the French were to give up—as they soon did. Following a protracted battle at Dien Bien Phu, the French were defeated and withdrew in May 1954, providing an opening for Dulles' agenda of US military involvement. Hồ Chi Minh was now an official enemy of the United States.

THE US TAKES OVER

When the Geneva Accords bisected Vietnam at the 17th parallel, the US placed the staunchly Catholic "anti-communist" Ngo Dinh Diem in Saigon as the leader of the predominantly Buddhist population of Vietnam's southern region. (This religious and spiritual mismatch would fester for nine years before exploding.) Unconditionally backed by the US government, Diem established autocratic control. The Defense Department's comprehensive history of the US involvement in

Indochina (the famous *Pentagon Papers*) refers to South Vietnam as "essentially the creation of the United States."[321]

Meanwhile, the future of US war industries remained bright. During and immediately following WWII, Hồ Chí Minh's army had been fully outfitted by the US. So the French and North Vietnamese had been battling each other with US manufactures' wares. Now, Diem's army in South Vietnam would also be equipped with US-manufactured weapons and matériel. The cash cow remained alive and well.

In August 1954 (under Air Force Lieutenant Colonel cover), CIA agent Edward Lansdale arrived in Saigon.[322] Ostensibly called to Southeast Asia to battle communists in *North* Vietnam, Lansdale's team proceeded to destroy the social integrity of *South* Vietnam. Through a covert psychological warfare operation, over one million North Vietnamese were induced to cross the 17th parallel and migrate south toward Saigon and the Mekong Delta. US Navy vessels and the CIA's Civil Air Transport enabled the massive, 1,500-mile migration.[323] It was a recipe for disaster.

By the hundreds of thousands, North Vietnamese arrived in South Vietnam with only meager possessions and were soon destitute. The immigrants became indistinguishable from Hồ Chí Minh's agents that were also known to have infiltrated the south during this time. Even basic communication with locals was challenging, because five different languages were spoken in Vietnam's various regions. This situation eventually led to the common understanding among US troops that the enemy was "anyone who ran."[324]

As the 1955 Geneva-mandated election drew near, all opinions predicted a country-wide landslide for Hồ Chí Minh. Diem's authoritarian control, which now involved manhunts and political re-education camps, was producing widespread resistance.[325] With his popularity declining in step with increasingly harsh rule, Diem brazenly announced that there would be no election. Were it not backed with the threat of US military intervention, Diem's refusal to allow this Geneva-mandated election would most likely have resulted in widespread insurrection, and Hồ's army would have abruptly overrun Saigon.[326]

Diem's autocratic rule did nothing to quell the tide of violence that followed the arrival of the CIA-transferred refugees from the north; the social fabric of South Vietnam slowly descended into a terrifying chaos. As the conflict escalated, large areas of South Vietnam were declared free-fire zones, meaning that *anyone* could be considered an enemy.[327]

Bombs began to fall; the aerial assault was devastating. Eventually, seven million tons of bombs fell on Vietnam—more than twice the total tonnage that fell on all Europe and Asia in WWII. USAF helicopters and fixed-wing aircraft sprayed twenty million gallons of herbicides and defoliants (including dioxin-laced Agent Orange) across Southeast Asia, deeply poisoning a geographic region the size of Massachusetts.[328] And at every turn, the military establishment in Washington advocated military escalation as the best response to the expanding calamity.

By the time the Kennedys were moving into the White House, the United States had been actively engaged in Southeast Asian conflict for over a decade. Immediately pressured by Pentagon advisors advocating military intervention, Kennedy dispatched Democratic Senate Majority Leader Mike Mansfield to Saigon. Mansfield and John Kenneth Galbraith (US Ambassador to India at the time) both advised Kennedy to withdraw from Southeast Asia. Robert Kennedy later told Daniel Ellsberg (of *Pentagon Papers* fame) that his brother became determined not to send ground troops to Vietnam, knowing that the US would be in the same predicament the French had finally broken free of.[329] Carefully negotiating his way through this conflict within his administration, Kennedy occasionally authorized an increase in the number of US advisors or helicopters; however, he steadfastly refused to deploy ground forces.[330]

In the spring of 1963, the simmering conflict between Catholic President Diem and the Vietnamese Buddhist majority began to boil over when (on the eve of the Buddha's birthday) Diem issued an edict against flying religious flags. Buddhists gathered on May 8 outside a government radio station to demand the broadcast of a Buddhist monk's reply to Diem's oppression. The CIA precipitated a full-blown crisis by covertly detonating two powerful explosives in the crowd. Seven demonstrators and a child were killed and over a dozen others were injured.

The CIA set off the bombs just as Diem's provincial security forces arrived on the scene; their surprised commander panicked and authorized the use of percussion grenades to disperse the crowd. This antagonistic action helped to mistakenly convince the Buddhist movement that the Diem government was responsible for the deadly explosions.[331]

On June 11, 1963, in a climate of increasing frustration, a Buddhist monk protested by setting himself on fire in Saigon. The story was headlined around the world, and made more shocking by Diem's sister-in-law, the "Dragon Lady" Madame Nhu, who publicly called the monk's self-immolation a "barbecue," and stated, "Let them burn and we shall clap our hands."[332]

Washington turned against Diem, publicly announcing support of the Buddhists against his government. In reply, Diem called for a complete US withdrawal from South Vietnam. Suddenly, the political landscape underwent a quiet but shattering alteration.

As with Hồ Chí Minh in the postwar era, Diem had outlived his usefulness; his anti-US stance was now an obstacle to those promoting the escalation of US involvement in Vietnam. Whereas US support had enabled Diem to survive a populist-supported military coup in 1960, the new US Ambassador to Vietnam, Henry Cabot Lodge, now facilitated a military coup that deposed and assassinated Diem on November 2, 1963.

President Johnson Sells the War

A persistent myth of the Vietnam War is that President Lyndon Johnson continued Kennedy's Vietnam policy. But records of the executive orders of Kennedy and Johnson now tell a different story.

Kennedy's National Security Action Memorandum (NSAM) 263 of October 11, 1963 ordered the withdrawal of 1,000 US military personnel by the end of 1963, and a nearly complete withdrawal by the end of 1965.[333] Kennedy was pulling out of Vietnam.

Four days after he was sworn in aboard Air Force One, however, President Johnson's NSAM 273 specifically and unilaterally *reversed* Kennedy's October 11 orders.[334] All that was then needed was an incident capable of activating Congress and galvanizing the populace for war. The incident occurred the following year.

In July 1964, the naval destroyer *USS Maddox* was prowling the North Vietnamese coastline. This aggressive posturing was timed to coincide with US-sponsored South Vietnamese raids along this same coastline, creating the impression that the *Maddox* was directing the onshore raids.[335]

The *Maddox* was chased off by North Vietnamese PT (torpedo) boats on August 2, and the front-page of the following day's *New York Times* announced, RED PT BOATS FIRE AT U.S. DESTROYER ON VIETNAM DUTY. The official story was that North Vietnamese torpedoes and shells had been hurled at the *Maddox* in an unprovoked attack. But North Vietnam's action was *not* an unprovoked attack, it was a *reprisal*. As officials in Washington understood, the August 2 attack was launched because the North Vietnamese believed that the *Maddox* was directing the commando raids onshore.

Following the incident, *Maddox* Captain John Herrick suggested that his ship's provocative mission be discontinued. Washington, however, not only ordered Herrick to continue the *Maddox* mission, but also ordered further onshore raids to coincide with *Maddox* maneuvers.[336]

The incident President Johnson used to rally the nation to war was an alleged second North Vietnamese attack on August 4. The record indicates, however, that this second attack never took place. The attack story was based solely on the report of the *Maddox*'s new sonar operator, on duty during the early morning hours of August 4. Whereas the rookie sonarman thought he detected torpedo after torpedo (none of which ever detonated), more seasoned members of the crew believed he had heard only the sound of the Maddox's own propellers.

Following this uncertain incident on a night with virtually zero visibility, Captain Herrick cabled Washington from the scene, "Review of action makes many reported contacts and torpedoes fired appear doubtful. . . . Freak weather effects and overeager sonarman may have accounted for many reports. No actual visual sighting by *Maddox*. Suggest complete evaluation before any further action."[337]

Many in Washington had doubts regarding the alleged Tonkin Gulf attack.[338] Nevertheless, Johnson discarded Herrick's cautions and summoned the press, proclaiming, "My fellow Americans, renewed hostile actions against United States ships on the high seas in the Gulf of Tonkin have today required me to order the military forces of the United States to take action in reply." The Tonkin Gulf deception enabled Johnson to rally the US electorate and extract the Tonkin Gulf Resolution from Congress, which began the escalation of US involvement that became the tragedy of the Vietnam War.

The US intervention in Vietnam was a massive and violent effort to subvert the independence movement of the Vietnamese people, similar to other nationalist and democratic movements that Washington crushed during the early Cold War years (chapters 1, 2, and 5). Over 2.5 million US troops rotated through service in Vietnam. Some 58,000 did not return alive. Approximately 375,000 veterans sustained physical injury and/or persistent psychological suffering; the postwar lives of over 100,000 have ended in suicide.[339] An estimated 2.3 million Vietnamese were slaughtered, the land deeply poisoned for those who survived. US engagements in Southeast Asia transferred some $220 billion ($1.5 trillion in 2010 dollars) from the US Treasury to the military-industrial complex.

THE KENNEDY ASSASSINATION

From the outset, the US citizenry was skeptical of the Warren Commission's Lee Harvey Oswald story. Fifty years on, only one in four or five still subscribe to the Oswald story.[340] And yet, while millions have long sensed the truth of Kennedy's assassination, there has not been a widespread understanding of *why* he was gunned down.

By the fall of 1963, President Kennedy's charismatic leadership was shifting the world away from the Cold War Worldview of irreconcilable conflict, toward a vision of world peace that he and Khrushchev were developing over the back-channel. The success of the nuclear test ban treaty and the electorate's expanding support of Kennedy's peace initiatives made the threat of his 1964 reelection a highly undesirable prospect for the military-industrial interests of war.

In Laos, at the Bay of Pigs, the Berlin Wall, and throughout the Cuban Missile Crisis, Kennedy's knack for diplomatic negotiation had precluded US military engagement—including the pre-emptive nuclear attacks on Cuba and the Soviet Union that his advisors repeatedly advocated. Kennedy had become a guardian of peace and democracy, and therefore the enemy of the powerful forces that were covertly overthrowing democracies and assassinating progressive leaders during this era. But to the power structure that was orchestrating these covert operations and steering US foreign policy in militarist directions, this United States President was the most threatening of all.

Whereas the U-2 Affair had effectively sabotaged Eisenhower's eleventh-hour peace initiative, Kennedy was outmaneuvering the militarists at every turn and gathering strong electoral support in the process. His likely reelection posed a solid and snowballing threat to the militarist establishment whose demonstrated priorities called for the suppression of the very measures Kennedy inspired. In different ways, Diem and Kennedy were both obstructing the war that Washington militarists wanted in Vietnam. Ambassador Lodge had overseen Diem's assassination. The die was cast. For the Vietnam War to unfold, John F. Kennedy had to be stopped.

THE WARREN COMMISSION: A KEY TASK

The seven separate bullet wounds of President Kennedy and Texas Governor John Connally were difficult to explain under the Oswald "lone assassin" story. Eventually, the Warren Commission attributed all seven wounds to what became known as the "magic bullet." In *Breach of Trust—How the Warren Commission Failed the Nation and Why*, Gerald McKnight provides a synopsis of this aspect of the Warren Commission's report:

> According to the report, CE 399 [Warren Commission Exhibit # 399] hit JFK in the back of the neck, then passed through the neck without striking any hard object and emerged at the front of his throat. It then entered Connally in the back of the right armpit and slid along his fifth rib, demolishing four inches of the rib before it exited the chest below the right nipple. The bullet then allegedly struck and shattered the radius of Connally's right wrist, one of the hardest bones in the body, located just above the wrist on the dorsal side, then exited at the base of his palm and entered his left thigh just above the knee. CE 399 then traveled about three inches beneath the surface of the thigh, hit the femur, and deposited a lead fragment on the bone. Sometime later, with a spasm of reverse kinetic energy, it spontaneously exited the hole in Connally's thigh and neatly tucked itself under the mattress of a stretcher parked in a hallway of the Parkland Memorial Hospital that the report asserted was linked to the wounded governor.[341]

An essential element of the magic bullet hypothesis was the *exit* of the bullet from the front of Kennedy's throat, because Oswald was alleged to have shot from *behind* the President's limousine. But at a press conference the afternoon of the assassination, Parkland Dr. Malcolm Perry stated that Kennedy's throat wound was an *entrance* wound (a fact subsequently corroborated by several other Parkland medical staff).[342]

Later testifying to the Warren Commission, Dr. Perry described his initial statement about the entrance wound as "inaccurate." But in 1975, witness Jim Gochenaur told the House Select Committee on Intelligence that his good friend, Dallas Secret Service agent Elmer Moore, had been "ordered to tell Dr. Perry to change his testimony." Agent Moore threatened Dr. Perry "on orders from Washington and Mr. Kelly of the Secret Service Headquarters."[343]

As the Warren Commission's staff council, Arlen Specter (later a US Senator) resolved the problem of the entrance wound in Kennedy's neck by asking the Parkland doctors, "Assuming . . . that the bullet passed through the President's body . . . and exited at a point in the midline of the neck, would the hole which you saw on the President' throat be consistent with an exit point, assuming the factors which [I] have just given you?"[344] The answer to Specter's hypothetical question was, of course, "Yes," and this allowed Specter to put the doctors' apparent retractions on record.

Kennedy's head wounds were a second problem that the Oswald story could not explain. In 1992, *JFK: Conspiracy of Silence* was published by Dr. Charles Crenshaw, who also attended Kennedy at Dallas' Parkland Memorial Hospital. Crenshaw reported that 21 out of 22 members of the Parkland ER staff confirmed that a massive wound was located in the right rear of Kennedy's skull. In the opinion of Crenshaw and other medical professionals, this wound was unquestionable evidence of a *frontal* bullet impact, an impossibility according to the official story which held that Oswald shot from behind the President's limousine.[345]

At Parkland, Dallas Coroner Earl Rose tried to enforce Texas state law that required an autopsy within the state's borders. But Rose was pushed aside by Secret Service agents who took possession of the body, and the autopsy was then managed by US military personnel at Bethesda Naval Hospital in Maryland.

As described by several participants at Bethesda, US Army Generals and Admirals closely supervised the doctors and pathologists who performed the autopsy. When the medical team prepared to examine Kennedy's neck wound, Admiral Calvin Galloway intervened, stating,

"Leave it alone. Don't touch it." Similarly, Admiral George Burkley prevented a close examination of a back wound.[346]

The JFK Records Act of 1992 released a flood of evidence including government documents and sworn testimonies of government agents and Mafiosi kingpins. This information indicates that the CIA was the chief architect of the Kennedy assassination. Insightful volumes have now detailed the complex and intricate plans to terminate the Kennedy Presidency.[347] Nothing was left to chance.[348]

Over the decades since the assassination, independent investigative efforts have increasingly concluded that indeed, the smoke seen rising from the fence behind the famous grassy knoll came from rifle shots that mortally wounded President Kennedy. Those works that still maintain the Oswald story typically ignore or distort information that contradicts it. For example, Vincent Bugliosi's three published works on the Kennedy assassination, including his 1,632-page *Reclaiming History*, do not mention the Parkland doctor's press statements about Kennedy's throat entrance wound or Arlen Specter's solution to that situation. Doctor Crenshaw's revelations are ignored entirely.

The assassination of John F. Kennedy was arguably the most brilliantly executed and audacious political maneuver of the 20th Century. Lee Harvey Oswald's CIA handlers groomed him in such a way that exposure of the Soviet and Cuban connections in his carefully developed background could have ignited international hostilities and precipitated World War III. Recognizing this possibility, Lyndon Johnson moved quickly to dismiss suggestions of a communist plot.[349] Both President Johnson and Robert Kennedy—although political enemies—participated in the Warren Commission's cover-up in order to avoid a superpower confrontation.[350]

Allen Dulles, whom Kennedy had forced out of the CIA two years prior, was Johnson's first pick for the commission to investigate the assassination. Dulles was passed over for the chair, but he did serve on the Warren Commission, where he controlled the roster from which those testifying to the commission were chosen. Dr. Crenshaw was not allowed to testify. Other Parkland medical professionals, including Dr. Perry, were forced to make statements that corroborated the Oswald story, even though they knew them to be false or contrary to their own medical observations.

The US citizenry has been either uninformed or misinformed regarding many national and world events. The following chapter examines the mass communications environment that has enabled these information failures.

Chapter Eleven

News, Propaganda, and US Foreign Policy

*The greatest test of a press system is how it empowers
citizens to monitor the government's war-making powers.
War is the most serious use of state power,
organized sanctioned violence;
how well it is under citizen review and control is not only
a litmus test for the media but for society as a whole.*[351]

Robert W. McChesney
2008

The Advent of Television

Network television news became a staple of US society at the dawn of the Cold War. There were only a few thousand television sets in the United States in 1945, but nearly 90 percent of households owned a television by 1960.[352]

During this era, a symbiotic partnership developed between government officials and network news producers. The stature of the emerging television industry was enhanced by frequent appearances of government officials who lent authority and prestige to the industry's news programs. The Truman administration used this free airtime to promote Cold War perspectives with unchallenged authority.

Early television news was often scripted and sometimes even produced by the military establishment, providing the networks with free news scripts and programming during their lean, startup years. This kind of collaboration shaped the relationship between the government and the television industry for decades.

For example, the Pentagon maintained five camera crews in Vietnam, and distributed several ready-for-TV pro-war stories to the networks weekly. This collaboration was exposed in 1970 when Senator J. William Fulbright[353] (D-AR) published *The Pentagon Propaganda Machine*. Fulbright's book detailed the development of a vast PR apparatus used to sell the public on the Department of Defense, the individual military services, and their budget appropriations. These efforts employed some 2,800 personnel and consumed $27 million in 1969 (over $150 million in 2010 dollars). All manner of pro-military propaganda emanated from this network, with virtually no oversight from any branch of the federal government.[354]

There was little room for journalistic dissent during this era. The networks, dependent on skittish corporate sponsors, required loyalty oaths from their employees and fired suspected leftists. Many reporters and editors fell in line with this new order and became insiders with ready access to government officials. But reporters and editors critical of the military or US foreign policy were sidelined or pushed out of the profession entirely.[355]

The following section discusses the media establishment's treatment of a foreign policy event of the Reagan era. This affair is a case study in the management of public opinion through information dominance, and also demonstrates the establishment's defense of the Beneficent Uncle Sam Worldview. Then, the two sections that follow survey the mass media's coverage of more recent US foreign policy events. The chapter concludes by examining the current state of our mass media and public information environment.

THE CIA-CONTRA AFFAIR

US-NICARAGUAN RELATIONS

When President Franklin Roosevelt's Good Neighbor Policy was ending the US occupation of Nicaragua in 1933, the US established the Nicaraguan National Guard, under the command of Anastasio Somoza. The Guard's violent repression of the masses enabled Somoza to seize the presidency in 1937, and subsequently, his two sons each served terms as president. The Somoza clan's plunder of Nicaragua's natural resources saw their net worth rise to a reported $900 million (over $2.5 billion in 2010 dollars) before the second of the Somoza sons was overthrown by Sandinista revolutionaries in 1979.[356]

The Sandinista government initiated a broad range of reforms to improve the People's standard of living. Meanwhile, in an attempt to oust the Sandinistas and restore the Somoza dynasty, the Reagan administration used the CIA to establish and supply a counterrevolutionary force they named the Contras. In efforts to destabilize the Sandinista government, the Reagan administration began blowing up oil pipelines, mining Nicaraguan seaports, and demolishing agricultural infrastructure.[357]

Between 1982 and 1984, Congress passed three pieces of legislation (collectively known as the Boland Amendment) that restricted US support of the Contras. The Iran-Contra Affair involved one of the Reagan administration's illegal circumventions of the Boland Amendment, and resulted in the criminal convictions of some administration officials.

Although less famous that the Iran-Contra Affair, the CIA-Contra Affair was another Reagan administration maneuver that illegally funneled cash into the Contra endeavor. In this effort, the CIA covertly facilitated the US importation of cocaine, precipitating the crack cocaine epidemic that devastated communities in South Central Los Angeles and elsewhere in the 1980s. During this time, infrequent reports of the CIA's Nicaraguan meddling appeared in *The Nation*, *In These Times*, and *Newsday*; however, these reports were denied or ignored with impunity by the nation's media establishment.[358]

Exposing the CIA-Contra Affair

On August 18, 1996, the *San Jose Mercury News* headlined *Dark Alliance* in the first of a three-part series exposing the CIA-Contra drug operation. The story's author, Gary Webb, was an investigative reporter with several journalistic awards.[359] Initially, *Dark Alliance* was greeted with silence by almost all of the nation's media. The television networks and the *New York Times* ignored the story entirely.[360] The story went viral, however, on the *Mercury News'* award-winning website, igniting protest rallies demanding an official investigation. A nationwide response occurred despite the corporate media's virtual blackout of the story.[361]

Then, in what was later described as one of the most venomous and factually inane assaults on a professional journalist's competence, the corporate media began to respond.[362] On October 1, *Washington Post* writer Howard Kurtz ignored Webb's evidence and attempted to portray the story as a he said-she said controversy. Kurtz stated that some journalists had "been trumpeting a *Mercury News* story that they say links the CIA to drug trafficking in the United States." Kurtz ridiculed Webb's story, stating that it had become "a hot topic" only on the unreliable mediums of the Internet and black talk radio. Attempting to reframe Webb's story as old news, Kurtz stated that Contra involvements in drug trafficking had been acknowledged by the Reagan Administration in the 1980s. Kurtz failed to mention that the *Post* had suppressed and disparaged the very reports that he now claimed were "known."[363]

On October 4, the *Washington Post* ran five articles that denounced Webb's story.[364] CIA AND CRACK: EVIDENCE IS LACKING OF CONTRA-TIED PLOT was one of two front page headlines. The other front page piece was a discussion of "black paranoia," which was claimed to be a factor in the popularity of Webb's story. In some reports, the *Post*'s writers cited statements of Adolfo Calero, a former Coca-Cola concessionaire in Managua. These reports did not mention that Calero was under tight CIA supervision, or that Webb had published a photo of Calero meeting with Contra drug traffickers. Nor was it revealed that California State University professor Dennis Ainsworth believed Calero to be a pathological liar.[365] *Dark Alliance* was anchored in documented evidence including federal grand jury testimony, interviews with guerrilla leaders, confidential FBI and US Drug Enforcement Administration reports, and congressional records. Some of the *Post*'s reporters, however, anchored their criticism of Webb's story in Calero's CIA-supervised statements.

Whereas Webb refused to use unattributed quotes in the *Dark Alliance* series, the *New York Times*' Tim Golden had no such scruples. In a piece entitled THOUGH EVIDENCE IS THIN, TALE OF C.I.A. AND DRUGS HAS A LIFE OF ITS OWN, Golden claimed to have interviewed over two dozen current and former rebels, CIA officers, and narcotics agents. However, all of Golden's sources had one thing in common: anonymity. In reality, Golden's story had no substance whatsoever.[366]

Webb's story was also portrayed as conspiracy theory. In an October 4, 1996 column headlined FINDING THE TRUEST TRUTH, the *Washington Post*'s Donna Britt distorted and mischaracterized Webb's story by attributing claims to Webb that he never made.[367] On November 15, 1996, commentator Andrea Mitchell announced on *NBC News in Depth* that Webb's story was a conspiracy theory that had been spread by talk radio.[368] Some arguments and evidence used to attack Webb bordered on the surreal.[369]

THE CIA INVESTIGATES...ITSELF

C.I.A. CLEARS ITSELF IN CRACK INVESTIGATION announced a *New York Times* headline on December 19, 1997. The absurdity of the CIA investigating itself was outdone by the fact that the CIA's report was not even available for public review.[370] In an article titled C.I.A. SAYS IT HAS FOUND NO LINK BETWEEN ITSELF AND CRACK TRADE, the *New York Times*' Tim Weiner used an anonymous source for comment on the event:

> In a still-secret report, the agency says it has found "no information to indicate that the C.I.A. coordinated or condoned drug trafficking or had dealings with crack dealers," said a Government official who would not allow his name to be used.[371]

Thus, the truth of the CIA-Contra drug connection that *Dark Alliance* exposed was overridden by anonymous quotes, statements of a CIA-controlled pathological liar, and unsubstantiated claims that the CIA had investigated itself and found itself innocent.

Mercury News editor Jerry Ceppos stood behind Webb's *Dark Alliance* series for months. Ceppos protested the *Washington Post*'s attack on Webb and exposed false statements made by the *Los Angeles Times* regarding Webb's story.[372] In the end, however, Ceppos could not bear the sustained attack of the nation's media establishment.

On May 11, 1997, the *Mercury News* published Ceppos' full retreat from the *Dark Alliance* story. The media majors were ecstatic. In four news articles with headlines such as THE MERCURY NEWS COMES CLEAN, the *New York Times* pronounced Ceppos' reversal as the definitive postmortem on Webb's story. Ceppos offered Webb a dead-end transfer to the paper's Cupertino bureau; Webb eventually resigned in frustration.

WEBB FULLY—BUT QUIETLY—VINDICATED

On October 8, 1998, the CIA released a declassified version of their Inspector General's report on Webb's allegations. Following two years of investigation, the CIA chose to release this report one hour after the House Judiciary Committee had issued articles of impeachment against President Clinton.[373] During the media frenzy over Clinton's circumstances, the cover letter and summary of the Inspector General's report was all the media found time to review. The cover letter and summary were consistently flattering to the agency and the media promptly conveyed this perspective to the public. The *body* of the report, however, contained evidence of criminal behavior on the part of the CIA and Vice President GHW Bush.[374] These aspects of the report were not mentioned.

Declassified government reports, congressional investigations, and the details of the Inspector General's report eventually corroborated nearly every detail of the *Dark Alliance* story. The *Los Angeles Times* and the *Chicago Tribune* eventually confirmed Webb's revelations along with the admission that they had failed to detect the truth earlier on.[375] But these meager revelations were insignificant compared to the national attention that the sustained attack on Webb had produced. The author himself eventually became a casualty of the story he exposed. Webb was unable to secure meaningful employment following his *Mercury News* departure and his marriage collapsed under the stress of the ordeal. Alone and broke, his career shattered, Webb took his own life in 2004.[376]

Gary Webb's career is a sad chapter in the history of US journalism. Unfortunately, more recent events indicate that our mass media system remains unable or unwilling to provide accurate and adequate public information regarding significant US foreign policy events.

In recent decades, strategies for maintaining Pentagon budgets have expanded beyond the advocacy of specific weapons programs and become directly involved in the formation of US foreign policy. These policies, in turn, can boost defense budgets and mandate military procurement programs. As evident in the next two sections, the US government's foreign policy apparatus has become increasingly influenced by unelected government officials employing sophisticated propaganda campaigns that have generally been carried by the mass media.

Iraq, 1991

Saddam Hussein: From Ally to Enemy

In November 1979, the Iranian Hostage Crisis (chapter 1) drew world attention to the Ayatollah Khomeini's call for Islamic unification against western powers. In need of Middle Eastern allies, the Carter administration reached out to Iraqi President Saddam Hussein. Eager to cooperate with US interests, Hussein launched a military invasion of Iran in September 1980.

When the Iranians appeared to be gaining the upper hand in 1983, presidential envoy Donald Rumsfeld (then CEO of Searle (chapter 6 and endnote 165)) was dispatched to Baghdad to assure Hussein of the Reagan administration's support.[377] (In 1984, while the United Nations was condemning Hussein's use of chemical weapons against Iranians, Rumsfeld returned to assure Hussein of the United States' full and continuing support.)

The tables turned when Hussein invaded Kuwait on August 2, 1990. In Washington's view, Hussein had suddenly become a dangerous renegade; the full force of the US military would be necessary to restore order in the Middle East.

Selling Military Intervention

The George H. W. (GHW) Bush administration began suggesting a military response to Hussein's Kuwait aggression, but polls indicated majority opposition to such an endeavor. Then a dramatic shift in public opinion coincided with an October 10, 1990 session of a Human Rights Caucus that included the testimony of a 15-year-old Kuwaiti girl identified as Nayirah. With teary and choking emotion, Nayirah stated,

> I volunteered at the al-Addan hospital [in Kuwait City]. While I was there, I saw the Iraqi soldiers come into the hospital with guns. They took the babies out of the incubators, took the incubators, and left the children to die on the cold floor.[378]

Following this introduction, Nayirah's story reverberated through the mass media echo chamber. Excerpts of Nayirah's address ended up on

Larry King Live and the story ran on the Associate Press newswire. President GHW Bush repeatedly referenced Nayirah's story, sternly informing reporters at one press conference ". . . kids in incubators, and they were thrown out of the incubators so that Kuwait could be systematically dismantled!"[379]

"Nayirah," it turned out, was the Kuwaiti Ambassador's daughter, and she had been scripted and theatrically coached by the giant New York public relations firm Hill & Knowlton.[380] Printed handouts supporting the fabricated story had been supplied to the press by Citizens for a Free Kuwait. This organization was actually a front group funded with some $11.9 million of the Kuwaiti Emir's vast oil wealth, $11.8 million of which went to pay Hill and Knowlton fees.[381]

The pro-intervention campaign achieved traction. Within weeks, public opinion shifted radically from majority opposition to 79 percent approval of US military intervention; Congress passed the Persian Gulf War resolution on January 12, 1991. *Seven* senators cited Nayirah's story in their speeches supporting the resolution—which passed by only *three* votes. The exposure of Nayirah's fabricated story could have helped senators recognize the extent to which public opinion was being skillfully manipulated to support military action.[382] So just how and when *was* the charade exposed?

THE TRUTH LEAKS OUT

The Canadian Broadcasting Corporation's December 1991 documentary *To Sell a War* gave the first public account of Hill and Knowlton's Nayirah scam, as well as other GHW Bush administration pre-war deceptions. The *New York Times* first acknowledged the Nayirah story on January 6, 1992. The *Times* piece was not an investigative news article, but rather a guest Op-Ed piece by *Harper's Magazine* President John R. MacArthur.[383] MacArthur's revelations were followed by one article that defended the fabricated story, one article that cited the documented evidence, and three letters to the editor, before the story quietly vanished.

Given the Senate's narrow three-vote margin on the Persian Gulf War resolution, it is very likely that Hill and Knowlton's Nayirah story changed the course of US-Middle East history. Yet the *New York Times* carried a total of only six pieces on this revelation, on back pages, half of which were letters-to-the-editor, before dropping it into oblivion.

IRAQ, 2003

SELLING ANOTHER WAR

The George W. (GW) Bush administration's campaign for the 2003 Iraq invasion engendered the largest anti-war demonstrations in history, including a worldwide protest in which an estimated 15 million people turned out in 60 countries on February 15, 2003. Efforts to mitigate this enormous resistance initially focused on claims that Hussein had stockpiles of weapons of mass destruction—the now-famous WMD and mushroom cloud threats emanating from White House, Pentagon, and Cabinet officials. The media establishment generally relayed the government's claims without question.

For example, Secretary of State Colin Powell's February 5, 2003 speech to the UN Security Council elicited a *New York Times* editorial the following day titled THE CASE AGAINST IRAQ. The tenor of the column was conveyed in its opening line:

> Secretary of State Colin Powell presented the United Nations and a global television audience yesterday with the most powerful case to date that Saddam Hussein stands in defiance of Security Council resolutions and has no intention of revealing or surrendering whatever unconventional weapons he may have.

While the *Times* and other mass media reported Powell's talking points as undisputed truth, independent (non-corporate) media outlets were questioning Powell's claims. *In These Times* editor Joel Bleifuss probed deeper:

> Powell told the world, "Iraq today harbors a deadly terrorist network, headed by Abu Mussab al-Zarqawi, an associate and collaborator of Osama bin Laden and his al-Qaeda lieutenants." This information, Powell said, came from "detainees." But American officials have admitted those very detainees are subjected to torture, raising questions about the reliability of that information.[384]

Bleifuss had it right. As later reported in *The Nation* (another independent publication), nine paragraphs of Powell's UN testimony were derived from information extracted through torture of an alleged al-Qaeda operative.[385]

Eventually, all of the administration's al-Qaeda and WMD allegations were discredited, including Powell's anthrax-waving proclamations before the UN Security Council. In 2014, the pro-war campaign was exposed as a deliberate deception to enable a secret neoconservative agenda of Middle East oil control.[386] But where did all these fabricated notions of WMD and Hussein-al-Qaeda connections come from in the first place?

THE OFFICE OF SPECIAL PLANS

The major source of the disinformation was a Pentagon unit called the Office of Special Plans (OSP), which had been created in September 2002. The Senate Intelligence Committee later reported that most of the administration's intelligence on Iraqi WMD had been manufactured by neoconservative officials in the Office of Special Plans.[387]

The OSP's role in the pro-war campaign began to surface after the Iraq invasion was launched. On July 17, 2003, the British national newspaper, *The Guardian*, published a report on the GW Bush administration's intelligence failures. The report described the OSP as an "ideologically driven network [that] functioned like a shadow government, much of it off the official payroll and beyond congressional oversight."[388]

Beginning January 2004, investigations of independent media source *Mother Jones* resulted in six articles that conveyed OSP revelations, and several independent web sources picked up the story as well.[389] In a *Salon.com* column posted on March 10, 2004, US Air Force Lieutenant Colonel Karen Kwiatkowski, who served in the OSP, described how Washington's policy-intelligence apparatus had been captured by neoconservatives within the OSP.[390]

With various foreign and independent media outlets sounding the alarm, what did the US mass media have to say?

The first *New York Times* article to mention the OSP appeared on May 11, 2003, carrying the title BLIND SPOTS; THE IMPOSSIBLE TASK FOR AMERICA'S SPIES. "Uncovering weapons of mass destruction has always been a tough job," the article's author, William Broad, stated in a leading paragraph. Broad's mention of the OSP was buried three-fourths of the way into his report:

> In last week's *New Yorker* magazine, Seymour M. Hersh argued that the Pentagon's Office of Special Plans led a campaign that distorted the appraisal of Iraqi unconventional weapons and misled the White House. Chief Diane Perry, a spokeswoman for the Defense Department, denied Mr. Hersh's charges. Ms. Perry said the Office of Special Plans does not have its own intelligence agents. "We do not produce intelligence reports," she said.

With this single he said-she said paragraph in his 650-word article, Broad dismisses Hersh's 5,500-word piece—which contained the emerging truth that Broad apparently failed to recognize.[391] Rather than offer any documentation or insight himself, Broad leaves readers with the suggestion that the WMD might eventually be discovered, by concluding, "On Iraq, the jury is still out."

The *Times* next mentioned the OSP a few weeks later on June 5, 2003, in an article by Eric Schmitt titled AFTER THE WAR: PREWAR INTELLIGENCE; AIDE DENIES SHAPING DATA TO JUSTIFY WAR. As the headline indicates, this article was essentially a forum for the administration's denial of evidence that independent journalists were then publishing. The dominant theme of the article was evident in its lead paragraph:

> The Pentagon's top policy adviser [Doug Feith] held an unusual briefing today to rebut accusations that senior civilian policy makers had politicized intelligence to fit their hawkish views on Iraq and to justify war on Saddam Hussein.

The text that followed provided Doug Feith (OSP chief and Undersecretary of Defense for Policy) an uncontested opportunity to refute evidence of the OSP's spurious intelligence. Feith was directly quoted 14 times on these issues, whereas Schmitt's article quoted only anonymous officials to counter Feith's assertions and denials. A typical account read, "One senior official, who said he was skeptical of Mr. Feith's account, was too angry to answer immediately. Another official said simply, 'There was a lot of doublespeak out there.'"

During this same time, *The Nation's* Robert Dreyfus chronicled the relevant history of the OSP, its questionable intelligence sources, and its role in the administration's overall pro-war campaign. Dreyfus revealed bogus WMD assertions and discredited the pre-invasion claim that the Iraqi people would welcome US troops with open arms.[392] The *New York Times* ignored the alarms independent journalists were sounding about the OSP's deceptions, choosing instead to print official talking points that defended the OSP and validated the administration's pro-war fabrications.

MULTIPLE INFORMATION FAILURES

The GW Bush administration's deceptive pro-war campaign was successful. Initially, most citizens opposed intervention, but a three-quarters majority supported the Iraq invasion by the time it began. As with the Nayirah scam, the truth was not disclosed until the war was a *fait accompli*.

Over time, numerous deceptions were uncovered, including the Judith Miller/Valerie Plame/Nigerian yellowcake scandal, the Jeff Gannon/Talon News fraud, Phil Donahue's termination from MSNBC for inviting anti-war guests on his show, and the relentless pronouncements of (non-existent) WMD from Dick Cheney, Donald Rumsfeld, and National Security Advisor Condoleezza Rice. Analyzing this phase of reporting in the *New York Times* and the *Washington Post*, Robert McChesney observes:

> Each newspaper implicitly acknowledged its role in leading the nation to war on bogus grounds, yet neither explicitly took responsibility. The confessions were halting and unenthusiastic... It was difficult to avoid [media analyst] Danny Schechter's conclusion that the mainstream press made minimum concessions on its Iraq coverage as a form of damage control. It had no interest in laying out the whole truth.[393]

When McChesney's litmus test (this chapter's epigraph) is applied to the 1991 and 2003 Iraq invasions, a serious failure of our nation's mass media is unmistakable. Strong public resistance to the 2003 invasion was derailed by a mass media system that obediently relayed the government's pro-war deceptions. Independent journalists who were exposing the true nature of these events were discredited or ignored by the corporate media. The militarized violence enabled by these information failures has now wasted large tracts of land in foreign nations and cost over a million human lives. This has all been carried out in our name, with our tax dollars.

Democracy requires an informed electorate, and the chief source of most citizen's information is the mass media. The character and quality of this system is examined in the following chapter.

CHAPTER TWELVE

United States Mass Media

The revolution in communication . . . makes the press, the [broadcast media], and other opinion-forming instruments far more important in the political process than ever before. Both press and [broadcast media] are, after all, "big business," and even when they possess the highest integrity, they are the prisoners of their own beliefs.

United States Congress
Temporary National Economic Committee
1940

Corporations are the predominant purveyors of public information in the United States. Mergers and acquisitions in recent decades have reduced the number of players and increased their size.

In radio, for example, the national ownership limit of 40 stations was eliminated by the 1996 Telecommunications Act, allowing Clear Channel Communications to acquire hundreds of stations nationwide. These stations were then stripped of local content, and fed generic, national programming that eventually allowed over 1,200 stations to be operated with only 200 employees.

Clear Channel's elimination of journalistic overhead and increased emphasis on advertising resulted in terrific profit margins—and also brought unprecedented programming and editorial control to radio. For example, the corporation removed the Dixie Chicks from station playlists following the group's mild disparagement of President GW Bush in 2003.[394] But when rock star Ted Nugent referred to the Obama administration as "vile," "evil," and "America-hating" in 2010, Nugent was given Clear Channel air time to defend his remarks.[395]

Together, Clear Channel and Viacom's Infinity are now larger than the next 23 firms combined. Other media sectors are now similarly concentrated, including television networks, cable systems and channels, music, book and magazine publishing, motion pictures, and newspapers.[396] So a small group of corporations dominate the US public information landscape. And as with all corporate ventures, the supreme objective of these entities is profit—*not* public information. The next sections discuss some ramifications of this corporate information dominance.

Corporate Television

Television in the United States is an almost entirely commercial enterprise, dominated by six conglomerates: Disney, Comcast, CBS, Time Warner, Viacom, and Rupert Murdock's News Corporation.[397] Broadcast networks' profits derive from paid advertising, and the networks tailor their programming to attract and retain their advertisers. The networks' programming can also be influenced by board interlocks that give corporations from other industries a voice in network policies and operations.

Despite the proliferation of new viewing platforms, the average US citizen still watches five hours of television a day. Watching television is the principal means by which many people interact with the world. Prior to the Internet, the propaganda and disinformation potential of television was unique and unprecedented.[398]

The current mass media system has been established as the foremost voice of news and information authority.[399] As discussed below, the social and political power of this information dominance is demonstrated through 1) the amplification of selected issues beyond any sense of public importance, 2) the systematic suppression of selected topics and events that *are* important to our society and our world, and 3) the framing and spin of editorial control.

Amplifying Some Voices, Ignoring Others

Renouncing corporate economic globalization and proclaiming *Another World is Possible*, the inaugural session of the World Social Forum drew 12,000 participants to Porto Alegre, Brazil in 2001, and by 2005, attendance had swollen twelve-fold to 155,000. The 2001 Forum was completely ignored by the *New York Times,* and the single *Times* article that mentioned the 2005 Forum focused exclusively on the controversial presidency of Brazil's Luiz Inácio Lula da Silva, with no mention of the Forum's global reform agenda or astounding attendance numbers.[400]

Here at home, the inaugural session of the United States Social Forum drew 15,000 progressives and civil rights activists to Atlanta in 2007—another civil society event that was completely ignored by the *New York Times.* That same year, however, when 2,500 of the planet's wealthy and politically connected gathered for the World Economic Forum in Davos, Switzerland, the *Times* featured or mentioned this Elite event in over 70 articles.

When the second session of the US Social Forum drew 18,000 people to Detroit in 2010, no major newspaper outside of Michigan mentioned the event. Not a single story ran on the Associated Press newswire. *Democracy Now!* host Amy Goodman mentioned the Forum as a guest on John King's CNN show, but the only other broadcast mention of the event came from Fox News' Glenn Beck. Beck warned viewers about "socialists and communists coming out of the woodwork to co-opt the youth and spread a dangerous disease."[401] When Tea Partiers showed up for a 2010 Convention in Nashville, however, it was big news.

The same corporate media outlets that completely ignored 18,000 progressive activists at the US Social Forum showered attention on 600 Tea Partiers in Nashville. The Tea Party event garnered 12 mentions in the *Washington Post,* 7 in the *Los Angeles Times,* 27 on *Fox News,* 19 on *MSNBC,* and a remarkable 71 mentions on *CNN.*[402] With front-page headlines such as LIGHTING A FUSE FOR REBELLION ON THE RIGHT and descriptions such as "a coming together for the conservative grassroots groups," the *New York Times* portrayed the Tea Party as a pervasive grassroots movement.[403] It was not.

A 2010 study by the *Christian Science Monitor* and the social analysis group Patchwork Nation concluded the Tea Party phenomenon was not a national movement as portrayed in the corporate mass media. Another Patchwork Nation study estimated that Tea Party membership constituted three hundredths of one percent of the US electorate at that time. Two Tea Party conventions scheduled in the fall of 2010 were cancelled due to dismal registration numbers. It took heavy promotion over the Fox network and the star power of Sarah

Palin to prompt a turnout at a Washington DC Tea Party rally in August 2010.[404]

While Tea Party events have been unjustifiably portrayed as part of a larger grassroots movement, the corporate mass media have been reluctant to recognize the *genuine* grassroots movements behind many populist events. For example, the WTO Ministerial Conferences in Seattle (1999) and Cancun (2003) attracted tens of thousands of protesters. However, no news feature of the *New York Times, Washington Post, Fox News,* or *MSNBC* portrayed those protests as part of a broader social movement.[405] Instead, the corporate media focused on a tiny minority of violent activists, which allowed these large and diverse crowds to be portrayed as dangerous fringe elements. The mass media generally ignored the core issue that was rousing protests worldwide: corporate economic domination.

Even huge crowds can fail to evoke a response from the corporate media. Over 100,000 citizens turned out in Washington DC for the 2009 National Equality March supporting sexual minorities' civil rights, but the event was largely ignored in the mass media. The 2011 Occupy Wall Street demonstrations were initially overlooked, receiving corporate media attention only when pepper-spraying and mass arrests began providing sensational news hooks.[406]

The corporate media has also ignored or downplayed stories and entire issue areas that threaten Elite power. For example, an exposé in *The Nation* broke the story of the American Legislative Exchange Council's leaked documents in 2011, and other independents including *In These Times* and *Democracy Now!* soon relayed the story. The *New York Times*, meanwhile, relayed none of this news.[407]

It was not until ALEC was widely exposed in connection with Stand Your Ground laws (implicated in the Trayvon Martin killing) that the *Times* began offering more relevant and important information about ALEC.[408] ALEC's government privatization agenda is a subject of vital importance to our democracy, yet as with the Nayirah, Office of Special Plans, and Iraqi WMD stories, the *Times* again failed to pioneer a story of vital importance to our democracy. When a news story threatens Elite power, the *Times* frequently does not report it until other media outlets have broken the story."

A Rancorous National Discourse

Pundit discourse has become a staple of talk radio and current affairs television shows. Our national discourse has been pushed to the right and increasingly confined to a narrow set of topics debated by a select group of experts and government officials. (Accused of drifting left in recent years, Bill Moyers responded, "I didn't drift; I moved left just by standing still.")[409] Public feedback mechanisms such as viewer call-ins and self-selected Internet polls emphasize the intense commitments of special interest groups, but this discourse is not representative of the public at large.[410]

National news commentators such as Rush Limbaugh and Bill O'Reilly routinely deal in character assassination and violent rhetoric. In January 2013, Limbaugh stated, "You know how to stop abortion? Require that each one occur with a gun."[411] Senator Claire McCaskill (D-MO) was the target of a vicious attack at a May 2012 Tea Party Express rally in Missouri. Calling McCaskill "an evil monster," Tea Partier Scott Boston told the gathering, "We have to kill the Claire Bear, ladies and gentlemen."[412] Such antagonistic and mean-spirited language compromises the public's access to meaningful news and information, and promotes a contentious and rancorous national discourse.

A mass media atmosphere of conflict and polarized animosity encourages divisions along our various demographic lines. Recent efforts to blame public sector workers' salaries and benefits for state budget crises are an example.[413] Such discord serves the Elite well: as people point fingers at each other, Elite-threatening issues such as economic inequality and money in politics are pushed aside. A national discussion of one of these unifying issues could precipitate the Elite's nightmare—the galvanizing of a movement that they do not condone and cannot control.

Given the *corporate* media system's shortcomings, it appears that we need a *public* media system whose top priority is reliable public information—not maximum profit or Elite propaganda. ("Reliable" in this context means *adequate* and *accurate* coverage of important public interest issues.) This chapter concludes with a look at the current state of our public broadcast media. Possibilities for improving our public media are discussed in chapters 18 and 19.

PUBLIC BROADCAST MEDIA—TRULY *PUBLIC*?

National Public Radio (NPR) and the Public Broadcasting Service (PBS) are commonly believed to be public-funded enterprises, largely independent of political and economic interests. But despite many years of valuable cultural and public-service programming, this is not the case.

Since the inception of radio (1930s) and then television (1940s), commercial interests have prevailed over public media efforts.[414] When the 1996 Public Broadcasting Act created NPR, PBS, and the Corporation for Public Broadcasting (CPB) a stable funding proposal for NPR and PBS was stricken from the final bill, and a discretionary funding system was established under the auspices of the CPB.[415] Today, for every dollar of US public media spending per capita, Canada spends $22, Germany $27, and the UK $80. Denmark and Finland spend $101 to the US public media dollar.[416]

The CPB's oversight has enabled politicians and appointed officials to police the ideological boundaries of public broadcasting and also prevent public broadcasting's direct competition with commercial media interests. This is one reason why some PBS stations' most popular programs are aired after 9:00 P.M., when they will not detract from the corporate networks' prime time viewership (and advertising revenue). Inadequate and unreliable federal funding requires our public media to conduct pledge drives and solicit advertisers ("underwriters"), with all the attached strings that those advertising contracts entail. "In short," Robert McChesney writes, "public media was set up in such a way as to ensure that it was feeble, dependent, and marginal."[417]

In 2003, federal subsidies covered only 15 percent of NPR's and PBS's expenses, yet even this level of funding was attacked.[418] Following his appointment as CPB's chair, right-wing Republican Kenneth Tomlinson proposed deep cuts in NPR and PBS allocations, alleging an intolerable liberal bias. He commissioned a secret investigation to document this alleged bias, focusing on the PBS program *NOW with Bill Moyers*. But contrary to his allegations, Tomlinson's investigators concluded that Moyers' programs were accurate and evenhanded. Tomlinson ignored his investigators and continued his war against public broadcasting.[419]

Tomlinson resigned as chair of CPB in 2005 amid accusations of improper conduct. Sixteen US Senators had signed an allegation charging that Tomlinson "seriously undermines the credibility and mission of public television."[420] Over the years, aggressive actions against public media by appointed ideologues such as Tomlinson have kept a short, conservative leash on NPR and PBS.

From anti-democratic CIA operations to deceitful war-promotion campaigns, We the People have frequently been uninformed or misinformed by the corporate mass media. The corporate media are also intertwined with the current political/electoral system, which is surveyed in the following chapter. Network television is particularly invested, if for no other reason than the billions of dollars that flow into their coffers with every election cycle.

CHAPTER THIRTEEN

Who Decides?

I am convinced that . . . a quasi-religious movement, one concerned with the need to change the values that now govern much of human activity, is essential to the persistence of our civilization.[421]

Paul Ehrlich
1986

Values are the enduring foundation of moral, ethical, and sometimes spiritual beliefs that anchor our decisions and priorities. Given our current ecological predicament, the decisions of present generations will influence the character of Life on Earth for millennia. These decisions will be guided by Values, and most will be made by politicians. This chapter examines the Values of the Democratic, Republican, and Green Parties to determine the kind of world their politicians are likely to work toward, the kind of future they will vote for.[422] Then, the US political/electoral landscape is surveyed, and possibilities for progressive change are discussed.

REPUBLICAN PARTY VALUES

The Republican Party's national website offers a page entitled "What we believe."[423] The Republicans' Values are evident in the key words and phrases that are emphasized by boldface at their web page (*italics* are used here). For example, "The Republican Party is inspired by the *power and ingenuity of the individual*," and "The Republican Party believes in the *value of voluntary giving and community support* over taxation and forced redistribution." Four additional phrases are emphasized: *government must be limited; low taxes; logical business regulations;* and *preserving our national strength."*

The first statement on the Republicans' page conveys a sense of nationalism: "The Republican Party believes that the United States has been blessed with a unique set of individual rights and freedoms available to all." This American Exceptionalism was evident in the foreign policy actions of the GW Bush administration, which demonstrated that individual rights and freedoms *are* sometimes "unique" to the United States, and often do not apply to citizens of other nations.

As an overarching theme, the Republicans' beliefs appear to reflect corporate goals and objectives, including limited government, low taxes, and "logical" business regulations. Limited government and low taxes also appear on the masthead of the Republican-sponsored group FreedomWorks (chapter 7), and wealthy Republicans are funding American Legislative Exchange Council (ALEC) efforts to eliminate government oversight and regulation. As the surveys and information in prior chapters indicate, Republicans' efforts to *limit* government are more about *corporate control* of government (privatization), and their recent efforts to lower taxes have primarily aided corporations and the wealthy.

DEMOCRATIC PARTY VALUES

The website of the Democratic Party offers a separate page to explain each of their 13 Values: civil rights; economy and job creation; education; energy independence; environment; fair elections; healthcare; immigration reform; national security; open government; science and technology; retirement security; and voting rights.[424]

The Democrats' Values are sometimes conveyed through the party's history and current reflections in a particular area. For example, their civil rights page begins, "Democrats have a long and proud history of defending Civil Rights and expanding opportunity for all Americans." Similarly, their retirement security page begins, "In 1935, Democrats and President Franklin Roosevelt created Social Security." These statements are sometimes short on substance and not particularly relevant to current affairs.

In some issue areas, the Democrats seem to define their position primarily in relation to the Republican stance. For example, under economy and job creation, we see that "Democrats are fighting to repair a decade of damage [presumably the GW Bush years] and grow an economy based on hard work and responsibility, not greed and reckless speculation . . ." But some specific actions are advocated, such as "ending tax loopholes that let corporations hide profits overseas" and a commitment to "strengthening the Employment Non-Discrimination Act."

The Democrats' pages also contain self-congratulatory platitudes such as, "Democrats have made historic investments in research for clean-energy technologies that are helping to create the industries of the future." Similarly, on their energy independence page, the Democrats state that they "believe that now is the moment for this generation to embark on a national mission to unleash America's innovation and seize control of our own destiny."

RED AND BLUE SHORTCOMINGS

Both Democrats and Republicans sometimes fall short of their stated Values. Under the Democrats' open government heading, for example, they mention their efforts to ensure "that government is open, transparent, and responsive to the needs of the people." During the Obama administration's pursuit of the Trans-Pacific Partnership trade agreement, however, over 600 business representatives had full access to the agreement's developmental proceedings, while representatives of the public interest were shut out entirely.[425]

The Democrats also state, "In 2010, despite unanimous opposition from Republicans, Democrats were finally able to pass comprehensive health reform into law." Unmentioned is the fact that the public option favored by 80 percent of the electorate was completely ignored in the Democrats' efforts. The Democrats' Patient Protection and Affordable Care Act left intact the insurance corporations' stranglehold on healthcare (chapter 7).

The Republicans state that they are "working to extend peace, freedom and human rights throughout the world." Yet this is the party that perpetrated the Nayirah hoax and the WMD lies. These deceptions were used to gather public support for the 2001 and 2003 invasions of Iraq—actions that did *not* extend peace, freedom and human rights.

The Republicans' statement regarding "the value of voluntary giving and community support over taxation and forced redistribution" is evident in their efforts to privatize Social Security and undermine Medicare and unemployment benefits. These efforts demonstrate a commitment to the concentrated financial wealth of the few, *not* "community support."

There are no statements related to ecological Balance in the Republicans' document. Neither party acknowledges the myth of infinite growth, and although the Democrats do mention the rights of future generations, they, too, want to "grow the economy." The Democrats' environment page does acknowledge the threat of global warming, and states that they are "working to develop comprehensive energy and climate legislation;" however, they suggest that it may be a long wait for "all of us acting together ... to finally address the challenge of climate change and seize our clean-energy future."

Regarding Peace, both parties support the Terror Worldview of a perpetually militarized planet—the polar opposite of world Peace. The Democrats are "committed to ensuring that our troops have [everything] they need when they are deployed," and the Republicans are "committed to preserving our national strength." Both parties ignore the global threat of escalating militarization spurred on by the United States' ongoing history of militaristic foreign policy actions. All in all, it appears that the Democrats' and Republicans' Values will not assist a shift toward ecological Balance or world Peace.

GREEN PARTY VALUES

The Green Party of the United States' website offers a page entitled "Ten Key Values of the Green Party." Their Values are: grassroots democracy; social justice and equal opportunity; ecological wisdom; non-violence; decentralization; community based economics; feminism and gender equity; respect for diversity; personal and global responsibility; and, future focus and sustainability.[426] A brief paragraph details each of their ten Values.

Under their ecological wisdom Value, the Greens state that "we are part of nature" and that humans "must maintain an ecological balance." Rejecting the concept of infinite growth, the Greens advocate "a sustainable economics that does not depend on continual expansion for survival." The Greens also state that we must "live within the ecological and resource limits of our communities and our planet," and they desire a society that "utilizes resources in such a way that future generations will benefit and not suffer from the practices of our generation."

With regard to Peace, the Greens' non-violence Value rejects and opposes the Terror Worldview. They aspire to "demilitarize, and eliminate weapons of mass destruction"[427] and promote non-violent methods "toward lasting personal, community and global peace." Additionally, the Greens "call for the replacement of the cultural ethics of domination and control with more cooperative ways of interacting that respect differences of opinion and gender."

The Greens identify the corporate economic system as a fundamental problem, stating, "Centralization of wealth and power contributes to social and economic injustice, environmental destruction, and militarization." To remedy this situation, the Greens support restructuring economic institutions "away from a system which is controlled by and mostly benefits the powerful few" and they specifically seek to "restrict the size and concentrated power of corporations. . ." The Greens recognize the danger that corporate power poses to our democracy and our world (chapter 7); they stand firm against this threat and advocate specific solutions.

GREENS REJECT PLUTOCRACY, PROMOTE DEMOCRACY

In a fundamental departure from politics-as-usual, Green political candidates do not accept corporate campaign donations. Over $6 billion was spent on political campaigns in 2012, and many multi-million dollar donors made large contributions to *both* Democrats and Republicans (chapter 7).[428] With the vast majority of these sums emanating from corporate enterprises, perhaps it should be no surprise that the Democrats and the Republicans have had little to say about the social power and political influence wielded by corporate interests today.[429]

The Greens specifically advocate the invigoration of our democracy, and are striving to "increase public participation at every level of government and to ensure that our public representatives are fully accountable to the people who elect them." The Greens also want to "expand the process of participatory democracy by directly including citizens in the decision-making process." Whereas this objective complements Deliberation Day and other pro-democracy initiatives will be discussed (chapter 19), the government privatization agenda of the Republican-dominated ALEC is Deliberation Day's polar opposite. The

Greens' democratic ambitions appear to move beyond anything the other parties envision.

The Greens' rejection of corporate contributions frees them of the ties that keep the other parties chained to corporate class backers, and their Values address the two most important crises of our time: the ecological unraveling of the Earth and the dismantling of our democracy. Additionally, the Green Party of the United States is a member of the Global Greens, a network with over 100 member parties. From Albania to Zambia, Green Parties are active on all continents (save Antarctica). Green Party successes in other nations indicate US possibilities.

German Greens led an effort to pass their Renewable Energies Act, which created over 300,000 jobs. The Germans now have three times the photovoltaic capacity of the US.[430] New Zealand Greens are acting to attain 100 percent renewable energy generation by 2030, and Greens in Australia shepherded the passage of a national Clean Energy Act. A greening of the United States government could integrate our nation into a worldwide community committed to Values of Balance and Peace.

A FAÇADE OF DEMOCRACY

> *One of our two major parties is dominated by extremists
> dedicated to destroying the social contract,
> and the other party has been so enfeebled by two decades
> of collaboration with the donor class it can offer only feeble resistance to
> the forces that are devastating everyday people.*[431]
>
> Bill Moyers
> 2014

For decades, a myth has beset progressive electoral politics: a belief that the right Democrat in the Oval Office will put the nation back on track. Yes, controlling interests of the Republican Party have become the corporate class' political partner. But recent Democratic presidencies have not interrupted Elite agendas of corporate power and economic dominance.

Bill Clinton used fast track authority to push the North American Free Trade Agreement (NAFTA) through Congress in 1993. This deal boosted transnational corporations' profits, but cost the US workforce at least 700,000 jobs, as factories relocated to the Global South.[432] Clinton also signed the Telecommunications Act of 1996, expediting the concentration of media empires and cross-ownership of television, radio, and newspapers. He also signed the Financial Services Modernization Act of 1999, a deregulation that allowed the conglomeration of banks, securities firms, and insurance companies (and the formation of Citigroup, the first too-big-to-fail financial conglomerate).

President Obama allowed the insurance industry to continue its stranglehold on healthcare,[433] he left the perpetrators of the 2008 Wall Street scam unscathed, and he pursued the (NAFTA-on-steroids) Trans-Pacific Partnership agreement.[434] Larry Summers was an architect of the deregulations that facilitated the 2008 financial crisis. Despite this and other shortcomings, Obama chose Summers to direct his National Economic Council, and then nominated him to head the Federal Reserve.[435] Obama continued GW Bush's dismissal of international treaties, refusing to join 150 other nations in banning landmines.[436] He signed legislation deregulating the oil pipeline industry, allowing these accident-prone corporations to self-monitor their construction standards.[437] Obama has also expanded Bush's drone program, authorizing hundreds of strikes in Pakistan, Yemen, and Somalia that killed at least 2,400 men, women, and children, including four US citizens.[438]

It does not appear that just having a Democrat in the Oval Office will turn the country around.[439] While neoconservatives have pushed the Republicans further to the right in recent decades, the Democrats have been following them. For 25 years beginning in 1985, the business-funded Democratic Leadership Council (DLC) pushed the Democratic Party to the right on several corporate issues, including the adoption of deregulation and privatization policies, reduction of business tax rates, and the promotion of free trade agreements.

Both political parties of the United States' two-party system are beholden to the corporate class for the funding now essential to political participation. So regardless of which party has majority standing, this system ensures Elite control. A shades-of-gray, two-party subterfuge maintains an illusion of choice; but in reality, the choice is only the *pace* of the Elite agenda.

A RIGGED SYSTEM

The US political system has been rigged to restrict political participation to the two major parties. For example, the Commission on Presidential Debates was jointly created by the Democratic and Republican Parties and remains controlled by them. Viewed by tens of millions of voters, these debates lend visibility and credibility to a candidate's campaign. Following Ross Perot's 1992 participation as an Independent presidential candidate, his popularity rose by 12 percentage points. Following Perot's performance, however, Democrats and Republicans revised the Commission's access rules, effectively excluding all third party candidates. Today, under these rules, Perot could not participate.[440]

Largely invisible in presidential election cycles, third party candidates are also absent on many state ballots, due to ballot access laws, registration fees, and petition requirements. Thus hindered and excluded, third party candidates have been blamed for spoiling efforts to elect what is often the least-bad of the major parties' candidates.[441]

This rigged political/electoral system is part of a broader reality that is seldom explicitly acknowledged: The United States of America, purported Beacon of Democracy for all the world, is *not* a democracy at this time. Corporate class *money* is in charge, not We the People. Corporations have captured regulatory agencies, and all three government branches increasingly comply with a corporate agenda of greed and power that now threatens all Creation.

Elected representatives are our primary link to government operations. But in recent decades, some *unelected* officials have influenced government policies and actions significantly. Surveying the current state of the US military-industrial complex, the following chapter examines the influence of unelected officials on US foreign policy.

CHAPTER FOURTEEN

The New Military Complex

One of the little known secrets of Washington is that policy isn't really generated very much within the policy apparatus. A great number of the ideas come from outside the government, from various think tanks.[442]

Joseph Cirincione
Carnegie Endowment for Peace, 2005

President Eisenhower's 1961 farewell address contained these famous lines:

> In the councils of government, we must guard against the acquisition of unwarranted influence, whether sought or unsought, by the military-industrial complex. The potential for the disastrous rise of misplaced power exists—and will persist.[443]

Although an early draft of Eisenhower's speech used the term military-industrial-congressional complex, the congressional reference was later deleted, and the term military-industrial complex entered the nation's lexicon. The two-component conception of this system has endured, but in several aspects, the configuration and scope of this assemblage has evolved substantially over the intervening decades.

I. INDUSTRY-GOVERNMENT INTEGRATION

Defense industry links to government have been fortified by the corporate-government revolving door. Rotations like Cheney's move from defense secretary to Halliburton CEO to the vice presidency are almost routine. For example, President Obama pulled William Lynn from his post as chief lobbyist for the defense giant Raytheon, to become Deputy Secretary in his Defense Department. And prior to his lobbying job at Raytheon, Lynn had served as Undersecretary of Defense during the Clinton administration.

II. CORPORATE NETWORKING

Board interlocks (chapter 6) have increasingly tied armaments industries to the larger corporate world. Interlocks with the defense contractor Honeywell, for example, include Boeing, Bank of America, Walgreens, General Motors, and Goldman Sachs.[444] The board of defense giant Northrop Grumman includes executives from Hilton Hotels, Wal-Mart, and Verizon, and former Joint Chiefs' Chair Richard B. Meyers.[445] Board interlocks give unrelated industries a voice in policies and management of armaments corporations.

III. PRIVATIZATION OF THE ARMED FORCES

US military forces and their ancillary services have been shifting into corporate hands in recent decades. For example, during the 1991 Gulf War, one in ten people deployed in the war zone was a private contractor. By the time US forces rolled into Baghdad in 2003, there were nearly equal numbers of corporate employees and US military troops. Overall, one third of Iraq War funding has gone to these corporations.[446] This increase in corporate-employed personnel evolved out of the 1992 contract that Dick Cheney awarded to Halliburton during his term as defense secretary.

Privatization of the military has funneled defense revenue streams into corporate coffers—a river of funding that is now as wide as it is deep. Currently, there are 183 private defense contractors, not counting the numerous subsidiaries of giants like Northrop Grumman.[447] These industries operate under the same corporate imperatives that govern all corporations. The military corporation Blackwater changed its name to Xe Services and then again to Academi, but its purpose remains unchanged: it exists to maximize profit for its investors. And its business? War.

IV. URBAN WARRIOR

Three efforts have been shifting the US legal and law enforcement landscape to democracy's disadvantage. First, the 1878 Posse Comitatus Act (that prohibits US military actions against US citizens) has been under assault for decades. In what has been called an urban warrior initiative, the Posse Comitatus line separating domestic police departments from the US military has been blurred if not erased entirely. An overarching police state apparatus has been quietly evolving, superimposing US military command over state and local law enforcement.[448] The Homeland Security Department has been sponsoring an annual Urban Shield conference, where armaments makers unveil their latest technologies to state and local police representatives. Homeland Security has issued grants totaling $41 billion since 2002 to help state and local police units purchase tanks, helicopters, armored Humvees, and other weapons of war.[449]

V. UNITARY EXECUTIVE

In a second and related effort, an ideology called "unitary executive theory" has pushed to expand unilateral presidential authority and abandon the balance between the governmental branches.[450] These revisions allow federal executive command of domestic policing forces in a way that jeopardizes our constitutional rights. For example, the Military Commissions Act of 2006 subverted Geneva Conventions to hand the president unconditional authority to define what is—and what is not—torture, and to imprison US citizens indefinitely, without any specified charges.[451] All that is necessary to activate these sweeping presidential powers is a president's own proclamation of a national emergency.

VI. CONTINUITY OF GOVERNMENT

The third effort that poses a threat to our democracy is a so-called "continuity of government" (COG) scheme, initiated during the Reagan administration.[452] As with the Posse Comitatus and unitary executive strategies, this effort has also found new expression since 9/11. Anchored in COG ideology, the Patriot Act has subjected US citizens to warrantless eavesdropping, arbitrary detention, and deportation on grounds of mere association—all supposedly to enhance our national security. In 2012, TransCanada corporation cited Patriot

Act provisions to suggest that Keystone XL pipeline protesters be prosecuted under anti-terrorism laws.⁴⁵³

With measures including martial law, COG ideology appears to be virtually boundless. In August 2002, Attorney General John Ashcroft proposed that on his authority alone, a US citizen could be deemed an enemy combatant, stripped of constitutional rights, and incarcerated indefinitely.⁴⁵⁴

<u>VI. PRIVATIZATION OF US FOREIGN POLICY</u>

In addition to military, industrial, and congressional factors in Eisenhower's analysis, there is now a fourth component: think tanks. While progressive think tanks exist, they are outnumbered and out-financed by their conservative and neoconservative counterparts. This imbalance arose in the 1970s, when wealthy conservatives began funding efforts to publicly promote right-wing worldviews through the creation and funding of private institutes, university professorships, foundations, and think tanks.⁴⁵⁵ An investment of over $4 billion has produced dozens of right-wing think tanks (e.g., the Heritage Foundation and the Cato Institute).⁴⁵⁶ These entities promote conservative worldviews both publicly (often through in-house studios linked to corporate media networks) and privately through personal conduits into the governmental policy apparatus. In 2003, these interconnections enabled a single think tank to activate a predetermined agenda of Middle East oil domination through a deceptive campaign orchestrated by appointed government officials. Briefly, details of this story conclude this chapter.

Privatized Foreign Policy in Action

In 1998, a neoconservative think tank calling itself the Project for the New American Century (PNAC) delivered an unsolicited advisory letter to President Clinton. This letter declared, "The only acceptable strategy is one that eliminates the possibility that Iraq will be able to use or threaten to use weapons of mass destruction." In what would become a call to arms, the letter concluded, "We urge you . . . to turn your Administration's attention to implementing a strategy for removing Saddam's regime from power."⁴⁵⁷

Clinton ignored PNAC's advice, but three years later, thirteen of this letter's eighteen signatories, including Donald Rumsfeld and Paul

Wolfowitz, were *appointed* to positions of power and influence in the GW Bush administration.[458] PNAC's Iraq agenda then began to unfold.

Often regarded as the ideological father of PNAC, Paul Wolfowitz (a disciple of radical right political philosopher Leo Strauss[459]) influenced the policy positions of the neoconservative movement during this period. As the Undersecretary of Defense for Policy from 1989 to 1993, Wolfowitz and I. Lewis "Scooter" Libby co-authored the 1992 Defense Planning Guidance, later known as the Wolfowitz Doctrine. This document advocated a dramatic increase in US defense spending to leverage the nation's lone superpower status toward domination of Persian Gulf oil. Moreover, the Wolfowitz Doctrine promoted controversial policies such as pre-emptive military action against possible rivals to US military power.[460]

Then on June 1, 2002, in a brash pronouncement defying Article 51 of the UN Charter, the Wolfowitz Doctrine became official US policy. President GW Bush announced in a West Point commencement address that the United States would now conduct pre-emptive wars of aggression as it saw fit.[461] As summarized in the documentary *Hijacking Catastrophe*, the GW Bush speech "marked the culmination of a relentless campaign by radical conservatives to change the very nature of American foreign policy; to use unrivaled American military power to shape the globe and the 21st century itself in the image of the United States; to create—in their own words—a New American Century."[462] The deceptions then perpetrated by the Rumsfeld Pentagon and Office of Special Plans enabled the invasion of Iraq, activating PNAC's agenda of Persian Gulf oil control.

The United States is a global military empire that divides the planet into six geographic zones called "combatant commands." With military expenditures four times that of China, the number two spender, the US Defense Department is the largest employer in the world, with over three million active service, private, and civilian workers. The US military burns 12 million gallons of fossil fuel *daily*.[463] The maintenance of the empire requires it:

On the ground, the US has at least 800 foreign military bases scattered over 130 countries, including all Middle East nations except Iran. (These numbers are likely understated.[464])

In the air, the Defense Department's own airline, Air Mobility Command, shuttles military personnel around the empire. The secretary of defense travels in a Boeing 757, generals and admirals use business class jets, and the Air Force has over 5,600 other aircraft in service.

Afloat, eleven aircraft carrier task forces patrol the planet's major ports and shipping lanes, along with destroyers, amphibious assault ships, submarines, and other naval assets. (China has one aircraft carrier.)

The following chapter examines how terrorism has become the principal enemy of the US military empire and a central organizing principle of US international relations.

Chapter Fifteen

From Cold War to Terror War

*They hate our freedoms: our freedom of religion,
our freedom of speech, our freedom to vote and assemble and
disagree with each other.*

George W. Bush
Congressional address, September 20, 2001

At the close of WWII, a contraction of the war industries was avoided when the Truman administration established the Cold War Worldview and rallied around NSC-68's theme of expansionist communism. These efforts poured trillions of dollars into military preparedness and worldwide anti-communist endeavors for decades.

When the Soviet Union collapsed in 1989, a new enemy was not on the horizon. But the Wolfowitz Doctrine identified a new military mission: military control of Persian Gulf oil. Acknowledging public resistance to such an agenda, Wolfowitz suggested that support could be rapidly galvanized by "some catastrophic and catalyzing event—like a new Pearl Harbor."[465] Just such an event occurred in September of the following year.

The events of 9/11 were used by the GW Bush administration to initiate the Wolfowitz agenda of Middle East oil control. A new and nebulous enemy, terrorism, renewed enthusiasm for foreign invasions beginning with Afghanistan. An "Osama bin Laden and the Terrorists" (OBL&TT) narrative of 9/11 was immediately established as an unquestionable truth; however, during the 14 months that the administration stymied a formal investigation of 9/11, no credible evidence was put forth to substantiate the OBL&TT story. Regardless, President Bush announced at the United Nations, "Let us never tolerate outrageous conspiracy theories concerning the attacks of September the eleventh; malicious lies that attempt to shift the blame away from the terrorists themselves, away from the guilty."[466] But never mind outrageous conspiracy theories, what was the *evidence* for the OBL&TT story?

Although Osama bin Laden was listed on the FBI's Most Wanted web page in connection with 1998 bombings of US foreign embassies, bin Laden's FBI page never mentioned the crimes of 9/11. In June 2006, when asked why 9/11 was not included in the FBI's charges against bin Laden, the FBI's chief of investigative publicity, Rex Tomb, said that the FBI had no hard evidence connecting bin Laden to 9/11.[467] And yet, the Final Report of the official 9/11 Commission portrays bin Laden as the mastermind of 9/11. What evidence did the 9/11 Commission have of bin Laden's guilt?

THE OFFICIAL INVESTIGATION

In January 2008, NBC News reporters found that some of the 9/11 Commission's information about the 9/11 attacks was derived from interrogations of high-ranking al-Qaida operatives. All of these interrogations had employed "enhanced interrogation techniques," sometimes including waterboarding, which simulates drowning. The report further stated that the information derived from these torture interrogations anchored the chapters of the 9/11 Commission's Report that detailed the planning and execution of the 9/11 attacks.[468] How did the members of the 9/11 Commission regard this evidence derived from interrogations?

In *Without Precedent: The Inside Story of the 9/11 Commission*, the Commission's co-chairs, Thomas Kean and Lee Hamilton, explain that the al-Qaeda detainee testimony information was passed from the detainee, to the interrogator, then to a person who wrote up the interrogation report. Then, these reports, with no transcripts, were passed to the Commission's staff, who often took six weeks to process the reports before finally making them available to the commissioners.

Kean and Hamilton concluded that they "had no way of evaluating the credibility of detainee information."[469] But in the end, these convoluted and torture-induced reports became the anchors for the Commission's OBL&TT story of 9/11. (A Bush administration insider orchestrated and supervised the 9/11 Commission's investigation—see Appendix IV, Who Ran the Investigation?)

The credibility of the 9/11 Commission Report is undermined by this methodology of tortured interrogations. The following sections examine two other aspects of 9/11 that the 9/11 Commission Report did not adequately address or explain: the collapse of World Trade Center Building Seven and the paralysis of US air defenses during the 9/11 emergency.

THE MAGIC BUILDING

The 9/11 Commission Report completely ignores the collapse of World Trade Center Building Seven (WTC 7)—the third tower that collapsed on September 11th. (Numerous videos of the collapse are posted on the Internet.[470]) WTC 7 was not hit by an airplane, and stood outside the area impacted by the Twin Towers' collapses. But the destruction of this 47-story skyscraper was included in the World Trade Center ownership's insurance claim as a loss of 9/11, resulting in an $861 million award in February 2002.[471] Thus, as with the Twin Towers, the destruction of this building was formally recognized as an event of 9/11.

Initially, *New York Times* writer James Glanz reported that structural engineering professionals were perplexed over WTC 7's collapse.[472] Whereas the collapses of the Twin Towers could be attributed to the effects of the airliner impacts and ensuing aviation fuel fires, WTC 7 was *not* hit by an airplane; these explanations could not be applied to WTC 7's free fall collapse at 5:20 P.M. on 9/11.

The Bush administration initially asked the Federal Emergency Management Agency to investigate WTC 7's collapse. FEMA's 2002 report was inconclusive, stating that even their best possible explanation of WTC 7's collapse had "only a low probability of occurrence."[473] Prior to FEMA's report, however, the task of explaining the collapse had already been passed to a second government agency, the National Institute of Standards and Technology, a division of the Commerce Department.

NIST's investigation suffered repeated delays, cancellations, and inconclusive reports before finally advancing their Final Report in November 2008. Small fires had become visible in WTC 7 around noon on 9/11, and NIST's six year investigation concluded that these fires caused a "thermal expansion of key structural members" that brought down the entire building.[474]

AN ALTERNATIVE HYPOTHESIS

No steel-frame skyscraper had ever collapsed due to fire until the three WTC towers came down on 9/11. Every other occurrence of such an event has been a controlled demolition.[475] And in fact, the collapse of WTC 7 *is* consistent with the known and observed characteristics of controlled demolitions, including:

1. the building collapse started at the bottom;
2. the onset of the collapse was sudden (not gradual or halting);
3. the building came down totally, leaving none of its steel columns erect or intact;
4. the building came straight down, symmetrically;
5. it came down at virtual free fall speed;
6. much of the building's concrete was literally pulverized, producing a huge dust cloud; and
7. the building's remains collapsed into its own footprint, leaving a relatively small, compact pile of rubble.[476]

Over the six years of NIST's investigation, it repeatedly asserted that explosives did *not* cause WTC 7's sudden collapse. For example, at the unveiling of a draft report in August 2008, NIST's lead investigator, Shyam Sunder, stated, "Before I tell you what we found, I'd like to tell you what we did not find. We did not find any evidence that explosives were used to bring the building down."[477] But as it turns out, NIST did not *look* for evidence of explosives.

In January 2008, *Hartford Advocate* reporter Jennifer Abel questioned NIST spokesperson Michael Newman on recent revelations that NIST had not looked for evidence of explosives at the site of the World Trade Center destruction. Newman replied, "Right, because there was no evidence of that." When Abel questioned Newman as to how NIST knew there was no evidence if they had not looked for it, Newman replied, "If you're looking for something that isn't there, you're wasting your time . . . "[478]

Subsequently, a team of nine professional scientists, including chemists and physicists, *did* look for evidence of explosives in the WTC debris. They found it. In 2009, the peer-reviewed *Open Chemical Physics Journal* stated that dust from the WTC destruction contained chips of nano-thermite—a highly explosive compound used in controlled demolition.[479]

Over 1,700 architects and engineers have questioned the official explanation of the collapses of all three WTC skyscrapers.[480] Another group that disputes the official OBL&TT story is *Patriots Question 9/11*, a group of three thousand government officials, professionals, and academicians of all stripes who are calling for a new and independent investigation of September 11th.[481]

After initially announcing the mystery of WTC 7's collapse, the *New York Times* seemingly lost interest in the event. The *Times* devoted one article to the release of NIST's Draft for Public Comment in 2008 but made no mention of their Final Report. The sudden collapse of this 1.8 million square foot skyscraper has been allowed to fade into oblivion.

Why did NIST so strenuously deny the possibility that explosives brought down WTC 7? Any serious consideration of an explosive-driven collapse of WTC 7 would immediately cast suspicion onto the Twin Towers, which collapsed in the same manner as WTC 7. Furthermore, the implosion of a skyscraper requires weeks of on-site preparations—access that bin Laden's foot soldiers would not have had. Demolition preparations would have also required the knowledge and cooperation of the World Trade Center's security agency—again, not the haunt of Muslim terrorists.[482] Serious consideration of an explosive-driven demolition of WTC 7 threatens the credibility of the entire official story of 9/11.

What Paralyzed US Air Defenses?

Boston air traffic control was the first to report a hijacked aircraft on the morning of 9/11. When northeast air defense offices in Rome, NY, received this information, the agent taking the call asked, "Is this real-world or exercise?" The reply from Boston was, "No, this is not an exercise, not a test."

The 9/11 Commission Report quotes this brief conversation as part of the morning's sequence of events, and drops an endnote before continuing on. The endnote states, "On 9/11, NORAD [North American Aerospace Defense Command] was scheduled to conduct a military exercise, Vigilant Guardian, which postulated a bomber attack from the former Soviet Union."[483] The endnote then states the Commission's opinion that this military exercise probably enhanced the nation's response to the 9/11 emergency. This is all that is mentioned of the matter. Here is what the Commission's report did *not* discuss:

Four months prior to 9/11, an executive order of the Bush administration placed Vice President Dick Cheney in charge of a new branch of FEMA called the Office of National Preparedness.[484] The order gave Cheney direct supervision of all preparedness training throughout the federal government.

Under Cheney's supervision, FEMA scheduled four military exercises (known as war games) for September 11, 2001. The morning of 9/11 (while Bush was in a Florida classroom), Cheney was in the President's Emergency Operations Center in Washington, overseeing both the war games and the unfolding emergency.[485]

The war games conducted on 9/11 were Vigilant Guardian (mentioned in the Commission Report), as well as Vigilant Warrior, Northern Vigilance, and Northern Guardian (not mentioned). Some of these exercises involved military aircraft simulating hijacked commercial airliners. Others involved the insertion of phantom aircraft images on Federal Aviation Administration (FAA) and NORAD radar screens.[486] As a result of these simulated hijackings and false radar insertions, there were reports of between 11 and 21 hijacked airliners at any one time during the 9/11 emergency.

The Northern Vigilance and Northern Guardian exercises deployed many of the northeast air corridor's fighter jets to air bases in northern Canada and Alaska, rendering them unavailable to respond to the 9/11 emergency. Similarly, a number of fighter jets from the Washington DC area were on training drills over North Carolina the morning of 9/11, compromising the defense of the airspace surrounding the Pentagon.[487]

The National Reconnaissance Office (NRO) headquartered in Chantilly, Virginia, is a US intelligence agency that monitors the Earth's airspace from satellites. During the confusion that the 9/11 war games produced on FAA and NORAD radar screens, the NRO's real-time tracking of planes in the northeast air corridor could have helped resolve the confusion. However, a fifth exercise was taking place on the morning of 9/11: an emergency preparedness drill that simulated an airplane crashing into NRO headquarters. Before the 9/11 emergency began, NRO had been shut down and evacuated.[488]

The 9/11 Commission's brief mention of Vigilant Guardian does not even begin to explain the complexity of the war games that coincided with the 9/11 emergency. Nor does the Report mention the uncanny resemblance between some of the games' airliner-hijacking scenarios and the reported hijackings that comprised the emergency. The FAA and NORAD confusion, as well as the deployment of defensive fighter jets to other regions, combined to play a significant role in the paralysis of US air defenses.

Moreover, the Commission's contention that Vigilant Guardian actually *facilitated* the nation's defense on 9/11 is not supported by the available evidence. On the contrary, the war games were the primary reason why US air defenses completely *failed* to respond to the 9/11 emergency. As with the tortured interrogation reports and the omission of the WTC 7 event, the false portrayal of Vigilant Guardian and the complete omission of the other 9/11 war games and the NRO drill jeopardizes the credibility of the Commission's entire report.

Growing Skepticism

Less than half the world population believes al-Qaeda was behind the 9/11 attacks, and fifteen percent think the US government was involved.[489] Germans are particularly skeptical. The Emnid Institute has found that 89 percent of Germans believe the US government has not told the truth about 9/11, and that one-fourth of these Germans think the US government perpetrated the 9/11 attacks.[490] What might account for these Germans' beliefs and suspicions?

In *The Rise and Fall of the Third Reich*, William Shirer recounts the February 1933 fire that destroyed the Reichstag building, seat of the German Parliament in Berlin. Only four weeks into his tenure as Weimar Germany's Chancellor, Adolf Hitler and his fellow Nazis immediately framed the inferno as a communist crime.[491] A feeble-minded Dutch communist was apprehended and proclaimed to be the arsonist, and over four thousand communist officials, Social Democrats and liberal leaders were arrested. Hitler exploited the Reichstag fire politically, urging President Hindenburg to sign a decree ("for the Protection of the People and the State") which suspended seven sections of the German constitution that guaranteed individual and civil liberties.

Those questioning the suspicious fire were sidelined, as was the mystery of how one arsonist could simultaneously ignite major fires throughout the Reichstag's imposing, three-story structure. Indeed, the Nuremberg Trials found that a small detachment of Nazi storm troopers had accessed the building through an underground passage from the Presidential Palace. Once inside, they started fires in several places and then took the underground passage back to the Palace.

The Dutch communist *did* have a passion for fire, and had made his way into the Reichstag that same evening, setting some fires of his own. Shirer explains, "This feeble-minded pyromaniac was a godsend to the Nazis. He had [come to the attention of Nazi Storm Troopers] a few days before, after having been overheard in a bar boasting that he had attempted to set fire to several public buildings and that he was going to try the Reichstag next."

The Nuremberg Trials proved that the Nazis orchestrated the Reichstag fire to activate a political agenda. So perhaps the German citizenry's awareness of the Nazis' Reichstag deception (and its dire consequences) has influenced their present-day suspicions regarding the events of September 11th. Indeed, the parallels are haunting:

> In 1933, an ambitious Nazi minority had managed to place Adolf Hitler into the Chancellorship and elect a substantial Nazi contingent to parliament. Blaming the Reichstag fire on the communists, the Nazis pushed a pre-formulated decree that severely restricted civil rights, condoned repressive actions previously beyond the legal limits of government, and launched the aggressive military campaign that led to World War II.
>
> In 2001, what the late Gore Vidal called the Cheney-Bush Junta came to power through Supreme Court fiat, and numerous neoconservatives were appointed to powerful government positions. Osama bin Laden was fingered within two hours of the 9/11 attacks, and the War on Terror was announced. Congress swiftly enacted the civil rights intrusions of the Patriot Act by supermajorities. The rush to invade Afghanistan was followed by a deceptive campaign promoting the invasion of Iraq, all of which ushered in the War on Terror, forecasted not to end in our lifetimes.[492]

While Germans' 9/11 suspicions rank among the highest in the world, the OBL&TT story is also floundering here at home. A 2006 Zogby International poll found that 42 percent of US citizens believed that the US government and the 9/11 Commission concealed information in a cover-up, and an equal number want to see a new investigation of 9/11.[493] These are substantial numbers; some 90 million US adults do not believe that we have heard the truth about 9/11.

Fabrications and deceptions have frequently been employed to justify foreign invasions and promote military budgets at key junctures in our nation's history. These enduring and interwoven themes of war and deceit have recently attracted the attention of a group of concerned social scientists.

UNCLE SAM'S SECRETS: STATE CRIMES AGAINST DEMOCRACY

The February 2010 issue of *American Behavioral Scientist* examined the post-WWII emergence and persistence of a group of events the journal identified as state crimes against democracy (SCADs). SCADs are "concerted actions or inactions by government insiders intended to manipulate democratic processes and undermine popular sovereignty."[494] The journal's contributors addressed two categories of events: 1) events whose investigations resulted in criminal convictions of high government officials; and 2) events whose investigations (if any) have not resulted in criminal convictions, but for which significant evidence of criminality has been documented.

The Watergate break-ins and cover-up, the Iran-Contra affair, and the outing of CIA agent Valerie Plame-Wilson were included as examples in the first group —all resulted in prison sentences for high government officials. The Tonkin Gulf incident, the assassinations of John and Robert Kennedy, the events of September 11th, and the intelligence manipulations used to justify the 2003 Iraq invasion were cited as examples of the second category—events without conclusive investigations or criminal convictions.[495]

There is an established category into which suspicions and/or evidence of SCADs have been routinely filed. We will call it the conspiracy theory repository (CTR). The CTR has perhaps been most rigorously deployed to defend the Oswald story of the Kennedy assassination. Anyone questioning one of this story's anomalies—such as the Warren Commission's magic bullet hypothesis—has been branded a conspiracy theorist.

The Kennedy assassination still serves as a benchmark. GW Bush's Press Secretary Ari Fleischer derided Congresswoman Cynthia

McKinney's questioning of the official 9/11 story by stating, "She must be running for the hall of fame of the Grassy Knoll Society."[496] Fleisher used the conspiracy theory framing not to challenge McKinney's evidence or argument, but to shunt her into the CTR and close down the conversation entirely.

The CTR has been established as the home of all manner of cranks and crackpots, and those speculating (or offering proof of) Elite complicity in suspicious events have been routinely ridiculed and diverted into the CTR. By establishing the CTR as the only appropriate home for their detractors, the perpetrators of SCADs created a social convention that it is impolite, uneducated, or somehow demented to speak truths that challenge the official version of events.[497] Facts are not considered, because the entire topic is taboo; the conversation is summarily ended.

But many events that have been relegated to the CTR *have* been conspiracies. A small group, secretly plotting or carrying out assassinations, coups d'état, or war-promotion deceptions meets any standard definition of conspiracy. The CIA's Latin American overthrows, Johnson's Tonkin Gulf deception, the Nayirah caper... all of the secret and deceptive events surveyed in prior chapters meet this definition. Uncle Sam has been planning and orchestrating conspiracies for decades.

One episode of Uncle Sam's conspiratorial history is particularly relevant to present day perspectives of 9/11: Operation Northwoods (chapter 9). The Joint Chief's conspiracy advocated US government perpetration of some of the very elements of the 9/11 emergency, including airliner hijackings and sacrificing US citizens' lives to advance a foreign policy agenda. Numerous violent scenarios were proposed to frame Cuba as a terrorist enemy in order to launch the Chiefs' long-standing goal of militarily overthrowing the Castro government. President Kennedy's unwillingness to support Operation Northwoods may have been the only thing that stopped it.

Whatever the whole truth of 9/11, the event was utilized to launch the neoconservative's agenda of Middle East oil control and a torrent of related mischief: the Patriot Act's infringement on civil rights; torture and murder in violation of international convention; and the death of over a million people, including thousands of US citizens.

The foregoing chapters have examined our history and current affairs in an effort to discover and understand the forces now dismantling our democracy and driving the unraveling of the Earth. The following chapter concludes this effort.

CHAPTER SIXTEEN

Facing the Rascal

*We have to learn to look at things as they are,
painful and overwhelming as that may be,
for no healing can begin until we are fully present to our world,
until we learn to sustain the gaze.*[498]

Joanna Macy
1991

Our Ecological Imperative calls us to chart a course toward a healthy world. But there is a group of forces obstructing this path, herding us in the opposite direction toward an ecological cliff. This chapter introduces and examines the concept of the *Rascal*, a metaphor that can help us comprehend the complexity and character of the forces we are up against. As used here, the term *Rascal* encompasses behaviors and worldviews that are detrimental to humanity's relationship with the Earth. The remaining chapters then discuss the initiation and encouragement of a Democracy Movement, an effort to curtail the *Rascal's* influence and enable us to respond to our Ecological Imperative.

RECOGNIZING ADDICTION

In North America and other affluent regions, few have been unaffected by the abundance of the industrial age. It has been easy to get hooked; to varying degrees and in various ways, we have all become attached to the material riches of this era—we are loath to give them up.

For some, however, the abundance has been extreme, and excessive affluence has spawned destructive addictions to money and power. The late Scott Peck, psychiatrist and author of *The Road Less Traveled*

(1978), warned that addictions to money and power can be more powerful than the worst forms of substance abuse, and that the ramifications of these personal addictions can be devastating to an entire society.[499]

This seems to be precisely our situation. As the Earth unravels and the majority slide down socioeconomic charts, billionaires are funding all manner of efforts to increase corporate hegemony and personal fortunes, in a seemingly unquenchable thirst for money and power. The *Rascal* is evident in the "thirst for exclusive privilege" and "concentration of economic power" that Presidents Jackson and Roosevelt warned of in centuries past.[500] Billions of dollars flow into lobbying and political campaigns—why? To tilt the system against democracy and enable the accumulation of ever larger financial fortunes. This is avarice, addiction to money.

RECOGNIZING CORRUPTION

Many have observed that power tends to corrupt, and that absolute power corrupts absolutely. In our present situation, *money* is power. Corporate fortunes are being leveraged into political/electoral control, regulatory capture, and manipulative propaganda. This is a recipe for absolute corruption.

Governmental corruption assumed new form and strength in the postwar era, when a national security apparatus was established beyond the eye of the electorate or the supervisory reach of Congress. The CIA's secret overthrows and assassinations have been some of the most corrupt and anti-democratic conspiracies in history; the agency's efforts to prolong and exacerbate the Cold War were surveyed in chapter 8. Although quietly established over six decades ago, the machinations of the National Security Agency have only recently attracted public attention.

The *Rascal* has been involved in many of the US foreign policy events that have been discussed. In the Guatemala event, for example, wealth, power, and corruption are all evident. Sam Zemurray was a very wealthy man, even before he took control of United Fruit Company. But Zemurray kept pushing; he manipulated the resources of the US government into the overthrow of Guatemala's democracy. This was a morally bankrupt endeavor, funded by US taxpayers who never even knew it happened.

Moral misbehavior in the fossil fuel industry is now a major obstacle to our Ecological Imperative. Faced with a scientific consensus over global warming, the fossil fuel industry has funded multimillion dollar propaganda campaigns to neutralize public alarm over global warming.[501]

In the 2014 election cycle, the energy and natural resources sector spent $103 million on political campaigns, and over $340 million lobbying Congress.[502] Through their indentured politicians, these industries have encouraged the construction of urban infrastructures that depend on fossil fuel transportation, and killed or lethally underfunded public transportation initiatives. Fossil fuel industries have also used the American Legislative Exchange Council to reverse state legislatures' renewable energy mandates. Given the role of global warming in the looming ecological crisis, these actions are utterly corrupt and morally unconscionable.[503]

EVIL AND THE TERROR WAR

"Evil is opposition to life. . . . It has, in short, to do with killing," wrote Scott Peck in *People of the Lie* (1983). In addition to killing, a second hallmark of evil is dishonesty—lies. The US war on Iraq was exemplary in both regards, where Pentagon deceptions led to the death of hundreds of thousands; simply put, lies and killing.

Peck further states that evil is usually accompanied by a desire to appear as good.[504] This, too, was evident in the Middle East invasions, where the carnage was camouflaged under Beneficent Uncle Sam banners of Operation Enduring Freedom and Operation Iraqi Freedom.

To claim that evil is afoot is not to suggest that it is lurking around every corner. What *is* warranted, however, is mindfulness of this telltale pair of symptoms: where lies are found in the company of killing, evil is to be suspected.

The Terror War was launched by 9/11, and the official story of that day suffers credibility issues (chapter 15). Post-9/11, there was the rush to invade Afghanistan, where the US oversaw the immediate restoration of opium poppy production (which the Taliban had curtailed), while bin Laden, the announced target of the chase, somehow just disappeared. (See Afghanistan Revisited, Appendix V.) Then came the lies to justify the invasion of Iraq (chapter 11). So from the start, the

Terror War has been anchored in deceptions and lies, and over a million people have been killed.

There has been little or no evidence of the government's claims that torture produces intelligence of terrorist plots. But what the torture program *has* produced is radical hatred of the United States, *increasing* the likelihood of anti-US terrorism. So while the torture program purports to be a response to terrorism, this program is *itself* terrorism, and it encourages terrorism in reply. This program violates international human-rights law; over 100 detainees have been tortured to death.[505] But when Congress moved to prohibit the most heinous torture techniques, President Bush promised a veto.[506]

CIA Director John Brennan has said that the US drone bombing program applies "targeted, surgical pressure to the groups that threaten us."[507] But the body counts do not support Brennan's claim. Drone bombings targeting just 41 men have now killed an estimated 1,147 civilians, including 12 members of a Yemeni wedding party in February 2014.[508] The US drone program is state-sponsored terrorism. Like the torture program, it enflames anti-US sentiment and elicits terrorism in reply.[509] These policies are a pernicious aspect of the *Rascal*; their pretenses and killing suggest evil is involved.

THE RASCAL'S WORLDVIEWS

The *Rascal* includes the addiction, corruption and a potential for evil that have been discussed. But the *Rascal* is also a group of problematic worldviews, some of which have deep roots established over generations in our collective consciousness. Through these worldviews, the *Rascal* has become a part of most all of us.

For example, a preoccupation with economic growth is anchored in the unsustainable paradigm of infinite growth. Sustainable economic models have been proposed and demonstrated, but the *Rascal* remains singularly focused on growth, encouraging the unchecked avarice of the already wealthy.[510]

The material aspirations encouraged by the Land of Desire Worldview (Appendix VI) are beyond the carrying capacity of the Earth. Worldviews and belief systems that disconnect humanity from the Earth's web of Life have encouraged the overexploitation of natural resources. Here again, these worldviews enable the *Rascal's* greed but obstruct our Ecological Imperative.

The Beneficent Uncle Sam Worldview continues to shield US foreign policy from critical review. Somehow, under this worldview, freedom and democracy are delivered by military invasions and occupations. Only when camouflaged by the Beneficent Uncle Sam Worldview can the United States' preemptive wars of aggression be sold as the actions of a "Defense" Department.

The Cold War Worldview served the *Rascal's* agenda of greed and power for over four decades, but the irony at the foundation of this worldview has seldom been acknowledged. Before the Cold War even began, the US had instigated a war against Mexico that appropriated half of that country as our own. We had ousted Spain from the hemisphere in order to take control of Cuba, Puerto Rico, and the Philippines. US agricultural interests had overthrown the Hawaiian monarchy and appointed Sanford Dole President of Hawaii.[511] US Marines and gunboats had escorted US industries into Latin America, and we had pried Panama loose from Columbia in order to create an inter-oceanic canal, that we then controlled with military bases.[512]

The Cold War Worldview emphasized a Soviet agenda of world domination, while ignoring the United States' history of geographic and economic expansion. But revelations of the CIA's anti-democratic operations now undermine both the Cold War and Beneficent Uncle Sam Worldviews. The Soviet Union was not without fault, certainly, but the CIA's democracy-suppression operations show that United States' foreign policy had more to do with the global expansion of US corporations and military installations than with fending off communist takeovers and spreading democracy.

We are now in a similar situation with the Terror Worldview. The United States' torture and drone programs are actually exacerbating the terrorism we are supposed to be eliminating. And ultimately, the Terror and Cold Wars have yielded the same result: global expansion of the military-industrial complex and corporate commandeering of global natural resources.

The Rascal's Agents

The *Rascal* has morphed, mutated, and metastasized for millennia. Currently, the *Rascal's* inner circle includes a cabal of corporate Elite who exemplify the *Rascal's* avarice and hunger for power. Promoting the corporate-government merger, they stand opposed to basic principles of democracy.

For the Earth, corporations engaged in natural resource extraction are a most troubling component of the *Rascal*. Given the Sun's energy, the Earth is the ultimate source of the financial wealth emanating from extractive corporations. Under the *Dodge* profit imperative, corporations are conducting a liquidation of Creation (chapter 6). With fossil fuels as a leading example, natural resources are being stripped of their cash value, sacrificing the future of Life to quarterly profit goals.

The Elite are easy targets for blame here, and yet, some of those at the tiptop of the economic pyramid are trapped in positions and lifestyles that have become an ordinary part of our society. Yes, evil seems to be involved in some cases; but good people, too, have been drawn in by the *Rascal's* temptations, becoming addicted to wealth and/or corrupted by power dealt to them by their life circumstances. But similar to other afflictions, an intervention is needed to stop this behavior.

A Democracy Movement can, as Swami Byondananda says, feed two birds with one scone. It can both resuscitate our democracy and enable us to chart a course toward a sustainable future. The following chapter discusses the launching of this Movement.

CHAPTER SEVENTEEN

Launching a Movement

*All great reforms, great movements,
come from the bottom and not the top....
Wherever there is a wrong, point it out to all the world,
and you can trust the people to fight it.*[513]

John Peter Altgeld
Governor of Illinois, 1893-1897

*[I]f Americans take personal ownership of the Constitution and
the Bill of Rights, they can push back any darkness....
We need the next revolution.*[514]

Naomi Wolf
Give Me Liberty
2008

We are approaching a Tipping Point, a phenomenon that journalist and author Malcolm Gladwell describes as a moment when sudden change is possible, a "moment of critical mass, the threshold, the boiling point."[515] Spontaneous eruptions like Occupy Wall Street and the Wisconsin Uprising have made discontent and animosity more visible.[516] Progressive multimillion-member netroots groups like MoveOn and thousands of organizations opposing the *Rascal's* mischief all indicate a hunger for revolutionary change.

Frustration has now permeated the upper middle class; even the top forty percent are increasingly aligned against the top one percent, a trend related to the emergence of a precariat class.[517] The membership of the precariat has long included blue collar workers, but corporate downsizing and globalization have now eroded the security of the managerial and professional class, shifting formerly upper-income workers into precariat conditions of temporary jobs or underemployment.

The People are restless. Dissatisfaction is growing deeper and wider. This chapter discusses opportunities to use the approaching Tipping Point as a means to launch a Democracy Movement.

STORIES AND TIPPING POINTS

Stories can shape public opinion and influence the worldviews that guide our society. The introduction of a *new* story can push a society to a Tipping Point and change the course of history. The Elite have used deceptive stories to gather public support for wars; the Tonkin Gulf, Nayirah, and WMD deceptions were stories that vilified enemies and launched wars against them (chapters 10 and 11).

A story with the right timing and characteristics could push us to a Tipping Point that pivots our society toward democratic renewal. What kind of story could precipitate a Tipping Point and galvanize a Democracy Movement?

Compelling stories usually engage people emotionally, even viscerally. *Dark Alliance* (the CIA-Contra story, chapter 11) touched people's lives, stirred emotions, and ignited protests. The story linked the horrors of a crack cocaine epidemic to an illegal conspiracy of the Reagan administration, eliciting outrage, not only in the neighborhoods the drugs had ravaged, but all across the nation. Similarly, the Occupy Wall Street (OWS) protests had an emotional component: while home foreclosure rates soared to over 3 million a year, Wall Street bankers walked away with fortunes. Even those unaffected by the crash were agitated and disgusted.

A story like *Dark Alliance* or OWS could have become a Tipping Point and launched a movement. But these possibilities were precluded by Elite control of public information. Recall how the media establishment mobilized to destroy Gary Webb's career and discredit *Dark Alliance*'s revelations. Information control was also evident in the OWS protests. The *New York Times*' initial headlines offered only warnings and discouragement, day after day:

WALL STREET PROTEST BEGINS, WITH DEMONSTRATORS BLOCKED
PROTESTERS FIND WALL STREET OFF LIMITS
WALL STREET PROTESTS CONTINUE, WITH AT LEAST 6 ARRESTED
WALL STREET PROTESTS CONTINUE, WITH 7 MORE ARRESTED
WALL ST. PROTESTS CONTINUE, WITH ARRESTS AT MORNING MARCH
PROTESTERS ARE GUNNING FOR WALL STREET, WITH FAULTY AIM[518]

Throughout the OWS demonstrations, the establishment media largely ignored the protests' core issue of Elite economic domination, preferring stories of citizen powerlessness: protesters being monitored, herded, and arrested by state-backed power.[519] In this information environment, protesters did not see an accurate reflection of themselves; there was an emphasis on fringe elements, violent incidents, and police repression. People are reluctant to feel kinship with a group that is demonized (or a movement they can't see) in their daily news.

The corporate media have frequently ignored progressive events and failed to convey the true nature of various national and world situations. Independent (non-corporate) media outlets, on the other hand, have often announced progressive trends and exposed the true nature of government deceptions. Unfortunately, the voice of the independents has generally not been sufficient to overcome (or even balance) the power and reach of the corporate media. But if the independents' voices could be adequately amplified, they could announce a new story capable of pushing us to a Tipping Point.

ANNOUNCING A NEW STORY

Uniting and coordinating the voices of independent media outlets could produce a chorus strong enough to effectively announce a new story. This could be accomplished by an organization like the Media Consortium, a networking group of dozens of progressive, independent media outlets: print publications such as *The Nation, Mother Jones,* and *In These Times*; broadcast ventures like *Free Speech TV* and *Democracy Now!*; and websites such as *Truth-Out, AlterNet,* and *Workers Independent News.*[520]

With a combined audience in the tens of millions, the Media Consortium's membership would avail the independent media of an advantage the corporate media system has utilized for decades: an echo chamber for high priority news and information. As a story echoed through the independent media's print, broadcast, and online outlets, each voice would join an information environment filled with the supportive voices of other outlets.

A surge of Internet attention could also reach a large audience and help overcome corporate media blackouts or distortions. The memberships of on-line activist groups such as Free Press and Media Matters for America could make a new story go viral. These groups' members could also bury the corporate media in a torrent of demands for adequate and accurate coverage of the story.

The information environment created by actions like these could push our society to a Tipping Point. Those initially involved in the Movement could see the larger whole of which they were a part, and sympathetic bystanders would be more inclined to join a movement they could see and understand. This could all happen.

Readily available, accurate news is crucial to the launch, expansion, and ultimate success of a Democracy Movement. Every step of the way, We the People will need to know what is really going on. All the news power we can muster—public and independent media, Internet commentary and social media networks, and door-to-door citizen action—could be needed to expose the right story at an opportune moment.

STORIES WITH POTENTIAL

In a congressional address, President Franklin Roosevelt proposed the Monopoly Investigation of 1938, stating:

> The liberty of a democracy is not safe if the people tolerate the growth of private power to a point where it becomes stronger than their democratic state itself. That, in its essence, is fascism—ownership of government by an individual, by a group, or by any other controlling private power.[521]

"Fascism" is a foreign and frightening term for many, but essentially, as Roosevelt observed, fascism involves the convergence of corporate and governmental power. Corporate-government synergy is precisely what the CIA's covert operations have facilitated since its inception—a global effort to suppress democracy and support corporate-friendly autocracies.

A comprehensive corporate-government merger is now underway in the United States. In recent decades, the corporate Elite have tightened their grip on our political/electoral system, our government and regulatory agencies, and our financial/economic and public information systems. The corporate-government revolving door and the government privatization agenda of the American Legislative Exchange Council have been facilitating this merger, and corporate money now largely controls both wings of the two-party political system.

This trend toward tyranny is occurring largely through careful control of what is reported by the corporate media. A case in point is the framing of NSA whistleblower Edward Snowden as a traitor, when in reality, he is a patriot exposing the vast corporate-government surveillance network now watching our communications over Verizon, Microsoft, Yahoo!, Facebook, Skype, and other networks.[522]

Political scientist Laurence Britt has analyzed several fascist regimes in history, including Mussolini's Italy, Hitler's Germany, and Suharto's Indonesia. Britt found that several characteristics were common to all these regimes, including: supremacy of the military; controlled mass media; expansion of corporate power; suppression of organized labor; fraudulent elections; and nine other features.[523] From urban warrior measures to corporate hands in the ballot box, these characteristics are now evident in the United States.[524]

Naomi Wolf draws on world history to chronicle our situation in *The End of America*.[525] Wolf surveys ten steps that have established autocratic rule in other nations, and details evidence of these steps in the United States. In 2007, Joe Conason concluded a study of authoritarian and dictatorial measures in the United States by stating, "Yes, it can happen here."[526] This is a defining story of our time. Adequately exposed, it could spark a Tipping Point and spawn a revolution.

When a Democracy Movement becomes visible, the Elite may respond with a state crime against democracy—another story with Tipping Point potential. A new SCAD could enable the declaration of a national emergency, thereby activating repressive measures like continuity of government. Dangerous as this could be, rapidly and thoroughly exposing the true nature of this story could galvanize the populace and expand our efforts into an unstoppable Movement.

A provoking story could also be made of the Elite's history of accusing their enemies of exactly the mischief that *they* have been up to:

> While Senator McCarthy announced groundless claims that communist agents had infiltrated the State Department, the CIA's Operation Mockingbird was placing undercover agents throughout the federal government.
>
> Cold War accusations of "expansionist communism" obscured the global expansion of US corporate capitalism.
>
> "Vote fraud" has been portrayed as a national electoral problem, but in reality, the infractions of voters are a miniscule problem compared to the irregularities that have been documented on corporate-programmed voting machines.
>
> The conspiracy theory repository (CTR) has shielded Elite conspiracies such as the Tonkin Gulf incident and the 2003 pro-war deceptions from serious investigation.
>
> Notions of a "vast right-wing conspiracy" have been shunted into the CTR, but in reality, Elite-perpetrated SCADs are by definition conspiracies, and they have frequently changed the course of world history.
>
> The characterization of the mass media as the "liberal media" is a complete reversal of the true situation. The corporate media have obediently relayed government deceptions and ignored information that seriously exposes or threatens Elite control.
>
> Elite pundits assert that progressive changes in tax codes are "class warfare," while efforts to privatize social security and dismantle public safety nets are portrayed as responsible reforms necessary to national fiscal stability.[527]
>
> Washington's declared enemy is "terrorism." But the United States' preemptive wars of aggression, routine use of torture, and undiscriminating drone killings all indicate that Uncle Sam is a terrorist.

Each of these maneuverings serves to reinforce the fallacy of the others. Combining them into a narrative could expose the ongoing deceit involved in Elite portrayals of reality. This, in turn, could provoke animosity and increase skepticism of their current assertions.

Stories with Tipping Point potential already exist, and others will most likely appear. Choosing a compelling story is important but the *key* to encouraging a Tipping Point is the *amplification* of the story by multiple sources. When the right story becomes visible, we need to jump on it, loudly and repeatedly, with all our information power.

There will likely be a critical moment following the Tipping Point, when the *Rascal* acts to defend the status quo and quash our Movement. The following chapter discusses strategies and actions to help ensure the nascent Movement's expansion at this critical juncture.

CHAPTER EIGHTEEN

Sustaining a Movement

*An invasion of armies can be resisted;
an invasion of ideas cannot be resisted.*[528]

Victor Hugo
La Chute, from "*Les Misérables*," 1877

Our democratic and ecological circumstances are both urgent crises; time is of the essence. We cannot afford to let an opportune moment pass by. Anticipating a Tipping Point, we can contemplate plans and strategies to ensure that when an opportunity is identified, we are ready and able to subdue the *Rascal* and resuscitate our democracy.

FOCUSING ON DEMANDS

Our Movement needs to focus on what we *demand*, rather than what we oppose. Although most people understood the grievances that inspired the Occupy protests, for example, the movement's goals and objectives were not clear. Even sympathetic commentators criticized the movement for not advocating actions to reform corporate financial wrongdoings.[529] Focusing on strategic demands can concentrate the Tipping Point's energy and initiate an avalanche of democratic renewal. The exact nature of the Tipping Point may suggest specific demands, but other demands could be considered in advance.

For example, we could immediately demand full funding for our public media. No delays, no excuses; vote yes. Recognizing their own stake in this demand, PBS and NPR affiliates would be likely to support this initiative. Stations could preempt routine programming and make the Movement high-priority news. Primetime panel discussions and feature programs could force the core issues of the Movement into the national discourse, altering the information landscape to democracy's advantage. This would enhance the visibility and legitimacy of the Movement and expand its support. Gathering momentum, another demand or two could be announced, targeting system changes that further tip the field in favor of democracy.

Protesters in the streets—even millions—will not change the systems that sustain the Elite power structure. But millions of citizens *demanding specific actions* of their elected representatives could initiate system changes that turn the tide. For instance, a specific effort could publish the position of every member of Congress regarding the public media funding initiative mentioned above. Activist networks could target recalcitrant senators and representatives, organizing on-line campaigns to unseat them in the next election.

It is difficult to estimate the character of a confrontation with the *Rascal.* But we would likely do well to stop and hold to our initial demands until they are met. We may need to bring all resources to bear, from impeachment petitions to general strikes. This would clearly demonstrate that We the People are taking charge; the status quo will not continue. No delays, no excuses; keep the pressure on.

Rascal Watch

The Elite will attempt to crush a potential threat to their wealth or power. A dangerous confrontation could be avoided if we anticipate this reply and plan ahead. The prompt exposure of a state crime against democracy (SCAD) has been discussed, but there are other considerations.

For example, the initiation of a Democracy Movement could provoke another repressive government response like the Patriot Act. In the post-9/11 atmosphere of ultra-patriotism, this Act (its 342 pages clearly drafted prior to 9/11) was swiftly enacted by supermajorities before all but a few members of Congress had even *seen* the document.[530] Similar to the Espionage and Sedition Acts that quashed public dissent during World War I (chapter 3), this Act's provisions eroded our civil rights and public safeguards. Here again, targeting members of Congress with specific demands could help derail another legislative maneuver like the Patriot Act.

The Elite's response to rebellion can also be seen in Washington's reply to the Chilean government's progressive reforms in the 1970s (chapter 1). In response to this uprising, US-Chilean Ambassador Edward Korry proclaimed, "We shall do all within our power to condemn Chile and the Chilean people to utmost deprivation and poverty."

Elite regard for the US citizenry is no different than Ambassador Korry's attitude toward the Chilean People. Our middle class is being hollowed out and millions have been evicted from their homes by the financial Elite's 2008 machinations.[531] And our health as a nation is no more of an Elite priority than it was in Chile, Guatemala, Iran, and other nations condemned to economic servitude and social devastation. As the corporate-government merger progresses, our nation is moving in this direction.

Defensive responses to recent civil disobedience demonstrations have included technological tactics such as the interruption of cellular and internet services used to organize these events.[532] This can provoke a disconcerting train of thought. The Elite now control corporate transportation lines delivering vital resources to all corners of the nation, agribusinesses that direct much of the nation's food supply, and privatized energy grids and communications networks that supply power and connectivity to entire regions. Particularly in conjunction with a new SCAD or widespread grassroots demonstrations, the Elite might well exercise this control by attempting to condemn us to "utmost deprivation." Planned, organized pressure can help ensure that whatever obstacles we encounter, our democratic efforts prevail.

PRECLUDING VIOLENCE

Violence is a principal tool of the *Rascal*. We are dealing with a force that has crushed democracies, assassinated uncooperative leaders, and now commands a global military empire. Elite operatives are well-versed in violence-based control; they introduce violence to their advantage.[533] The People would almost certainly lose in a contest of brute force.

Street demonstrations are particularly vulnerable to manipulation. There are now documented instances of agents provocateurs inciting violence at otherwise peaceful civil disobedience demonstrations.[534] Even huge peaceful rallies can be portrayed as violent events when the corporate media focus on a handful of agents provocateurs.

However initiated, acts of violence may be falsely attributed to our Movement, enabling the *Rascal* to portray our efforts as lawless anarchism and order a government crackdown. It would be to our advantage to preclude the introduction of violence, and focus on democratic processes to achieve the transformation we desire. Violence is not our ally.

PUTTING TIME ON OUR SIDE

The Elite use time to maintain an information environment conducive to their continued control. Government classification of records can buy time—often decades—during which silence or deception can prevail. The Operation Mockingbird media network may still exist, helping to suppress Elite-threatening information and thereby enhance government deceptions.

For example, early exposure of the Tonkin Gulf deception could have energized the anti-war movement of the 1960s and altered the course of world history. But that information was suppressed for years, and then typically presented as a debate as to what really happened. The emotive power of such events diminishes over years and generations.

The omissions and distortions of the 9/11 Commission's Final Report indicate that 9/11 may have been the Terror War's Tonkin Gulf incident. The Commission completely ignored the mysterious collapse of World Trade Center Building Seven and distorted the extent and the effect of the 9/11 war games. But a new investigation that addressed these events could prompt an indignation of unprecedented magnitude. Perhaps 9/11 is already too far in our past, but the immediate exposure of a new SCAD could push us to a Tipping Point and energize a Movement.

When our government becomes more responsive to the will of the electorate, what kind of changes would we like to make? How can we extend a Movement's initial momentum and bring our democracy to its full expression? The following chapter suggests plans and actions to make this happen.

Chapter Nineteen

Democratic Strategic Initiatives

*The most powerful form of thinking is strategic.
It is not just a matter of thinking ahead....
It is a matter of setting many things in motion by
setting one thing in motion. It is a matter of
reconfiguring the future by doing one thing in the present.*[535]

George Lakoff
2006

As long as the Elite control our political/electoral and governmental systems, reform efforts will be largely confined to protests and appeals—with marginal results.[536] We need to change the structure and nature of this contest. We need to alter our governmental and political/electoral systems in ways that encourage public participation and democratic self-rule. Strategic Initiatives can help us achieve these changes.

A Strategic Initiative is a single action that produces many results. President Franklin Roosevelt's New Deal was a Strategic Initiative that altered the nation's entire socioeconomic condition, creating the Social Security and Works Progress Administrations, and other progressive innovations. This chapter proposes some Strategic Initiatives to strengthen our democratic processes and amplify the electorate's voice in political/governmental affairs.

Deliberation Day: Tapping the Wisdom of Crowds

One promising example of a progressive Strategic Initiative is Deliberation Day, a concept developed by Yale law professor Bruce Ackerman and Stanford communications professor James Fishkin.[537] On a national holiday held during presidential election years, millions of randomly selected voters would participate in community discussions about the upcoming elections (and be financially compensated for their time). These meetings would bring voters together to discuss candidates' positions on issues and also pose questions and raise issues that candidates might rather ignore. A consolidated report of voter input would be supplied to candidates and the mass media. The candidates' responses to the People's questions and issues would inform voters' ballot decisions.

As an important national event, the media would presumably cover Deliberation Day's proceedings and conclusions. This would enable the voice of the People to shape the national discourse, forcing candidates to address the People's high priority issues. This information landscape would help prevent paid advertising and propaganda from dominating the political/electoral process.

Years of research and experiments convinced Ackerman and Fishkin that ordinary citizens can think through complex public issues and discuss them productively with each other.[538] In *The Wisdom of Crowds* (2004), James Surowiecki reached a similar conclusion. As individuals, we all have our limitations of knowledge, foresight, and reasoning ability. But Surowiecki found that when all our imperfect judgments are aggregated in the right way, we are collectively capable of excellent decisions. And as it turns out, all of Surowiecki's requirements for effective group decision-making are satisfied in Ackerman and Fishkin's concept of Deliberation Day.[539]

Deliberation Day is a Strategic Initiative; it could shift the entire political/electoral landscape and re-engage tens of millions of citizens who now do not even vote.[540] Ackerman and Fishkin estimate the total expense of a Deliberation Day event with 70 million participants at $2.5 billion—roughly a day-and-a-half of US military spending, one-fifth of US automakers' annual advertising budgets—a small price to pay for the reinvigoration of our democracy.[541]

LEGISLATIVE AGENDAS

Every Deliberation Day could produce a Legislative Agenda—a list of national priorities and actions the electorate favors. Issued to our elected representatives, the collective wisdom of the People could direct the actions and priorities of our government.

The electorate could, for example, instruct Congress to dismantle the CIA or facilitate the termination of corporate personhood by constitutional amendment. Other directives could change the mandate of the Commerce Department from promoting unlimited growth to developing community-supported agriculture and sustainable local economies.

An elected representative failing to support a Legislative Agenda could be ejected in the next election and replaced with one who did. As a routine outcome of every Deliberation Day, Legislative Agendas could help put the electorate in charge of our government.

DIRECT DEMOCRACY OPTIONS

The official actions of congressional representatives too often disagree with the opinions and desires of the majority in their constituencies. For example, a majority of the electorate favors a public option for health care; the two major political parties won't even discuss it. Meanwhile, the *Rascal* is spreading $3 billion a year around the capitol to ensure that our legislators respond to *its* voice (chapter 7). We need to fix this.

From city councils to the Oval Office, the voice of the People needs to be heard more clearly by elected representatives. Moreover, it should be routinely evident whether or not our elected representatives are responsive to their constituencies. Applying current communications tools to the electorate-representative relationship could make this happen. Just how might this work?

Voter registration rolls could be used to compose a program we will call Direct Democracy. Choosing between telephone, Internet, and US mail options, all voters could set up secure accounts in a Direct Democracy network. Through this network, voters could receive reports similar to the voter information guides that most states now provide, and routinely inform their representatives of their wishes regarding pending legislation. The record of representatives' adherence to their constituents' wishes would be available to voters at every election. Those representatives not responding to the majority of their constituents could be voted out of office.

With a few days' Pentagon spending, a Direct Democracy pilot network could be designed and installed in one state. A nationwide expansion of this network would provide an inexpensive means to ensure that elected representatives are responsive to their constituencies.

No doubt, others could devise a Direct Democracy system far beyond these musings. (The Bill and Melinda Gates Foundation seems the perfect steward for such an endeavor.) Some might envision a Network that would enable the entire electorate to vote on certain bills of national importance. But whatever its eventual design, a Direct Democracy system could enable the People to more effectively supervise their elected representatives, and have a stronger voice in legislation that affects their lives and our collective future.

EXECUTIVE BRANCH OVERSIGHT

Currently, electoral campaigns of the executive branch are inordinately focused on the race for the presidency. But Cabinet Secretaries can exert an equal or even greater force on the fate of our nation than the occupant of the Oval Office.[542] As Defense Secretaries, for example, Dick Cheney and Donald Rumsfeld had enormous impact on the course of world history and the lives of millions. Cheney's Defense term precipitated the wholesale privatization of the US armed forces (chapter 6), and Rumsfeld's Pentagon led our nation to war under false pretenses (chapter 11).

The heads of Cabinet-level *agencies* wield similar influence. Recall FDA Commissioner Arthur Hayes' unilateral action approving the public release of aspartame (endnote 165 from chapter 6). Perhaps the CIA's covert operations need no further mention. Clearly, the leadership of Cabinet-level entities can affect vital aspects of our society, including foreign policy, public health, and ecological safeguards. And yet, these top-level executive branch offices are appointed without the electorate's comment or participation. Cabinet nominations and agency appointments are frequently predicated on corporate backgrounds or personal financial wealth, rather than public service backgrounds or relevant expertise.[543]

Broadening the scope of presidential campaigns could strengthen the electorate's oversight of the executive branch. Imagine a presidential election *not* obsessed with the presidential horserace, but focused instead on a broader evaluation of the executive branch each presidential candidate would bring into office. Beyond choosing a vice-presidential running mate (the only pre-election choice now routinely announced), a presidential candidate's Values and leadership direction would become evident through his or her Cabinet and agency nominations. This would provide a more adequate understanding of the overall direction that any presidential administration would lead the nation. (In cases where nominations have not been announced, presidential candidates could publish the criteria they would use to select their nominees.)

BREAKING THE TWO-PARTY LOCKOUT:
AN EXECUTIVE BRANCH SLATE

A presidential campaign setting forth an executive branch slate could pioneer the political/electoral changes described in the prior section. Nominations for Cabinet and agency heads could stress *accomplishments* over titles, emphasizing the Values that have guided each nominee's working life. These accomplishments could then be contrasted with the deeds and endeavors of past officials, those currently in office, or other nominees in the upcoming election.

For example, Andrew Bacevich, retired US Army Colonel and Boston University professor of international relations, could be the slate's defense secretary nominee. Bacevich, author of several critiques of militaristic US foreign policy, has called the US occupation of Iraq "immoral, illicit, and imprudent." Placed in a context that included the Office of Special Plans' deceptions that *facilitated* the occupation of Iraq, Bacevich's nomination could be seen by many as a move toward honesty and integrity in US foreign policy.

An executive slate campaign could initiate a discussion of Values in the national discourse. This shift could give the electorate a stronger voice in the Values that would guide the next presidential administration.

Public Information Initiatives: Reviving the Federal Communications Commission

> *Now is the time for America to dramatically expand the existing public-broadcasting system, re-envisioning it as truly public media.*[544]
>
> Robert W. McChesney and John Nichols
> 2010

Reliable public information is a fundamental requirement of democratic self-rule. The electorate needs adequate and accurate information about our history, current events, and a broad range of national issues. Full funding of PBS and NPR could enable these assets to produce adequate and accurate public information. If action has not already been demanded in this arena (chapter 18), a Legislative Agenda could direct Congress to ensure full funding of our public media and sever the "underwriting" agreements that now obligate PBS and NPR to corporations. Funding the US public media at the per capita level of the UK would amount to about $24 billion annually—just eleven days of Pentagon spending.[545] We could further demand the dismantling of the Corporation for Public Broadcasting, unleashing our public media to address vital local, national, and global issues during prime time.

It is not widely understood that the radio and television frequency spectrum is the public property of the US citizenry. The Federal Communications Commission (FCC) was created to regulate broadcast operations in the public interest; broadcasters must pass FCC licensing requirements to begin and maintain operations. But in reality, the FCC has been a casualty of the same political pressure and corporate capture that has compromised other regulatory bodies (chapters 6 and 7).

Legislative Agendas and Direct Democracy could pressure Congress to restore the FCC to its original mandate, including enforcement of standards of accuracy, civility, and public service programming. A record of distortion, deception, or disregard for the truth on important public issues could result in the revocation of a broadcaster's license.

Specifically, the FCC could be instructed to revive the Fairness Doctrine, a former FCC policy that required broadcasters to present issues of public importance, and to do so in an honest and evenhanded manner. This policy was attacked during the deregulatory frenzy of the Reagan era and discontinued in 1987. A revival of the Fairness Doctrine could force broadcasters to air topics and voices that the *Rascal* would rather ignore. Those long-absent from important conversations could elevate public awareness and understanding of issues such as renewable energy and foreign policy.

ENLISTING MULTIPLE COMMUNITIES; ADDRESSING THE NGO DILEMMA

There are thousands of non-governmental organizations (NGOs), spiritual, religious, and ecological groups, and independent media outlets currently battling the *Rascal.* All these entities would have a stake in a Democracy Movement. Many will benefit from stronger democratic oversight of government policy, for example. Internet campaigns and inter-organizational networking could enlist millions from these organizations, expanding the Movement exponentially. The leaders of these groups could be featured on public media programs, building cohesion between and within their various sectors.

But as a Movement progresses and our government becomes more responsive to the People, these same groups may lose their raison d'être. We would do well to proactively establish options to transition the staffs of these groups into new opportunities. This program could provide scholarships for retraining into fields that will be expanding in the new era, coordinate early retirement options, and government job placement programs. Whatever the details, achieving positive outcomes for those who have done valuable public service work would help keep these valuable workers involved and contributing to the new democratic era—and it's the right thing to do.

Most likely, none of this will be easy. The Elite will rigorously defend the political/governmental and economic systems that sustain their power and wealth. But we have one advantage that can win the day: we are the majority. When we cross the Tipping

Point, we must all join the Movement to make our majority evident. From phone calls to general strikes, we will need all who are able to press for the initial demands of the Movement. Our strength will be in our number. Like a giant but gentle dragon, we can sit down at the *Rascal's* table and calmly announce the dawn of a new democratic era.

Afterword

What I Believe

Nothing in this world is so powerful as an idea whose time has come.

Victor Hugo
1852

We are all here for such a brief moment; our legacy is our response to the trials of our time. For current generations, a trial of extraordinary consequence has appeared: the *Rascal* is plundering our children's future. We must revive our democracy in order to subdue the *Rascal* and chart a course toward a healthy planet and a vibrant society. Otherwise, the *Rascal's* overindulgence will continue pushing us toward an ecological cliff. Launching a Democracy Movement is the most important action we can take to ensure a brighter future.

The key to the success of our Movement is reliable public information. With it, awareness of our democratic and ecological crises will expand, and citizens will be more likely to rise up and demand change. With it, We the People can recognize the power of our majority and coalesce into an unstoppable force. The Elite fear these things may happen; hence their enormous propaganda efforts to deny the ecological unraveling and obscure the advancing corporate-government merger.

Yes, we need reliable information in order to recognize our democratic and ecological crises. But at some point, more information is not necessarily beneficial. A sustained diet of political or ecological news can be debilitating, and we can also fall into "paralysis by analysis." So once we comprehend the crises, shifting our focus toward positive change can be an energizing and important step.

We can encourage this shift by tuning out the corporate media's rancorous discourse, sensationalism, and selective reporting. We can cancel subscriptions to corporate publications, turn off corporate broadcast stations, and block their internet propaganda. Instead, we can network with friends and neighbors to discuss local opportunities for progressive change. Seattle's networking group Inspire is an outstanding example of this (www.inspireseattle.org). We can organize a potluck. As Liz Carpenter once said, "Lots of solutions happen around a casserole."[546]

Once our Democracy Movement gets started, I think reliable public information will be even more critical. As in the past, the corporate media will attempt to demonize our Movement or render it invisible. More dangerously, they will likely exploit (or stage) opportunities to attribute violence to our Movement, which would allow the *Rascal* to unleash its full arsenal of repression. Reliable information will enable us to refute corporate media propaganda and keep the focus on the Movement's demands.

United under a vision of a healthy and vibrant world, We the People can build a progressive foundation for our children's future. We can reject war and insist on diplomacy. We can refuse violence and choose deliberation. We can disallow the *Rascal's* ruinous greed and encourage a global effort to restore the ecological Balance. We the People can make this happen. We need to do it now.

APPENDIX I

Current Ecological Trends

This supplement surveys the global ecological unraveling mentioned in the Introduction. The twelve topics discussed here are adapted from Jared Diamond's *Collapse—How Societies Choose to Fail or Succeed* (2005 Viking).

1. NATURAL HABITAT DISINTEGRATION

The expansion of the human enterprise continues to convert natural ecosystems into human-made systems such as cities and farmlands. Tropical rainforests are a sobering example of the loss. Hailed as Earth's headquarters of global biodiversity by the eminent biologist Edward O. Wilson, these complex ecosystems formerly occupied some four billion acres. They have now shrunk by one-half, and will vanish within the next fifty years at current rates of destruction.

Rainforest statistics from *The Future of Life* Edward O. Wilson (2002 Random House) 59

A brief but illuminating portrayal of habitat disintegration is contained in *The Song of the Dodo—Island Biogeography in an Age of Extinctions* David Quammen (1996 Scribner) 9-13

Habitat issues on Madagascar (among the last large land masses on Earth to be inhabited by humans) are discussed in *The Eighth Continent—Life, Death, and Discovery in the Lost World of Madagascar* Peter Tyson (2000 HarperCollins)

For an artistic interpretation of these concepts, listen to the British musical group Seize the Day's "Temples of Rain Are Burning" at
http://www.seizetheday.org/music.cfm?albumID=2&trackID=20

2. DIMINISHING WILD FOODS

One example is fish. Hydroelectric dams have adversely impacted the migratory requirements of anadromous fish (those that live at sea, but reproduce in fresh water), including many species of salmon. In addition, industrial harvesting has precipitated the collapse of one-third of the Earth's oceanic fisheries, and the rate of this decline has been accelerating. This is an alarming trend, given that one-third of humanity is dependent on oceanic fish to meet its protein needs.

The impact of Columbia River hydroelectric projects is discussed by the Northwest Power and Conservation Council at
http://www.nwcouncil.org/history/DamsImpacts.asp
See "The Oceanic Crisis" *Monthly Review* July-August 2008 91-111
See the BBC's '*Only 50 Years Left' for Sea Fish* at
http://news.bbc.co.uk/2/hi/science/nature/6108414.stm

3. DIMINISHING GENETIC DIVERSITY

A mass extinction event is in progress on planet Earth. It is estimated that 50 species a day quietly disappear, without the isolated media attention sometimes given to polar bears, tigers, and other charismatic megafauna. Yes, species have come and gone over the eons; however, as David Quammen explains to those untroubled by the current trend, "And there has always been a pilot light burning in your furnace. So why worry when your house is on fire?"

The David Quammen quote is from *The Song of the Dodo—Island Biogeography in an Age of Extinctions* (1996 Scribner) 605

For an overview of extinction events see *The Future of Life* Edward O. Wilson (2002 Random House) Chapter 4 "The Planetary Killer"

Regarding the rate of species extinction, see the PBS website at http://www.pbs.org/wgbh/evolution/library/03/2/l_032_04.html

See also paleontologist Niles Eldredge's *The Sixth Extinction* at http://www.actionbioscience.org/newfrontiers/eldredge2.html

For a discussion of human impact on the biosphere prior to the Industrial Age, see Tim Flannery's *The Eternal Frontier* (2001 Grove Press), or David Suzuki's *Earth Time* (1998 Stoddart) esp. 113

Ethnobotanist Mark Plotkin's *Medicine Quest—In Search of Nature's Healing Secrets* (2000 Viking) discusses the human health implications of species extinctions, including the extinctions of human tribes and cultures that have been the repositories of generations of medicinal knowledge. Forest-derived medicines are also discussed in Plotkin's *Tales of a Shaman's Apprentice* (1993 Viking).

4. Soil Erosion

Geneticist and agricultural author Wes Jackson believes that the loss of topsoil is the single greatest threat to our food supply and the continued existence of civilization. The farming state of Iowa, for example, has lost roughly half its topsoil to agriculture-induced erosion over the past 150 years. The time required to restore topsoil, however, is a geologic process measured in thousands of years. Is topsoil important? Jared Diamond found that soil erosion (as well as deforestation) contributed to the decline of all of the collapsed societies that he examined.

Wes Jackson quote from *The Sun* (October 2010); Jackson offers his vision for sustainable agriculture in *Consulting the Genius of the Place: An Ecological Approach to a New Agriculture* (2010 Counterpoint)

For details on soil erosion rates and mechanisms, see Diamond's *Collapse—How Societies Choose to Fail or Succeed* (2005 Viking) 489-490

5. Fossil Fuel Depletion

US oil reached peak production around 1970, and then entered a permanent phase of decline. Today, all the Earth's oil reserves have peaked—but humanity's reliance on petroleum continues to increase. For example, the industrial food system now requires the input of seven to ten energy calories to produce one food calorie. The dramatic food-production gains of the Green Revolution (that coincided with a doubling of the human population) were derived from the intense application of petroleum-based fertilizers and pesticides, delivered through petroleum-driven farm machinery. As food journalist Michael Pollan concisely explained to Bill Moyers, "we are eating oil." Indeed, oil depletion may play the largest single role in bringing the age of industrial expansion to a close.

In 1956, without naming it as such, the geoscientist M. King Hubbert famously predicted that US oil production would peak between 1966 and 1972 before entering a permanent phase of decline—exactly the reality that transpired in 1970.
Food-calorie information is from Michael Pollan's *The Omnivore's Dilemma—A Natural History of Four Meals* (2006 Penguin) 41-47
Michael Pollan quote from *Bill Moyers Journal—The Conversation Continues* Bill Moyers with Michael Winship (2011 New Press) 12
On the oil-prompted close of the industrial era, see "The Peak Oil Scenario" in *The End of Growth—Adapting to Our New Economic Reality* Richard Heinberg (2011 New Society Publishers) 15-17 Heinberg's updates are at http://richardheinberg.com/

6. Fresh Water Depletion

Agricultural, industrial, and residential demand now exceeds the Earth's sustainable supply of fresh water. Some of the Earth's rivers, including the Colorado at times, have run dry due to withdrawals. Groundwater reserves have also been drying up. The Ogallala Aquifer of the Great

Plains region (source of 30 percent of US agricultural irrigation) has been in decline since high-volume withdrawal began in the 1950s.

Maude Barlow discusses planetary water issues in *Blue Covenant: The Global Water Crisis and the Coming Battle for the Right to Water* (2007 New Press) (This work is articulately excerpted in *Monthly Review* July-August 2008 125-141)
Aquifer information is at
  http://en.wikipedia.org/wiki/Ogallala_Aquifer#Aquifer_water_balance
Updates on global water issues by Blue Planet Project are at
  http://www.blueplanetproject.net/

7. THE PHOTOSYNTHETIC CEILING

Ultimately, the Sun's radiant energy drives all the metabolic chemical reactions of life on Earth. Even exclusively carnivorous animals sit atop food chains anchored in photosynthetic—sunlight-driven—reactions. Our food, clothing fiber, and timber, are all derived from the Sun's energy. Even our hydroelectric dams are powered by the Sun, whose radiant energy drives the planet's hydrosphere, forming the clouds that deliver water to turbine-driven power generators. In 1986, Stanford University researchers estimated that our human civilization was appropriating some 40 percent of the Earth's total photosynthetic production—an estimate that has subsequently risen to 50 percent. Trends in population, technology, and land use indicate that the human enterprise may appropriate the Earth's entire photosynthetic capacity (reach the photosynthetic ceiling) by the middle of the current century. This scenario, although disputed by some, would leave virtually no photosynthetic production available for any species not integral to an exclusively human-centered biosphere.

Photosynthetic capacity was first explored in *Human Appropriation of the Products of Photosynthesis* Peter M. Vitousek et. al, in *Bioscience* V36 N6 368-373, on line at
http://www.biology.duke.edu/wilson/EcoSysServices/papers/VitousekEtal1986.pdf

Controversy about and interpretations of these concepts is at
http://environmental-issues.wikispaces.com/Photosynthetic+ceilings

8. INCREASING TOXIC CHEMICALS

Chemical pollutants concentrate toward the top of food chains, rendering carnivorous predators the final repositories of environmental pollution. Bald eagles, for example, were a focus of Rachel Carson's seminal work *Silent Spring* (1962) because they had become the final repositories of DDT that had concentrated up aquatic food chains into the staple of their diet: fish. The resulting concentrations of DDT in the eagles' bodies caused reproductive failures that drove them to the brink of extinction. Biologists today attribute the worldwide decline in human male sperm count to the synthetic chemicals now circulating throughout the Earth's hydrological and atmospheric systems. Even more sobering is the worldwide occurrence of synthetic chemicals in human breast milk, for as biologist and author Sandra Steingraber has observed, "adult humans are not at the top of the food chain; breast-feeding infants are."

A synopsis of food chain (biomagnification) principles is at
http://en.wikipedia.org/wiki/Biomagnification

For the results of national testing for chemical contaminants in the US population, see the Centers for Disease Control and Prevention's *Fourth National Report on Human Exposure to Environmental Chemicals* (December 2009) at
http://www.cdc.gov/exposurereport/

Some three decades after Carson's *Silent Spring*, the focus of chemical environmental hazards shifted from Bald eagles to human beings with the publication of *Our Stolen Future* by Theo Colborn, Dianne Dumanoski,

and John Peterson Myers (1996 Penguin Books). Then Deborah
Cadbury's *Altering Eden—The Feminization of Nature* (1997 St.
Martin's Press) drew specific attention to the developmental
complications of endocrine (hormone) disrupting chemicals. See also
Sandra Steingraber's *Having Faith: An Ecologist's Journey to Motherhood*
(2001 Perseus Books)

Updates on human sperm count decline are at
http://www.ourstolenfuture.org/newscience/reproduction/sperm/sper
m.htm

Regarding the disproportionate toxic burden shifted to and borne by Native
North Americans, see Rex Weyler's *Blood of the Land* (1992 Capitol City
Press) Chapter 5 & p154

9. Translocation of Alien Species

Plants and animals can cause serious disruptions when they are relocated to ecosystems where they have not existed previously. For example, mosquitoes were introduced in the Hawaiian Islands in 1826, arriving as larvae in the bilge water of a ship. The mosquitoes carried the infectious agents of avian malaria and the bird pox virus—diseases with which Hawaii's bird species had no evolutionary association, and therefore no innate immunity. Following the mosquito's introduction, the Hawaiian Islands became the avian extinction capital of the world. Commensurate with the globalization of trade and travel over the past few centuries, devastating planetary migrations of flora and fauna have proceeded apace, resulting in a worldwide endangerment or extinction of native species. Worldwatch author Chris Bright has referred to this phenomenon as evolution in reverse.

The Song of the Dodo—Island Biogeography in an Age of Extinctions David
Quammen (1996 Scribner) 316-17

Life Out of Bounds—Bioinvasion in a Borderless World Chris Bright (1998
Worldwatch Institute)

See also "Cheat Takes Over" in *A Sand County Almanac* Aldo Leopold (1949
Oxford University Press)

10. GLOBAL WARMING

There is broad scientific consensus that global warming is in progress, and that increasing greenhouse gasses are the chief culprit. Edward O. Wilson observes that the Earth's surface temperature has fluctuated in lockstep with CO_2 concentrations for the past 400,000 years and that CO_2 has risen by over 30% since the dawn of the Industrial Age (and continues to rise by over 2% annually at humanity's current rate of emissions). Many scientists now believe that a global climate crisis will unfold well before 2050, and could destroy human civilization.

Atmospheric history and statistics from *The Future of Life* Edward O. Wilson (2002 Knopf) 67 and *Now or Never—Why We Must Act Now to End Climate Change and Create a Sustainable Future* Tim Flannery (2009 Atlantic Monthly Press) 14-26

Ross Gelbspan's *The Heat is On: The high stakes battle over the Earth's threatened climate* (1997 Addison-Wesley) exposes the fossil fuel industry's financial sponsorship of skeptical "experts" who created the "debate" over global warming in the face of overwhelming scientific consensus.

Gelbspan's updates are at http://www.heatisonline.org/main.cfm

Naomi Oreskes details the scientific consensus on global warming in *Science*, December 3, 2004 at
http://www.sciencemag.org/content/306/5702/1686.full

Greenpeace International carries updates on industry funding of climate-denial at http://www.greenpeace.org/usa/en/campaigns/global-warming-and-energy/polluterwatch/koch-industries/

Updates from the Intergovernmental Panel on Climate Change (IPCC) are at http://www.ipcc.ch/index.htm

Scientists dissenting from the IPCC's conclusions are at http://en.wikipedia.org/wiki/List_of_scientists_opposing_the_mainstream_scientific_assessment_of_global_warming

11. Human Overpopulation

Having been relatively stable at one million [-BILLION?] for millennia, the past two centuries have seen a seven-fold increase in human population. In various ways, this expansion has driven the current mass extinction event; in part, we are squeezing other species off the face of the Earth. The mid-range estimate of the United Nations Population Division is a population of nine billion in the year 2050.

See current estimated human population statistics at
http://www.worldometers.info/world-population/

David Suzuki discusses exponential population growth in *Earth Time* (1998 Stoddart) Chapter 3

United Nations World Population projections appear in *Peak Everything— Waking Up to the Century of Declines* Richard Heinberg (2007 New Society Publishers) 11

12. Human Environmental Impact

The global increase in humanity's standard of living has forced the Earth to accommodate not just more people, but effectively larger people. It is estimated that four planet Earths would be required to support the current human population at a US standard of living.

Paul Ehrlich and John Holdren coined the formula I=PAT ("eye-pat"), where overall human Impact is a function of Population, Affluence, and Technological capability. See http://www.eoearth.org/article/IPAT_equation or more concisely in David Suzuki's *Earth Time* (1998 Stoddart) 20-21. I prefer to think of the relationship simply as I = PC (Impact equals Population times Consumption).

Jim Merkel discusses consumption issues and alternatives in *Radical Simplicity—small footprints on a finite Earth* (2003 New Society Publishers) esp. Chapter 2. See also Merkel's Global Living Project at http://www.radicalsimplicity.org/

The "larger people" concept is from *Overshoot: The Ecological Basis of Revolutionary Change* William R. Catton (1980 University of Illinois Press).

The Ecological Footprint concept debuted in *Our Ecological Footprint* Mathis Wackernagel & William Rees (1996 New Society Publishers).

Mathis Wackernagel explains the ecological footprint concept in 5 minutes at http://www.youtube.com/watch?v=94tYMWz_Ia4

Calculate your own ecological footprint on Wackernagel's Global Footprint Network at http://www.footprintnetwork.org/en/index.php/GFN/page/personal_footprint/

Appendix II

The Cold War Worldview

This supplement discusses the development of the Cold War Worldview. In addition to other events surveyed in chapters 4 and 5, Washington's early Cold War foreign policy stance is demonstrated here by the Truman administration's actions in Italy.

There were two opposing views of the Soviet Union within US policy circles at the close of WWII. At the heart of the first view was an image of the Soviet Union as a world revolutionary state, intent on world domination.[547] Charles Bohlen, who became US Ambassador to the Soviet Union in 1953, was an advocate of this view.

The roots of this perspective stretched back to the 1917 Bolshevik Revolution which overthrew the cruel and inept autocracy of Czar Nicholas II, famous for pogroms and financial policies that led to national economic ruin. Washington had no problem with the overthrow of Czar Nicholas, but was alarmed by the Bolsheviks' denouncement of capitalist ideology and their formal establishment of socialism in the new Union of Soviet Socialist Republics.[548] Twelve thousand US troops were dispatched to counteract the Bolshevik revolution.[549] Two years and thousands of US casualties later, the troops were withdrawn, having failed to "strangle at its birth the Bolshevik state," as Winston Churchill put it.[550] In post-WWII United States, those with memories of the Bolsheviks' socialist intentions believed that the Soviet Union was still the wolf, perhaps in a new dress, and were adamantly opposed to all things Soviet.

The alternative postwar perspective of the Soviet Union held that it was behaving like a traditional Great Power *within* the international system, rather than trying to overthrow it. Advocates of this view regarded détente with the Soviets as a distinct possibility. In the early postwar years, however, the Soviets-as-dominators perspective became the official stance of US foreign policy. This position misinterpreted both the range and degree of the Soviet challenge and also downplayed the possibilities for diplomacy and accommodation.[551]

The Soviets had suffered twenty *million* casualties in the war as well as significant destruction of infrastructure. Military strategists from all corners had concluded that their ability to wage war would be severely compromised for many years. Nevertheless, President Truman and State Secretary Marshall believed the Soviet Union was an aggressive military state intent on world domination. As discussed in chapter 4, the communists' 1948 passage through the "already half open" Czech door was amplified to crisis proportions. President Truman and others may have intended these actions to be short-term remedies for immediate political and economic problems; but once established, the Cold War Worldview of the Soviet Union as an Evil Empire persisted for decades.

The US response to Italy's 1946 election was an example of the anti-communist stance that the new Truman administration would take. In this election, the three major parties (and their seats won in the Assembly) were the right-leaning Christian Democrats (207), the Socialists (115) and the communists (104). Subsequently, the Socialist and Communist Parties merged into the Popular Democratic Front, shifting the Christian Democrats into minority status. Although the Italian Communist Party was only a minority within the Popular Democratic Front, Cold Warriors in the Truman administration viewed its very existence as tantamount to a communist takeover. Suddenly, Italy's next (1948) election became a top priority for the Truman administration; they believed a US intervention was needed to ensure the Christian Democrat's victory.

In January 1947, Italian Premier (and founder of Italy's Christian Democratic Party) Alcide de Gasperi appealed to the Truman administration for economic assistance toward Italy's war recovery efforts. A period of political chaos followed this request, during which de Gasperi and his cabinet resigned twice. Following the chaos, de Gasperi formed a Cabinet that excluded all socialists and communists, and Washington approved de Gasperi's aid request. Then, in the run-up to the 1948 election, the Truman administration ramped up support to the Christian Democrats:

The State Department announced that if the communists should win, Italy would receive no further US aid.

Washington's dire predictions of communist dictatorship and horror stories of life behind the Iron Curtain were broadcast in Italy.

The CIA funneled $1 million to communist opposition and supplied pamphlets that scandalized Communist Party members' sex lives and accused them of being fascists and atheists.

In the final month before the election, President Truman pledged the return of 29 Italian vessels seized during WWII.

The House Appropriations Committee approved $18.7 million in Italian aid, followed by a $4.3 million payment to former Italian war prisoners. The State Department pledged $31 million in gold as compensation for Nazi looting during the war, and large shipments of food (including $8 million in grain) were approved just four days before the election.[552]

Not surprisingly, the Christian Democrats won the 1948 Italian election, and Washington Cold Warriors breathed a sigh of relief. From their perspective, a communist takeover had been averted.

Appendix III

Bay of Pigs

> This supplement recounts the US-sponsored invasion of Cuba by a Cuban exile brigade in 1961. Other aspects of this event are discussed in Chapter 8.

It had become an enormous flotilla—an *armada*. Four US Navy destroyers escorted the aircraft carrier *USS Essex*, staffed with 3,200 men and a squadron of 12 Skyhawk fighter jets. The submarines *USS Cobbler* and *USS Threadfin*, and the helicopter assault carrier *USS Boxer* carrying two thousand marines were all steaming toward Rendezvous Point Zulu, 50 miles south of Cuba. At Zulu, these naval assets joined a CIA-trained Brigade of 1,543 Cuban exiles preparing to launch their long-awaited invasion of Cuba in an effort to overthrow the island's new revolutionary leader, Fidel Castro. Most members of the exile Brigade were quartered on five CIA-chartered freighters of the García Line, a family-owned shipping enterprise sailing from Miami under the command of Eduardo García. Seven additional US Navy destroyers escorted the García fleet, as well as two armed CIA support vessels, the *Blagar* and the *Barbara J*. As evening arrived, the flagship *Blagar* began leading the invasion fleet single file toward Cuba's southern shore. While still 12 miles from land, the 500-foot landing ship dock, *USS San Marcos*, pulled alongside the fleet to disgorge the contents of her enormous hold: seven landing craft vessels loaded with tanks, trucks and other heavy equipment that was to be ferried to the beaches along with the troops. The resulting column was now well over a mile in length. By all appearances, no expense had been spared. It was Sunday, April 16, 1961.

Shortly after 10:00 p.m., the *Blagar*'s commander, CIA agent Grayston Lynch, and five Cuban frogmen piled into a catamaran for an advance mission to lay out marker lights on Blue Beach, one of the three stretches of shoreline in the *Bahía de Cochinos* (Bay of Pigs) where the Brigade was planning to put ashore. Lynch stood watch as twin outboards thrust the landing party into the night, towing a rubber raft that would set the frogmen on the beach, which CIA intelligence had said would be quiet. When the beach slowly came into view, however, it appeared to be anything but quiet. Tall high-intensity vapor lights lit an extended stretch of the shoreline; Lynch later said it looked like Coney Island. A *bodega* (outdoor bar) was alive with locals enjoying the tropical evening. Contrary to CIA briefings, the area appeared to be wide awake.

Under these unanticipated circumstances, the relative darkness toward the center of the beach seemed to offer the best opportunity for an undetected landing, although the deep woods behind that stretch of shoreline made Lynch uneasy. Anchoring the catamaran a few hundred yards out, the frogmen transferred to the rubber raft. Motioning toward the dark woods, Lynch announced, "I'm going with you," as he jumped into the raft, "I want to know what's inside there." Engaging the raft's silent-running outboard, the frogmen's leader, José Alonso, set course for shore.

Dismissing contrary opinions including those of native Cubans, CIA experts had assured all involved that the dark areas in the U-2's Bay of Pigs photographs were seaweed. But the skeptics were right. The CIA's seaweed was in fact a coral reef. To no one's surprise aboard the rubber craft, the outboard hit the reef sharply and died some eighty yards offshore. Peeling over the side, the frogmen began the tedious process of walking the raft to shore, waist-deep in the surf.

Finally making the shoreline, the frogmen were placing the Brigade's landing lights when a radio message came from the *Blagar* out in the bay. "There's a truck coming toward your position!" The landing party took cover behind a jetty, and as the truck discharged thirty militiamen, the full battery of the *Blagar*'s armament opened up, raking the beach in heavy gunfire, scattering the militiamen into the woods.

Back in their flippers, the frogmen located a break in the coral that would allow limited landing access, but in the chaos and excitement, the boundaries of the channel were not adequately communicated. As two landing craft vessels steamed full-tilt for shore, their double-hulls were ripped open on the coral. As the landing crafts' passengers waded ashore, their communication radios were ruined by salt water. Once ashore, a squadron of the Brigade's fourth battalion commandeered an old Chevrolet they found behind the *bodega* and headed for a nearby airstrip, which was to become the Brigade's air base.

Shortly after midnight, Lynch received the alarming news that the Brigade's air cover scheduled for the coming dawn had been cancelled. "Castro still has operational aircraft. Expect you to be hit at dawn. Unload all troops and supplies and take ships to sea as soon as possible," read the communiqué from Washington. The coral reefs, having already delayed landing maneuvers and claimed important Brigade assets, now presented a critical obstacle to the success of the entire mission. Alonso questioned a local fisherman, discovering that the high tide necessary for the deep draft of the landing craft vessels would not arrive until dawn. Lynch broke from Washington's orders, cancelled the planned invasion of a third beach, and stationed the *Blagar* offshore. Her .50-caliber machine guns and 75-mm anti-aircraft cannon would offer the Brigade's best defense against Castro's air force at dawn.

Presiding over the Brigade's invasion force at Red Beach (18 miles further into the bay from Blue Beach) was CIA agent William "Rip" Robertson. As with Blue Beach, Red Beach maneuvers were not going well. Frogmen had come under small arms fire on the beach, and the García Line freighter *Houston*, carrying the second and fifth battalions, found that seven of its nine landing craft were not serviceable—the long troop-shuttle to shore would be dangerously prolonged. When finally on the beach, the second battalion discovered a microwave radio station with its equipment still warm. The battalion commander had not been briefed on the radio station's existence, and he wondered how the CIA planners could have missed it. By this time, there was also mutiny. The commander of the fifth battalion had become so disillusioned that he ordered his men not to disembark the *Houston*.

At dawn, the Brigade's situation deteriorated dramatically. As Washington's midnight message had warned, Cuban B-26's began strafing the beaches, sending the Brigade scrambling for cover. Even more menacing were Castro's British-built Sea Furies with their wing-mount missiles. The *Houston* (the recalcitrant fifth battalion still aboard) was hit amidship by a Sea Fury missile at 6:30 a.m., and immediately began taking on water as fire broke out below decks. "Give me all you got!" Captain Luís Morse commanded the engine room. This quick action prevented the full loss of the vessel by ramming it onto a sandy beach. Nevertheless, 28 men drowned or suffered fatal shark attacks attempting to make shore.

Due to the extended delay of landing maneuvers, morning found the García Line's *Río Escondido* floating in the bay off Blue Beach. She was a disaster waiting to happen. Carrying the Brigade's sixth battalion, she was also fully loaded with matériel. Large quantities of ammunition and 54,000 gallons of fuel were stowed below decks, and highly visible topside were another 200 55-gallon drums of aviation fuel.

At 9:30 a.m., Cuban Air Force Captain Enrique Carreras came barreling down on the *Río Escondido*, firing all four of his Sea Fury's missiles. "Abandon Ship!" hollered Captain Gus Tirado as fire engulfed the 200 fuel drums and flaming rivers poured below decks. All aboard jumped into the waves as every available watercraft raced to the scene and began plucking men from the bay. Miraculously, all escaped shark attack and had retreated to a safe distance before three huge explosions engulfed the ship in an enormous fireball. "God Almighty!" shouted Rip Robertson from twenty miles away at Red Beach, as a spectacular mushroom cloud rose in the sky. "Fidel got the A-bomb?"

The *Houston* and the *Río Escondido* lost, Eduardo García could stand no more. He ordered his three remaining freighters full-throttle into the Atlantic, their holds packed with the Brigade's ammunition. Continued aerial attacks forced the remaining invasion fleet's retreat from the bay by afternoon, leaving Brigade forces stranded and ill-equipped on the beach.

Word of the shortages on the beaches reached the CIA's airstrip in Nicaragua, where an effort was mounted to resupply the invasion force. Captain Eddie Ferrer's C-46 transport was loaded with 20,000 pounds of ammunition. Sensing imminent danger, Ferrer instructed his small crew to tie machine guns at the doors and windows of the cabin; all ports would remain open for the entire mission. The gravity of the situation moved the air contingent's chaplain, Father Cavero, to appeal to Ferrer for inclusion in the mission. Ferrer conceded, "Climb in."

Nicknamed "watermelon," the C-46 was a big, bulky cargo plane, and Ferrer's had been loaded to the hilt. Barely clearing the trees at the end of the runway, it lumbered off over the Caribbean. Approaching Cuban airspace, Ferrer's radio suddenly came alive, "May Day! May Day! This is Puma One!" Ferrer's fellow pilot, José Crespo, had been hit; a Sea Fury was on his tail. Just then, all firearms opened up in the rear cabin; Ferrer turned to see that even the priest was on his knees, emptying a submachine gun out a window. Ferrer turned back to sight the approaching plane and was horrified. "Cease fire! They're our friends!" (Both Brigade and Castro forces were flying B-26s with Cuban insignia, providing a constant source of confusion throughout the invasion.)

Their missions aborted in the face of Castro's air power, Ferrer and Crespo banked for Nicaragua. The badly needed ammunition would not reach the Brigade. Over the course of an agonizing two hours over the Caribbean, Crespo's B-26 gradually lost altitude due to engine damage sustained in the earlier skirmish. Father Cavero came to Ferrer's forward cabin and donned the radiophone to hear Crespo's and his co-pilot's confessions just before the bomber plunged into the sea. A four-aircraft search and rescue mission was immediately launched and continued throughout the following day. No trace was found.

Following these inauspicious beginnings, the plight of the men on the beach grew worse by the hour under dwindling ammunition supplies and increasing pressure from Castro's ground and air forces. Plans for the closure of the land routes to the bay were not realized, and these roadways conveyed Castro's steadily advancing forces. By Wednesday, the invasion had completely collapsed. Those Brigade forces that had not been captured scattered into the surrounding swamp, a morass of crocodiles, snakes, and mosquitoes amid dense tropical vegetation.

Searching the bay on Friday morning, a US destroyer picked up 12 survivors from the shoreline near the *Houston*'s wreckage. As rescue operations were plucking more survivors from the beach the following day, a Castro helicopter swooped down and opened fire. All present watched in amazement as a US Navy rescue plane appeared and (under strict "no fire" orders) repeatedly charged the helicopter in a contact run—a valiant attempt to literally knock the chopper out of the sky. Rescue efforts resumed when the helicopter retreated over the island.

All told, exile invasion forces suffered 114 casualties, and 1,201 were captured and imprisoned in Cuban jails. Four US pilots were killed in crashes and over 4,000 of Castro's soldiers were reported dead, missing, or wounded.

There are numerous accounts of this event. These five sources provided most of the details contained in this summary:

CIA agent Grayston L. Lynch's *Decision for Disaster—The Battle of the Bay of Pigs* (2003 Pocket Books)

Historian and Kennedy aide Arthur M. Schlesinger, Jr.'s *A Thousand Days—John F. Kennedy in the White House* (1965 Houghton Mifflin)

History professor Howard Jones' *The Bay of Pigs* (2008 Oxford University Press)

National Security Archive Director Peter Kornbluh's *Bay of Pigs Declassified—The Secret CIA Report on the Invasion of Cuba* (1998 The New Press)

Peter Wyden's *Bay of Pigs—The Untold Story* (1979 Simon and Schuster)

Appendix IV

Who Ran the Investigation?

> This supplement examines the structure and supervision of the National Commission on Terrorist Attacks Upon the United States, commonly known as the 9/11 Commission. Other aspects of 9/11 are discussed in chapter 15.

When the Bush administration finally (November 2002) conceded to an investigation of 9/11, an administration insider, Philip Zelikow, was appointed as the Commission's executive director. David Ray Griffin, emeritus professor at Claremont Graduate University, has documented the extent to which the independence of the 9/11 commission was compromised by Zelikow's connections to the Bush administration.[553] What did Zelikow do as the executive director?

One of the first things Zelikow did was draw up an outline of the 9/11 Commission's Final Report. As author and *New York Times* reporter Philip Shenon writes in *The Commission: The Uncensored History of the 9/11 Investigation*, Zelikow and a former Harvard associate set to work on the outline. By March 2003, with the commission's staff barely in place, their outline was complete.[554] It appears that what Zelikow needed was not an investigation, but a literary staff to supply the narrative for his outline. As the Commission's co-chairs, Thomas Kean and Lee Hamilton, later explained, Zelikow assigned one team of the Commission's staff to "tell the story of al-Qaeda's most successful operation—the 9/11 attacks."[555]

Kean and Hamilton were privy to Zelikow's advance outline early on, but they agreed not to share the outline with the commission's staff. To no avail; the staff eventually learned of Zelikow's preordained outline. As initial alarm gave way to cynicism, a parody entitled "The Warren Commission Report—Pre-emptive Outline" began circulating.

One of the parody's chapter headings was indicative of the mood: Single Bullet: We Haven't Seen the Evidence Yet. But Really. We're Sure.[556]

While the public face of the 9/11 Commission consisted primarily of its ten commissioners, all 85 members of the Commission's staff reported directly to Zelikow. Zelikow's executive actions insulated the commissioners from the staff, who witnessed Zelikow's increasing control over the investigation. Essentially, Zelikow became an eleventh commissioner, in many ways more powerful than the other ten. In short, Zelikow was in charge.[557] And the final stop in the processing of tortured al-Qaeda testimonies that anchored the Commission's OBL&TT story? The executive director's office.

Appendix V

Afghanistan Revisited

> This supplement examines the US invasion of Afghanistan, as mentioned in chapter 15.

The 2003 invasion of Iraq was justified by spurious notions of WMD and Iraq-al-Qaeda links (chapter 11). What was the invasion of Afghanistan really about? If history is any indication, it was about drugs and money.

Recall that the CIA orchestrated a Nicaraguan Contra fundraising endeavor that involved the US importation and retailing of cocaine in the 1980s. The CIA's drug-running history is not confined to Nicaragua; it appears to include Afghanistan.

During the 1980s and 1990s, the CIA oversaw the transfer of several C-130 Hercules transports from US government ownership to private contractors. These four-engine turboprops (capable of taking off and landing in fields and pastures) kept turning up in Latin America, Africa, *and the* Middle East. A C-130 linked to CIA affiliate T&G Aviation of Arizona was seized in 1994 with a billion dollars' worth of cocaine on board.[558]

In 2000, Afghanistan was supplying some 70 percent of the global opium market, topping world production charts. Then in June 2000, the Taliban issued a ban on opium production which initiated a precipitous (94 percent) drop in 2001 production.

When US forces invaded Afghanistan in late 2001, CIA and US military agents wasted no time liberating a number of known opium warlords who, they said, would assist US troops. The following year, Afghanistan again topped world charts as the planet's largest opium producer.[559]

During this time, a kilogram of heroin (a narcotic derived from raw opium) was fetching US $150,000 in Moscow. Following the money and knowing the CIA's history of involvement in drug trafficking, it appears that Operation Enduring Freedom was more concerned about liberating Afghan opium warlords and restoring opium poppy production, not so much about tracking down Osama bin Laden, who somehow managed to escape.

Appendix VI

The Land of Desire: From Citizens to Consumers

Chapter 3 examines government efforts to gather public support for wars. This supplement surveys the US government's early 20th century efforts in an entirely different arena: the stimulation of public demand for mass-produced goods. This effort encouraged the rise of materialism, and resulted in a cultural transformation during which the United States became the Land of Desire.[560]

*We talk about the American Dream, . . .
but what is that dream, in most cases,
but the dream of material things?*[561]

Eugene O'Neill

The last thing a fish would ever notice would be water, observed anthropologist Ralph Linton (1893-1953). From Linton's perspective, the last thing we humans would ever notice would be our culture—the ever-present and overarching context in which we live our lives; what George Orwell called the air we breathe. The United States today is often characterized as a consumer culture—with good reason: per capita, we have the largest ecological footprint on the planet. And yet, as the "air we breathe," this culture is all but invisible. How did this consumer culture become established?

At the turn of the 20th century, the mechanized manufacturing of the industrial revolution began flooding retail markets with mass-produced goods. The purchase of these goods soon became paramount to continued industrial expansion. Commercial interests, including national retailers, investment banks, and the entertainment industry, coalesced to encourage the consumption of industrial products. One of the most influential constituents in this web became the US Department of Commerce, created in 1913 as a Cabinet-level entity, singularly focused on the needs of the business sector.

The Commerce Department's largest spinoff, the Bureau of Foreign and Domestic Commerce (BFDC), attracted generous congressional appropriations and its staff mushroomed to 2,500 employees by 1930. BFDC provided the business community with advice, including how best to deliver goods, widen streets, and present merchandise in tempting ways. For several years, BFDC administrator Julius Klein coached the business community in a weekly radio broadcast from the White House. "Advertising is the key to world prosperity," Klein announced on air in 1929.[562]

Whereas land, livestock, and food crops had been the prized commodities of prior centuries' agrarian lifestyles, *money* now became the primary focus of an increasingly cash economy. The worth of almost anything came to be seen as the price it could fetch in the marketplace. Gradually, goods offering comfort and luxury became the cardinal feature of a new culture that increasingly regarded the new and the stylish as important and desirable.[563]

New York's Times Square exemplified the new commercial emphasis, and in 1917 was home to the world's largest electrified sign: an 80-foot high, 200-foot long, 17,000-lamp outdoor advertisement for Wrigley's Spearmint chewing gum. The advent of air conditioning and central heating in the 1920s introduced year-round shopping comfort, and Macy's led the New York department stores in extending shopping time to nine o'clock two nights a week.

A specific back-to-school market was created, and new marketing efforts expanded the most elaborate of all sales promotions: Christmas. By the late 1920s, annual Santa Claus appearances and holiday parades were being staged all across the nation, and Macy's had incorporated giant helium-inflated characters into the ever-swelling spectacle of its Thanksgiving Day parade. In 1928, thousands of balloons were released as Santa Claus glided onto the Macy's marquee in a Zeppelin dirigible.[564] The *sky* had become the limit.

The public responded to the new *zeitgeist*, embracing their role as consumers with an enthusiasm that soon exceeded their financial means. Bankers came to the rescue, offering easy credit with installment buying and a range of small loans that became a multibillion-dollar financial industry.[565] The charge customer was born.

In 1921, with the national economy in a dire post-WWI slump, President Warren G. Harding appointed Herbert Hoover as secretary of commerce. Hoover believed that the cause of the sluggish economy was insufficient consumption, and he set about stimulating consumer demand. Hoover's goal of a full-growth economy was achieved during the Roaring Twenties. But just when many believed that the nation had reached a state of permanent prosperity, the bubble burst, and Hoover's 1929 presidential inauguration coincided with the onset of the Great Depression.

During the 1930s, economist John Maynard Keynes advanced new ideas that were thought to be the answer to the Great Depression. Keynes discarded prior economic concerns such as wealth distribution and the productive limits of land, and portrayed economic growth as a panacea.[566] Keynesian economists later asserted that economic growth had pulled the nation out of the Depression era, but in reality, the economic stimulus of WWII had driven the economic recovery. Nevertheless, a growth-as-cure-all paradigm became established as conventional wisdom. The companion concept of *infinite* growth soon followed, promising that the growth paradigm could be sustained indefinitely.[567]

Keynesian economists introduced new concepts of substitutability and efficiency to defend the tenet of infinite growth against assaults from the natural sciences, the physical world, or common sense. The Green Revolution provides an example of the result. Initially portrayed as a permanent fix, the Green Revolution drastically increased our dependence on fossil fuels while postponing (but amplifying) humankind's reckoning with the carrying capacity of the Earth.[568]

The unlimited growth paradigm was enthusiastically embraced by business executives, and elected officials soon discovered that pro-growth policies were popular at the ballot box. The synergy of all these efforts established economic growth as the central tenet of national economic policy.

Economists critical of the infinite growth paradigm have been sidelined, their voices unheard by the vast majority. Keynesian economic assumptions have seldom been questioned in the mass media.[569] For example, one famous critic of the new consumer culture was sociologist and economist Thorstein Veblen, who coined the term "conspicuous consumption" in his 1899 classic *The Theory of the Leisure Class*. Veblen received a one-paragraph mention buried in the *New York Times*' only piece that mentioned his book. The *Times*' reported that Veblen's analysis threw a "curious light" upon many current practices and convictions, and concluded, "it is thought probable that Mr. Veblen's independent views will encounter a good deal of opposition."[570] Following this singular dismissal, the *Times* made no mention of Veblen for another four years.

Although largely unnoticed over time, the consumer culture spawned over a century ago became the air we breathe; the United States became the Land of Desire. The resulting economic activity has brought monetary prosperity to millions, but the attending emphasis on growth and consumption has also had negative consequences for our society and the Earth. Ecological footprint analysts estimate that four planet Earths would be required to support the current human population at a US standard of living.[571]

ENDNOTES

[1] "A Weakened World Cannot Forgive Us"
An interview with Kathleen Dean Moore *The Sun* (March 2001)

[2] UC-Berkeley distinguished professor of cognitive science and linguistics George Lakoff states, "if the facts don't fit the frames people have, they will keep the frames (which are, after all, physically in their brains) and ignore, forget, or explain away the facts." Lakoff is perhaps most famous for his *Don't Think of an Elephant—Know your values and frame the debate* (2004 Chelsea Green). Current cite is from his *Thinking Points—Communicating our American Values and Vision* (2006 Farrar, Straus and Giroux) 10, 40

[3] Once established, textbooks maintain their market standing through subsequent editions, so despite the older copyright dates of the texts Loewen surveyed, the myths and inaccuracies Loewen found persist. The US history text in current use at my local high school is the second edition of a 1994 copyright, *Fearon's United States History*, and it evidences the characteristics Loewen found in his 1995 survey.

The twelve textbooks Loewen examined were: *The American Adventure* Social Science Staff of the Educational Research Council of America (1975 Allyn and Bacon); *American Adventures* Ira Peck, Steven Jantzen, and Daniel Rosen (1987 Steck-Vaughn); *American History* John A. Garraty with Aaron Singer and Michael Gallagher (1982 Harcourt Brace Jovanovich); *The American Pageant* Thomas A. Bailey and David M. Kennedy (1991 D. C. Heath); *The American Tradition* Robert Green, Laura L. Becker, and Robert E. Coviello (1984 Charles E. Merrill); *The American Way* Nancy Bauer (1979 Holt, Rinehart and Winston); *The Challenge of Freedom* Robert Sobel, Roger LaRaus, Linda Ann De Leon, and Harry P. Morris (1990 Glencoe); *Discovering American History* Allan O. Kownslar and Donald B. Frizzle (1974 Holt, Rinehart and Winston); *Land of Promise* Carol Berkin and Leonard Wood (1983 Scott, Foresman); *Life and Liberty* Philip Roden, Robynn Greer, Bruce Kraig, and Betty Bivins (1984 Scott, Foresman); *Triumph of the American Nation* Paul Lewis Todd and Merle Curti (1986 Harcourt Brace Jovanovich); and *The United States—A History of the Republic* James West Davidson and Mark H. Lytle (1981 Prentice-Hall)

[4] *Lies My Teacher Told Me* James W. Loewen (1995 Touchstone) 220-226

[5] *Overthrow—America's Century of Regime Change From Hawaii to Iraq* Stephen Kinzer (2006 Times Books) 127

[6] *Killing Hope—U.S. Military and C.I.A. Interventions Since World War II* William Blum (2004 Common Courage Press) 72

[7] Amnesty International Secretary-General Martin Ennals, as cited in Amnesty's New York publication *Matchbox*, Fall 1976, Ibid., 72, 402n44

[8] *A People's History of the United States*
Howard Zinn (1980 Harper & Row) 431;
Killing Hope—U.S. Military and C.I.A. Interventions Since World War II William Blum (2004 Common Courage Press) 94-99; *Waging Peace 1956-1961* Dwight D. Eisenhower (1965 Doubleday) 264-269

[9] *The Political Economy of Third World Intervention: Mines, Money, and U.S. Policy in the Congo Crisis* David Gibbs (1991 University of Chicago Press) 100, Ibid. (Blum), 157, 414n6

[10] Ibid. (Blum), Chapter 26, 156-163
See also *In Search of Enemies—A CIA Story* John Stockwell (1978 W W Norton & Company); various entries for Lumumba and Mobutu.

[11] Political economist and media analyst Edward S. Herman has called Mobutu "possibly the greatest thief of the 20th century in ratio of loot to GDP." *Z Magazine* November 1996
(Herman is co-author (with Noam Chomsky) of *Manufacturing Consent*.)

[12] *Overthrow—America's Century of Regime Change From Hawaii to Iraq* Stephen Kinzer (2006 Times Books) 182

[13] Ibid. at 210-211

[14] What is *not* generally included in accounts of JFK's Alliance for Progress is that "it turned out to be mostly military aid to keep in power right-wing dictatorships and enable them to stave off revolutions." *A People's History of the United States* Howard Zinn (1980 Harper & Row) 430

[15] *Lies My Teacher Told Me* James W. Loewen (1995 Touchstone) 12, 16

[16] José Ortega y Gasset, Spanish philosopher, 1883-1955
The Great Thoughts Compiled by George Seldes with David Laskin and Henry Steele Commager (1996 Ballantine Books) 537

[17] Naomi Wolf discusses US citizen's naiveté vs. global awareness in *Give Me Liberty* (2008 Simon & Schuster) 197-199

[18] *Overthrow—America's Century of Regime Change From Hawaii to Iraq* Stephen Kinzer (2006 Times Books) 142

[19] *The CIA in Guatemala*
Richard H. Immerman (1982 University of Texas Press) 178

[20] This intergenerational resistance occurs when subsequent generations are unwilling or unable to challenge established legends that their elders still hold dear. For example, committees that choose history textbooks must answer to parents and teachers whose own worldviews are frequently a product of distorted versions of our history. When myths or legends conflict with documented history, these conflicts can become more than the members of textbook selection committees are willing to suffer. The adults on these committees may just want their children to adopt the same worldviews that they themselves have embraced since their own childhood. The end result, in any event, has been the perpetuation of inaccuracies,

omissions, and false legends in our nation's official history. (See James Loewen's account of a successful 1975 first amendment lawsuit that overcame Mississippi's rejection of a revisionist state history textbook in *Lies My Teacher Told Me* 17)

[21] *Blood of the Land—The Government and Corporate War Against First Nations* Rex Weyler (1992 New Society Publishers) 13-14
American Indian Holocaust and Survival
Russell Thornton (1987 University of Oklahoma Press) 42-43

[22] The estimated indigenous population of the contiguous United States declined from over 5 million in 1492 to a mere 250,000 by the close of the 19th century—a 95 percent reduction. This event in our history tends to be rationalized by Native Americans' possession of the "wrong" religious beliefs as well as their classification as primitives and savages. Similarly, the European invasion of the Americas has historically been framed as a "war" fought between adult male soldiers and warriors. In actuality, indigenous peoples were exterminated without regard to age or sex by intentional actions such as gifts of small pox-infected blankets and sneak attacks on villages or encampments to kill Native Americans of any age and either sex. This genocide in our past has typically been well-camouflaged in our official national history. *The Third Chimpanzee—The Evolution and Future of the Human Animal* Jared Diamond (1992 HarperCollins) 298-302

[23] In *War is a Force That Gives Us Meaning* (2002, Anchor Books, 77-78), Chris Hedges writes, "The reinterpretation of history . . . is the bedrock of the hatred and intolerance that leads to war." Hedges points to variations in the historical accounts of Bosnian Gavrilo Princip's assassination of the Austrian Archduke Franz Ferdinand in 1914 (oft-cited as the trigger that initiated World War I). Textbooks in the Serb-controlled region of Bosnia refer to Princip as "a hero and a poet," whereas in Croatian textbooks, Princip is "an assassin trained and instructed by the Serbs to commit this act of terrorism." And Muslims in the region offer a third version, describing Princip as "a nationalist whose deed sparked anti-Serbian rioting that was only stopped by the police from all three ethnic groups."

Hedges has discovered that the gap between these conflicting historical perspectives has continued to widen. "By the time today's books in the Balkans reach recent history, the divergence takes on ludicrous proportions; each side blames the others for the Bosnian war and makes no reference to the crimes or mistakes committed by its own leaders or fighters."

[24] Guatemalan history is primarily from
The CIA in Guatemala—The Foreign Policy of Intervention
Richard H. Immerman (1982 University of Texas Press).
Information also came from *Killing Hope—U.S. Military and C.I.A. Interventions Since World War II* William Blum (2004 Common Courage Press), and *Overthrow—America's Century of Regime Change From Hawaii to Iraq* Stephen Kinzer (2006 Times Books).

See also *Doing Business With the Dictators—A political History of United Fruit in Guatemala, 1899-1944* Paul J. Dosal (1993/1995 Scholarly Resources).

[25] Greg Grandin writes that "by 1930, Washington had sent gunboats into Latin American ports over six thousand times, invaded Cuba, Mexico (again), Guatemala, and Honduras, fought protracted guerrilla wars in the Dominican Republic, Nicaragua, and Haiti, annexed Puerto Rico, and taken a piece of Colombia to create both the Panamanian nation and the Panama Canal."
Empire's Workshop—Latin America, the United States, and the Rise of the New Imperialism (2006 Metropolitan Books) 3

[26] *Overthrow—America's Century of Regime Change From Hawaii to Iraq* Stephen Kinzer (2006 Times Books) 130;
The Father of Spin—Edward L. Bernays & the Birth of Public Relations Larry Tye (1998 Crown Publishers) 176

[27] Sulzberger was a member of the CIA's Mockingbird network (discussed ahead in chapter 8). A sampling of *New York Times'* 1954 headlines: "Guatemala Rally Reflects Red Grip" (February 21); "Communism in Guatemala: A Case History" (February 21); "Guatemalan Reds Exploit Reforms" (March 3); "Dulles Condemns Reds for Intrigue in the Americas" (March 6); "Red Defeat in Guatemala" (July 1); and a July 3 front page headline announcing the arrival of Castillo Armas, "Guatemala Gives Leader of Revolt Rousing Welcome."

[28] *Overthrow—America's Century of Regime Change From Hawaii to Iraq* Stephen Kinzer (2006 Times Books) 134-135

[29] This Peurifoy quote from Stephen Kinzer's *Overthrow* (137) agrees with Peurifoy's testimony before the House Select Committee on Communist Aggression: "I spent six hours with him one evening, and he talked like a Communist, he thought like a Communist, he acted like a Communist, and if he is not one, Mr. Chairman, he will do until one comes along."
The CIA in Guatemala The CIA in Guatemala—The Foreign Policy of Intervention Richard H. Immerman (1982 University of Texas Press) 181

[30] Phillips was sometimes quite innovative in his propaganda efforts. When a well-known Guatemalan fighter pilot defected, Phillips got him drunk at Opa-Locka and asked the pilot to act out the speech he would give to all his former colleagues if he were not concerned about his relatives still living in Guatemala. A dramatic recital calling for the defection of all Guatemalan pilots resulted, and Phillips' covert tape recording of the drunken tirade was subsequently broadcast over the Voice of Liberation network.

[31] *Overthrow—America's Century of Regime Change From Hawaii to Iraq* Stephen Kinzer (2006 Times Books) 140

[32] *Killing Hope—U.S. Military and C.I.A. Interventions Since World War II* William Blum (2004 Common Courage Press) 79

[33] To further demonize the Arbenz administration, UFCO's publicity office provided US journalists with photographs of mutilated bodies in a mass grave, ostensibly an example of the atrocities committed by the Arbenz "regime"—an accusation that was never substantiated. Ibid. at 78

[34] *Overthrow—America's Century of Regime Change From Hawaii to Iraq* Stephen Kinzer (2006 Times Books) 141

[35] When the Guatemalan Army Chief of Staff refused to step down, his resignation was obtained at gunpoint by a three-man junta formed under the CIA's handpicked pawn, Colonel Elfego Monzón. With President Arbenz out of the way and the military under control, Monzón's subordinates were each handed $100,000 and dismissed from further service. Monzón himself was retired within days, and Armas assumed power.

[36] *The CIA in Guatemala—The Foreign Policy of Intervention* Richard H. Immerman (1982 University of Texas Press) 198

[37] Consignment to Bernabe's list was to be taken seriously. Thousands were arbitrarily imprisoned, executed, or simply disappeared. As Ubico's enforcer, Bernabe reputedly submerged his suspects in electric shock baths or applied a head-shrinking steel skullcap in order to "pry loose secrets and crush improper thoughts." (Ibid. at 199)

[38] *Empire's Workshop: Latin America, the United States, and the Rise of the New Imperialism* Greg Grandin (2006 Metropolitan Books) 40-42

[39] Debs was arrested and imprisoned following this speech on June 16, 1918. *The Great Thoughts* Compiled by George Seldes with David Laskin and Henry Steele Commager (1996 Ballantine Books) 196

[40] *The Great Thoughts* Compiled by George Seldes with David Laskin and Henry Steele Commager (1996 Ballantine Books) 185

[41] John L. O'Sullivan's essay titled "Annexation" appeared in the July-August 1845 issue of *Democratic Review*, asserting that it was the "manifest destiny" of Anglo-Saxon Americans "to overspread the continent allotted by Providence for the free development of our yearly multiplying millions." (O'Sullivan's "Manifest Destiny" argument was subsequently employed in the dispute with Great Britain over the Oregon Country.)

[42] *A People's History of the United States,* Howard Zinn (1980 Harper & Row) 148

[43] Polk stated, "Mexico has passed the boundary of the United States, has invaded our territory and shed American blood upon the American soil. . . . As war exists, notwithstanding all our efforts to avoid it, exists by the act of Mexico herself, we are called upon by every consideration of duty and patriotism to vindicate with decision the honor, the rights, and the interests of our country."

The true nature of the event was recorded in Colonel Ethan Allen Hitchcock's diary while stationed at General Taylor's Rio Grande encampment prior to the Mexican attack. Hitchcock states, "I have said from the first that the United States are the aggressors. . . . We have not one particle of right to be here.... My heart is not in the business... but, as a military man, I am bound to execute orders." *A People's History of the United States* Howard Zinn (1980 Harper & Row) 148-150

[44] *The Great Quotations* George Seldes with J. Donald Adams (1966 Caesar-Stuart) 547

[45] Lincoln's speech included these lines: "The marching [of] an army into the midst of a peaceful Mexican settlement, frightening the inhabitants away, leaving their growing crops and other property to destruction, to you may appear a perfectly amiable, peaceful, un-provoking procedure; but it does not appear so to us." *People's History of the United States,* Howard Zinn (1980 Harper & Row) 149-151

[46] Ibid. at 152

[47] Ibid. at 302

[48] Norton was a Harvard professor and social critic whose intellectual endeavors earned him honorary degrees from Oxford, Columbia, and Yale. *The Great Quotations* George Seldes with J. Donald Adams (1966 Caesar-Stuart) 533

[49] *A People's History of the United States* Howard Zinn (1980 Harper & Row) 294-298

[50] http://www.pbs.org/crucible/bio_hearst.html See also *The Great Quotations* George Seldes with J. Donald Adams (1966 Caesar-Stuart) 305

[51] *A People's History of the United States* Howard Zinn (1980 Harper & Row) 301-302

[52] *The Great Quotations* George Seldes with J. Donald Adams (1966 Caesar-Stuart) 579-580

[53] *A People's History of the United States* Howard Zinn (1980 Harper & Row) 353-354

[54] In February 1915, the Imperial German government had declared the seas surrounding the British Isles to be a war zone, and that Allied ships in the area would be sunk without warning beginning February 18. Then on April 22, the German Embassy in Washington placed a notice in some four dozen US newspapers (often appearing next to Lusitania sailing announcements) warning that "vessels flying the flag of Great Britain, or any of her allies, are liable to destruction in those waters" and that "travelers sailing in the war zone on the ships of Great Britain or her allies do so at their own risk."

In this climate of hostilities, the Lusitania's name was removed from her hull, the Cunard Shipping Line colors on her funnels were blacked out, and on her final voyage, none of her flags were flown. Were these attempts to promote the ship's safe passage by concealing her national identity? Perhaps. But nevertheless, with German submarines lurking in British waters, the British Admiralty dispatched two destroyers to usher the Lusitania through British waters upon her return in March.

Then, in an increasingly hostile naval environment that included the sinking of Allied merchant vessels by the German submarine U-20 on May 5 and 6, British naval orders did not provide escort for the Lusitania's May

7 final and fatal return to the British Isles. Alone and stripped of her colorful identity, she became an easy mark for the U-20.

The controversy that subsequently arose as to whether or not the Lusitania was "unarmed" generally failed to distinguish between two separate questions. The first was whether guns were mounted on her decks. The ship had been constructed with cannon deck-mounts, but no artillery was ever installed. This fact was repeatedly cited as evidence that the ship was an "unarmed passenger liner."

The second question was whether she was carrying munitions and matériel. The answer is "yes." Falsified manifests concealed the Lusitania's cargo of over 1,000 cases of 3-inch shells and nearly five million rounds of US-made munitions. Furthermore, the Kaiser's Imperial German government knew this matériel was on board and en route to their war enemies.

Emphatic statements of the Wilson administration that the Lusitania was unarmed were duplicitous. William Jennings Bryan understood the deception. Stating that "passengers and ammunition should not travel together," Bryan resigned as Wilson's secretary of state, explaining that his continued service would be unfair to "the cause which is nearest to my heart, namely, the prevention of war." (Quotes from *New York Times* articles, June 1915.)

The national discourse throughout this event was predominantly a "Hawks vs. Doves" debate over the appropriate US response to the Lusitania's sinking, a debate that avoided any serious investigation of the liner's actual sinking.

[55] *Freedom of the Seas,* J. M. Kenworthy and George Young (1928 Hutchinson & Co.) *Room 40: British Naval Intelligence 1914-18* Patrick Beesly (1982 Harcourt Brace Jovanovich), as cited in *Towers of Deception—The Media Cover-Up of 9/11* Barrie Zwicker (2006 New Society Publishers) 272

[56] *World Crisis* Winston Churchill (1923 Thornton Butterworth), as cited in *Towers of Deception—The Media Cover-Up of 9/11,* Barrie Zwicker (2006 New Society Publishers) 272

[57] *A People's History of the United States* Howard Zinn (1980 Harper & Row) 355

[58] *A People's History of the United States* Howard Zinn (1980 Harper & Row) 355

[59] Text and video of the Roosevelt Pearl Harbor address at http://www.americanrhetoric.com/speeches/fdrpearlharbor.htm

[60] *Day of Deceit—The Truth About FDR and Pearl Harbor* Robert B. Stinnett (2000 Simon & Schuster) 256

[61] The McCollum Memorandum is at http://en.wikisource.org/wiki/McCollum_memorandum

[62] *A People's History of the United States* Howard Zinn (1980 Harper Colophon) 402

[63] *Day of Deceit—The Truth About FDR and Pearl Harbor,* Robert B. Stinnett (2000 Simon & Schuster) 9

[64] Ibid. at 18

[65] As Stimson's diary continues, his moral dilemma becomes apparent. "The question was how we should maneuver them into the position of firing the first shot without allowing too much danger to ourselves." Ibid. at 178

[66] An earlier, November 24th, memorandum stated, ". . . Statements of Japanese government and movements [of] their naval and military forces indicate in our opinion that a surprise aggressive movement in any direction." A memorandum three days later stated, ". . . an aggressive move by Japan is expected within the next few days. . ." At this juncture, military orders from Washington began repeatedly stressing the importance of Japan striking first. One dated November 27th read, ". . . United States desires that Japan commit the first overt act."

These memoranda appear in Appendix C, *Day of Deceit—The Truth About FDR and Pearl Harbor* Robert B. Stinnett (2000 Simon & Schuster)

[67] Ibid. at 144-145

[68] Transcript: Navy Court of Inquiry 1944 p1942, as cited in *Day of Deceit—The Truth About FDR and Pearl Harbor,* Robert B. Stinnett (2000 Simon & Schuster) 144, 349n10

[69] Ibid. at 144

[70] *The Reminiscences of Captain Joseph J. Rochefort* US Naval Institute Oral History Division 1970 163, as cited in *Day of Deceit—The Truth About FDR and Pearl Harbor* Robert B. Stinnett (2000 Simon & Schuster) 203, 361n2

[71] Upon Breen's death, the trade magazine *Variety* stated "More than any single individual, he shaped the moral stature of the American motion picture." http://en.wikipedia.org/wiki/Joseph_Breen and http://en.wikipedia.org/wiki/Propaganda_film#World_War_II

The Great Quotations, George Seldes with J. Donald Adams (1966 Caesar-Stuart) 113

[72] *All Governments Lie!—The Life and Times of Rebel Journalist I. F. Stone* Myra MacPherson (2006 Scribner) 246

[73] "Aviation RFC?" *Business Week* January 31, 1948, as cited in *Harry S. Truman and the War Scare of 1948* Frank Kofsky (1995 St. Martin's Press) 169, 345n1

[74] Some $175 billion (over $2 trillion in 2010 dollars) in war supply contracts went to private corporations; over $100 billion of this revenue went to the ten largest recipients. *The Power Elite* C. Wright Mills (1956 Oxford University Press) 100-101

A postwar Senate report noted that two thousand corporations had been contracted for scientific research during the war, but that 40 percent of the $1 billion spent had gone to the ten largest corporations. US Senate report,

"Economic Concentration and World War II" *A People's History of the United States* Howard Zinn (1980 Harper Colophon) 408, 416
Even prior to the US declaration of war, French and British military procurements had boosted the US aircraft makers' earnings to $21 million in 1939. By 1944, profits had soared to $52 million (over $6 billion in 2010 dollars). "Finance: War Baby in a Peace Economy," *Business Week* June 7, 1947 58, 63

Regarding tax-payer subsidies, Grumman Corporation, for example, was able to buy over $13 million worth of government-owned plants and tools for 30 cents on the dollar at war's end. *Harry S. Truman and the War Scare of 1948* Frank Kofsky (1995 St. Martin's Press) 9, 13, 310n7&9

[75] Ibid. (Kofsky) at 256
[76] "1949 in the Aircraft Industry" *Automotive Industries* January 1949 96; Ibid. at 12, 251, 363n22
[77] The 1936 edition of the Aircraft Yearbook observed that "among the disturbing factors in American aviation is an increased tendency in some official circles to consider seriously government manufacture of aircraft and engines."

During a December 1947 meeting of the President's Air Policy Commission, United Aircraft Corporation Chair Fred Rentschler stated, "There should be no reason whatever for considering this kind of assistance by government as coming within the scope of subsidy." And in a prophetic statement at this time, Secretary Symington explained, "The word to talk is not 'subsidy'; the word to talk is 'security.'" Perhaps this security perspective had been on Lockheed President Robert E. Gross' mind in January 1945—before the war's end—when he opined, "If we have a true and lasting peace, obviously the demand for military airplanes will be limited. On the other hand, if we have an armed truce, and it begins to look as though this may be the case, the demand for military airplanes might be very considerable." Ibid. at 48, 50, 251, 255

[78] *A People's History of the United States*
Howard Zinn (1980 Harper Colophon) 408, 409
[79] Marshall's term at State was bracketed by US military service. He was an Army General during WWII and became secretary of defense following his secretary of state post.
[80] *A People's History of the United States*
Howard Zinn (1980 Harper Colophon) 430
[81] *Harry S. Truman and the War Scare of 1948*
Frank Kofsky (1995 St. Martin's Press) 92
[82] EISENHOWER SCOFFS AT FEARS OF WAR STARTED BY RUSSIA
New York Times February 6, 1948
[83] Additionally, Commerce Secretary Averell Harriman told the President's Air Policy Commission that he was "convinced that [the Soviets] will not take any steps which they feel would bring them into a major conflict in the

foreseeable future." Proceedings of the President's Air Policy Commission, September 8 1947, as cited in *Harry S. Truman and the War Scare of 1948* Frank Kofsky (1995 St. Martin's Press) 83, 84, 328 n1,n4

[84] *Shattered Peace—The Origins of the Cold War and the National Security State* Daniel Yergin (1977 Houghton Mifflin) 351

[85] *The Forrestal Diaries* Walter Millis and E. S. Duffield, eds. (1951 Viking) 387, as quoted in *Harry S. Truman and the War Scare of 1948* Frank Kofsky (1995 St. Martin's Press) 104

[86] *The Papers of General Lucius D. Clay: Germany 1945-49* Jean Edward Smith (1974 Indiana University Press) 466-7 Ibid. (Kofsky) at 106-7
See also *Shattered Peace—The Origins of the Cold War and the National Security State* Daniel Yergin (1977 Houghton Mifflin) 351

[87] Ibid. (Kofsky) at 104-122

[88] *The Most Noble Adventure—The Marshall Plan and the Time When America Helped Rebuild Europe* Greg Behrman (2008 Free Press) 157

[89] The administration's stance on Czechoslovakia recognized that:
1) communists had made the strongest showing of any party in Czechoslovakia's 1946 elections; 2) a communist premier had recently been installed (Klement Gottwald); and 3) Czechoslovakia had followed the Kremlin's withdrawal from the Marshall Plan.

Also, the US Ambassador to Czechoslovakia cabled State Secretary Marshall during this time, observing the high probability of the Czechoslovakian Government soon becoming subservient to the Kremlin. Telegrams of September 29 and 30, 1947 *US Department of State, Foreign Relations of the United States* V4 Eastern Europe, The Soviet Union, 232-235

The Marshall statement was made in a telegram to the US Ambassador to France. *Harry S. Truman and the War Scare of 1948* Frank Kofsky (1995 St. Martin's Press) 94, 99

[90] In February 1948, Czechoslovakian President Eduard Benes was seriously ill and recovering from a major stroke of the prior summer that had left him impaired (he died in September). As part of a plan to force a reconstruction of the Czech Cabinet, twelve non-communist Cabinet members submitted their resignations to Benes on February 20, with the understanding that Benes would refuse their resignations. In an abrupt change of course, the ailing Benes accepted the non-communists' resignations, and allowed the reconstitution of a communist-dominated government on February 25. *Shattered Peace—The Origins of the Cold War and the National Security State* Daniel Yergin (1977 Houghton Mifflin) 347

[91] Robert Dallek has stated that Soviet agents murdered Masaryk, however he offered no evidence for this assertion. (*Harry S. Truman* (2008 Times Books) 73) Edward R. Murrow (Masaryk's friend of many years) seriously doubted the suicide story. (*The Polk Conspiracy—The Murder and Cover-up in the Case of CBS News Correspondent George Polk* Kati Marton (1990

Farrar, Straus & Giroux) 135) The timing of Masaryk's death, Murrow's doubts about suicide, the absence of a Soviet motive, and the extent to which the incident was unjustifiably amplified into the Reign of Terror crisis, all seem to make Washington the chief suspect in what was most likely Masaryk's murder.

[92] *New York Times,* March 11 & 12, 1948

[93] *Shattered Peace*
Daniel Yergin (1977 Houghton Mifflin) 354

[94] *Business Week* June 19 1948 26, as cited in
Shattered Peace—The Origins of the Cold War and the National Security State, Daniel Yergin (1977 Houghton Mifflin) 360

[95] *Harry S. Truman and the War Scare of 1948*
Frank Kofsky (1995 St. Martin's Press) 133

[96] On March 24, 1948 a *New York Times* front-page headline announced WARPLANE ENGINES SHIPPED TO RUSSIA. The article's lead paragraph stated, "Testimony that American warplane engines have been shipped to Russia within the last six months and that shipping boxes marked for Russia are lying 'All over the New York waterfront' was presented to Congress today." The article detailed Russian shipments of planes sold at "scrap prices, 'some of which were obviously new,'" and shipments of "everything from tractors and bulldozers to electric generators." Somewhat unbelievably, when the press questioned the President about these reports, Truman responded, "Russia is, at the present time, a friendly nation and has been buying goods from us right along." Public Papers of the Presidents of the United States: Harry S. Truman, 1948 (US Government Printing Office 1963) 193, as cited in *Harry S. Truman and the War Scare of 1948* Frank Kofsky (1995 St. Martin's Press) 149

[97] http://www.mtholyoke.edu/acad/intrel/nsc-68/nsc68-1.htm

[98] *Harry S. Truman* Robert Dallek (2008 Times Books) 102

[99] *U.S. Television News and Cold War Propaganda, 1947-1960* Nancy E. Bernhard (2003 Cambridge University Press) 83

[100] Acheson warned the editors, "We are faced with a threat not only to our country but to the civilization in which we live and to the whole physical environment in which that civilization can exist." Ibid. at 85

[101] Ibid. at 123

[102] *Shattered Peace—The Origins of the Cold War and the National Security State* Daniel Yergin (1977 Houghton Mifflin) 285

[103] Ibid.

[104] http://www.latimes.com/local/obituaries/la-me-david-greenglass-20141014-story.html#page=1

[105] *Witness to a Century*
George Seldes (1987 Ballantine Books) 357-361

[106] Representative Clare Hoffman's (R-MI) labeling of Seldes as a "Red smear artist" and a "mass producer of falsehood and vilification" was widely

reported, and Seldes was included in a Life Magazine photo essay that named dozens of US Citizens suspected of communist sympathies (including Leonard Bernstein, Albert Einstein, and Lillian Hellman).
See *TELL THE TRUTH AND RUN* Rick Goldsmith (2006 Never Tire Productions, Kovno Communications)

[107] Ronald Reagan was president of the Screen Actors Guild at this time, and testified as to the severity of the communist threat in the film industry.

[108] *The Culture of the Cold War*
Steven J. Whitfield (1996 John Hopkins University Press)

[109] Churchill is often credited with introducing the "Iron Curtain" into Cold War lexicon, however *Pravda* and the *Manchester Guardian* quoted Joseph Goebbels, German Reichminister of Propaganda, using the term in February 1945, and Senator Arthur Vandenberg used the term on the Senate floor on November 15, 1945.

[110] *Khrushchev Remembers—the Last Testament,*
Strobe Talbott, editor (1974 Little, Brown and Company) 355

[111] *The Polk Conspiracy—The Murder and Cover-up in the Case of CBS News Correspondent George Polk*
Kati Marton (1990 Farrar, Straus & Giroux) 23

[112] During the colonial period, approximately two percent of the Greek population came to control the vast majority of the nation's land, wealth, and resources. The majority of the population suffered all the consequences of severe and persistent poverty, and their misery was further aggravated by the mayhem and destruction of WWII.

[113] *The Polk Conspiracy—The Murder and Cover-up in the Case of CBS News Correspondent George Polk*
Kati Marton (1990 Farrar, Straus & Giroux) 80

[114] *The State of Europe* Howard K. Smith (Cresset Press 1950) 151 as quoted in *Killing Hope—U.S. Military and C.I.A. Interventions Since World War II* William Blum (2004 Common Courage Press) 35

[115] *Intervention and Revolution: The United States in the Third World* Richard Barnet (1970 Paladin) 109, as cited in *Killing Hope—U.S. Military and C.I.A. Interventions Since World War II*
William Blum (2004 Common Courage Press) 36

[116] Smith called the Athens government "the worst bunch I have seen at work anywhere," further stating, "The cruelty of its Nazi-trained police have forced honest men into the mountains. It seems to believe it needs no policy, except when the trough of foreign funds runs low, to shout, 'Communist,' and President Truman will send more." *The Polk Conspiracy—The Murder and Cover-up in the Case of CBS News Correspondent George Polk*
Kati Marton (1990 Farrar, Straus & Giroux) 89, 98, 118

[117] Ibid. at 91

[118] *Greece and the Great Powers, 1944-1947* Stephen G. Xydis (1963 Institute for Balkan Studies) 479, as cited in *Killing Hope—U.S. Military and C.I.A. Interventions Since World War II* William Blum (2004 Common Courage Press) 35-36, 396n11

[119] http://www.americanrhetoric.com/speeches/harrystrumantrumandoctrine.html

[120] A November 1947 memorandum of the American Mission to Aid Greece read in part, "We have established practical control . . . over national budget, taxation, currency, price and wage policies, and state economic planning, as well as over imports and exports, the issuance of foreign exchange and the direction of military reconstruction and relief expenditures."
American Foreign Policy in Greece 1944/1949: Economic, Military and Institutional Aspects Michael M. Amen 1978 Peter Lang Ltd.) 114-115, as cited in *Killing Hope—U.S. Military and C.I.A. Interventions Since World War II,* William Blum (2004 Common Courage Press) 38, 396n31

[121] Two-term Greek Prime Minister Andreas Papandreou (1981-1989 and 1993-1996) chronicled this era of US-Greek relations in *Democracy at Gunpoint: The Greek Front* (1970 Doubleday) Current cite from page 5.

[122] *The Polk Conspiracy—The Murder and Cover-up in the Case of CBS News Correspondent George Polk*
Kati Marton (1990 Farrar, Straus & Giroux) 89

[123] Polk further explained: "For example, consider the Liberty ships which the United States presented to Greece for re-creating the Greek merchant marine. After obtaining the ships, the Greek government promptly sold them to private Greek owners at extremely low prices."

The Liberty ships were large-capacity cargo vessels that rolled off US production lines by the hundreds during WWII. Some of the 2,400 that survived the war were sold to the Greek government to facilitate the reconstruction of their Merchant Marine; others were sold to individual Greek merchants (shipping magnate Aristotle Onassis' fleet began with Liberty ships).

The State Department grew concerned over public perceptions of Greek profiteering over the Liberty Ships program in 1947, and Acting Secretary of State Dean Acheson instructed the US Embassy in Athens to effect a solution to the matter, because "Failure to do so would adversely affect U.S. public opinion towards Greece." *The Polk Conspiracy—The Murder and Cover-up in the Case of CBS News Correspondent George Polk* Kati Marton (1990 Farrar, Straus & Giroux) 123

[124] *Harper's* December 1947 529-536

[125] *The Polk Conspiracy—The Murder and Cover-up in the Case of CBS News Correspondent George Polk*
Kati Marton (1990 Farrar, Straus & Giroux) Chapter 13

[126] To launch the story, an eleven-page coroner's report was immediately released, giving remarkable details of the crime itself, such as a claim that it

"took place in a rowboat." Sure enough, the "confession" of the eventually convicted "accomplice" to the crime stated that the murder had taken place in a rowboat.

The unjustified nature of the communist conspiracy claim did not go unnoticed by Edward R. Murrow, whose May 17, 1948 national broadcast included these lines: "According to the Associated Press, twenty or more communists have been questioned. The record does not show that any non-communists have been questioned. . . . [A leading government spokesperson] stated, 'We are one thousand percent sure it was the work of communists.' He offered no support for this statement." Ibid. at 183, 185, 218

[127] Staktopoulos' torture involved electric shocks to his feet (the scars from which he bore for the duration of his life), and beatings with truncheons (blows to his head produced permanent hearing damage), while his cries of agony were muffled by rags stuffed in his mouth. Ibid. at 275-280

[128] As Bill Moyers is fond to say of incredible anecdotes, *I'm not making this up.* Ibid. at 299, 309

[129] Rankin told Marshall that "they tend to restrain responsible Greek officials from taking necessary action for fear of further alienating opinion in the United States as created through the misinterpretations of local correspondents of influential American newspapers."

Rankin told Bigart, "Your inference that Mr. Tsaldaris is trying to set up a 'rightist police state' . . . could also harm the chance of further aid to Greece. Could it not? . . . In view of this delicate situation, I'm sure you will understand the danger of your sort of reporting." Ibid. at 130-134

[130] "Death in Salonika Bay: Who Pulled the Trigger?" *New York Times* September 17, 1977 See also Ibid. at 245

[131] Ibid. at 263

[132] *All Governments Lie!—The Life and Times of Rebel Journalist I. F. Stone* Myra MacPherson (2006 Scribner) 280

[133] Lippmann biographer Ronald Steel writes that despite expressing private doubts, Lippmann's adherence to this position "had the inestimable virtue of not upsetting cold war politics." *Walter Lippmann and the American Century* (1980 Vintage Books), Ibid. at 278-279

[134] Ibid. at 278

[135] *Witness to a Century* George Seldes (1987 Ballantine Books) 378-381

[136] For example, the return of the shah increased US oil corporations' share of Iran's oil reserves, the CIA restored order for United Fruit Company in Guatemala, and US-installed dictatorships in Congo and Chile assured corporate access to those nations' oil and mineral resources.

[137] *The Great Thoughts* Compiled by George Seldes with David Laskin and Henry Steele Commager (1996 Ballantine Books) 224

[138] The full quote reads, "The real difficulty is with the vast wealth and power in the hands of the few and the unscrupulous who represent or control capital.

Hundreds of laws of Congress and the state legislatures are in the interest of these men and against the interests of workingmen. These need to be exposed and repealed. All laws on corporations, on taxation, on trusts, wills, descent, and the like, need examination and extensive change. This is a government of the people, by the people, and for the people no longer. It is a government of corporations, by corporations, and for corporations."

[139] William Greider refers to the British Parliament as "a self-perpetuating 'committee of landlords' that for centuries protected propertied wealth against disenfranchised workers and peasants."
One World, Ready or Not—The Manic Logic of Global Capitalism William Greider (1997, Simon & Schuster) 38

[140] Mary Zepernick of the Program on Corporations, Law, and Democracy provides a concise history of early corporate developments in the documentary *The Corporation* (2003 Zeitgeist Films).

[141] The Court did not actually rule on the matter of corporate personhood; however. Justice Morrison Waite inserted a statement of opinion into the Court record that created an opportunity for corporate lawyers to then claim personhood status for corporations.
The Transformation of American Law 1870-1960—The Crisis of Legal Orthodoxy Morton J. Horwitz (1992 Oxford University Press) Chapter 3 "Santa Clara Revisited: The Development of Corporate Theory"

[142] *When Corporations Rule the World*
David C. Korten (1996 Kumarian Press) 59

[143] "Corporations are People Too"
Ben Manski and Lisa Graves *In These Times* March 2010

[144] Western Washington State University professor Daniel M. Warner observes: "The modern concept of Corporate Social Responsibility recognizes that the business firm has a range of 'stakeholders,' as they are called, all of whom are due fair consideration by the firm. The stakeholders are owners/managers, shareholders, employees, suppliers, government, community and -more recently- the environment and future generations." (Personal communication, 2008) Unfortunately, it appears that *stock*holders remain the primary *stake*holders in most corporate decision-making.

[145] http://motherjones.com/mojo/2010/04/west-virginia-mine-disaster and http://www.npr.org/templates/story/story.php?storyId=125864847

[146] *Mother Jones* September/October 2010 2

[147] In January 1989, the investigative television program *60 Minutes* discussed the health considerations of Alar (a brand name for the plant growth regulator Daminozide, once used extensively on tree fruit crops). With an audience estimated at 40 million people, this program elicited a public outcry that resulted in product recalls and serious financial repercussions for all levels of the food industry dealing in Alar-treated products.

Subsequently, corporate food and agribusiness lobbying resulted in the promulgation of food disparagement laws ("banana bills") in thirteen states

(Alabama, Arizona, Colorado (amended to allow *criminal* prosecution), Florida, Georgia, Idaho, Louisiana, Mississippi, North Dakota, Ohio, Oklahoma, South Dakota, and Texas), and such legislation is still pending in several other states (California, Delaware, Illinois, Iowa, Minnesota, Oregon, Pennsylvania, South Carolina, and Washington).

[148] Prior to the *60 Minutes* broadcast, 1) EPA scientists had classified Alar as a probable human carcinogen, 2) the American Academy of Pediatrics had urged the EPA to issue a ban on Alar, and 3) public concern had prompted six national grocery chains and nine major food processors to refuse apples treated with Alar.

Consistent with *Dodge*, however, it was not until the *60 Minutes* program caused serious financial repercussions that Uniroyal (Alar's sole manufacturer) finally discontinued the sale of Alar in the US. The public health consequences and the financial distress that farmers, orchardists, and grocers suffered following the Alar Scare could have been avoided entirely had Uniroyal heeded the EPA's warnings or the advice of the American Academy of Pediatrics. Unfortunately, it took the financial distress precipitated by the *60 Minutes* broadcast to elicit Uniroyal's response.

[149] http://www.freedomforum.org/packages/first/defamationandfirstamendment/Oprah.htm

[150] Other characteristics of psychopathy are: callous unconcern for the feelings of others; incapacity and/or inability to maintain enduring relationships; and the incapacity to experience guilt.

The Corporation documentary (2003 Zeitgeist Films) employed psychopathologist Robert Hare, University of British Columbia emeritus professor of Psychology, for this evaluation.

[151] The Institute for Legal Reform's web page states that it favors: arbitration over litigation; increased attorney–client privilege; reduced discovery; and statutory caps on damage awards.
http://en.wikipedia.org/wiki/Institute_for_Legal_Reform
Total annual Chamber of Commerce lobbying expenditures have been running between $44 and $125 million. (See endnote 181)

[152] http://en.wikipedia.org/wiki/Airline_deregulation#Impact

[153] http://en.wikiquote.org/wiki/Ronald_Reagan

[154] "Deregulation and the Financial Crisis" Robert Weissman January 22, 2008 Huffington Post Business

[155] Warren's concise synopsis starts about two minutes into the clip at http://www.thedailyshow.com/watch/wed-april-15-2009/elizabeth-warren-pt--2

[156] *When Corporations Rule the World*
David C. Korten (1996 Kumarian Press)177

[157] *Public Interest Laws as "Impediments" to Free Trade* Debi Barker and Jerry Mander, as cited in *Alternatives to Economic Globalization* The International Forum on Globalization (2002 Berrett-Koehler Publishers) 20

[158] "A Stealth Attack on Democratic Governance"
Lori Wallach *The American Prospect* April 2012 52
[159] http://www.fair.org/index.php?page=2870
[160] http://www.jwsr.org/wp-content/uploads/2013/03/jwsr-v12n2-staples.pdf
[161] *One World, Ready or Not—The Manic Logic of Global Capitalism* William Greider (1997 Simon & Schuster) 171
[162] In a tale of secrecy and intrigue (that would become a hallmark of the Cheney Vice-Presidency), GW Bush's vice-presidential search committee concluded that the committee's own chair—Dick Cheney—was the best candidate. Cheney avoided the extensive vetting that other candidates were subjected to by denying he was a candidate until his selection became a *fait accompli*. See Barton Gellman's *Angler—The Cheney Vice Presidency* (2008 Penguin Group)
[163] "Cheney Income At $36 Million; Bush: $894,880"
David Cay Johnson *New York Times* April 14, 2001
[164] Charles Lewis, founding director of the non-profit Center for Public Integrity, relates Cheney's revolving door career in the documentary *Why We Fight* (Eugene Jarecki 2005)
[165] The exceptionally sweet taste of aspartame (NutraSweet®) was discovered inadvertently during ulcer drug testing at Searle in 1965. Subsequently, numerous aspartame studies on animals reported severe reactions including death, which resulted in years of Food and Drug Administration rejections for public release. But the profit potential of a no-calorie all-purpose sweetener proved irresistible, especially when cyclamate—the industry standard of the day—was banned in 1970, and negative reports of saccharin were circulating as well.

Faced with continued FDA intransigence, Rumsfeld announced at a sales meeting in January 1981 that he would begin applying pressure for FDA approval through political connections rather than continued pursuit of conventional channels. As a member of President-elect Reagan's transition team, Rumsfeld facilitated the appointment of Arthur Hull Hayes Jr. as Reagan's Commissioner of the FDA. (Hayes resigned under ethics charges two years later and joined Searle's PR firm—yet another revolving door.) Hayes went to work on the aspartame issue, and within four months took unilateral action that granted FDA approval for the public release of aspartame. This astonishing action overruled the objections of FDA scientists, Hayes' subordinates, and a Public Board of Inquiry, and ignored 16 years of research-based opinions and actions that had continuously rejected the chemical as unfit for human consumption.

Searle's 1981 profits surged to over $130 million, and the company's sale to agribusiness giant Monsanto in 1985 netted Rumsfeld a reported $12 million. Rumsfeld's Searle parachute and other corporate ventures brought estimates of his personal wealth up to well over $100 million by the time he

spun back through the revolving door to become GW Bush's secretary of defense.
http://www.rense.com/general33/legal.htm
IT WAS TOUGH MEDICINE *New York Times* January 31, 1982
http://www.commondreams.org/headlines02/0918-06.htm

[166] Select "Montanto's government ties" at http://www.organicconsumers.org/monsanto/news.cfm

[167] Updates on farmers' battles with Monsanto are at http://www.organicconsumers.org/ge/prison051403.cfm

[168] http://en.wikipedia.org/wiki/Linda_Fisher

[169] In one instance, Bush appointed Daniel Troy as the FDA's general counsel. Troy was formerly a leading attorney for major drug companies who had repeatedly sued the FDA on his clients' behalf. One would like to believe that a person with relevant experience in a particular sector would provide especially insightful service to an agency regulating that sector. Once at FDA, however, Troy offered to use the agency's resources to help his former clients fight lawsuits by injured patients.
"When Advocates Become Regulators" Anne C. Mulkern *Denver Post* May 24, 2004, as cited in *It Can Happen Here—Authoritarian Peril in the Age of Bush* Joe Conason (2007 St. Martin's Press) 141

[170] "The Deep State Hiding in Plain Sight"
Bill Moyers & Company February 21, 2014
http://billmoyers.com/episode/the-deep-state-hiding-in-plain-sight/

[171] "Obama Admin's TPP Trade Officials Received Hefty Bonuses From Big Banks" Lee Fang *Republic Report* February 17, 2014
http://www.republicreport.org/2014/big-banks-tpp/

[172] http://www.youtube.com/watch?v=k5kHACjrdEY at 4:30

[173] *When Corporations Rule the World* David Korten (1995 Kumarian Press) Chapter 18 "Race to the Bottom" 229-237

[174] Quote from Roosevelt's acceptance speech at the Democratic National Convention, June 27, 1936 *The Great Quotations* George Seldes with J. Donald Adams (1966 Caesar-Stuart) 591

[175] At the age of 20, Brandeis graduated from Harvard Law School with the highest grade average in the college's history. He was a Supreme Court Justice for 23 years ending 1939. The quote is from the October 17, 1941 issue of *Labor. The Great Quotations*
George Seldes with J. Donald Adams (1966 Caesar-Stuart)

[176] See Senator Elizabeth Warren explain this system of wealth concentration at https://secure.actblue.com/contribute/page/warrenaflspeech/?refcode=CEW010715EJ
When Corporations Rule the World David Korten (1995 Kumarian Press)
Myth America—Democracy vs. Capitalism William Boyer (2003 Apex Press)

You Call This a Democracy? Who Benefits, Who Pays and Who Really Decides? Paul Kivel (2004 Apex Press)

The War at Home—The Corporate Offensive from Ronald Reagan to George W. Bush Jack Rasmus (2006 Kyklos Productions)

[177] The extreme financial wealth of this group is usually concealed within figures reporting larger group averages. For example, the highest income group delineated in Department of Labor reports is the top third, which merges incomes of approximately $75,000 with incomes into the tens of millions, designating the whole group as the rich. Similarly, national economic statistics often conceal wide disparities. Between 2002 and 2006, for example, US growth in real income was reported to be 2.8 percent; however, this 2.8 percent figure averaged the 11.0 percent gains of the top 1 percent with the 0.9 percent gain realized by the bottom 99 percent.

See the following reports and analyses:

"It's the Inequality, Stupid—Eleven charts that explain what's wrong with America." Dave Gilson and Carolyn Perot *Mother Jones* March/April 2011

"Survival" *Mother Jones* September-October 2014 32-35

Capital in the Twenty-First Century Thomas Piketty & Arthur Goldhammer (2014 Harvard University Press) Piketty sets today's economic inequality in a long history of economic disparity and demonstrates that increasing economic inequality is a built in feature of the capitalist system.

The War at Home—The Corporate Offensive from Ronald Reagan to George W. Bush Jack Rasmus (2006 Kyklos Productions) Rasmus' work summarized at http://www.kyklosproductions.com/posts/index.php?p=57

UC Berkeley economics professor Emmanuel Saez analyses are at:
http://www.econ.berkeley.edu/~saez/
http://www.econ.berkeley.edu/~saez/saez-UStopincomes-2006prel.pdf

[178] *Rich Media, Poor Democracy—Communication Politics in Dubious Times* Robert W. McChesney (1999 The New Press) 264

[179] For example, campaign strategy along with polls and voter mood were the dominant focus in three-fourths of the political segments on the nightly news broadcasts of network television during the 2008 presidential primary. In contrast, *issues* were the dominant frame in just five percent of the news segments.

In a total of 385 news segments during the 2008 presidential primary, the two categories of "campaign analysis and strategy" and "polls and voter mood" combined to be the dominant frame in 76 percent of the segments on the nightly news broadcasts of ABC, CBS, and NBC.

US citizens do not appreciate this coverage; nearly three-fourths of the electorate want more information on candidates' positions on domestic issues and foreign policy.

The Problem of the Media—U.S. Communication Politics in the 21st Century Robert W. McChesney (2004 Monthly Review Press) 126
http://www.fair.org/index.php?page=3368

[180] http://usatoday30.usatoday.com/news/politics/story/2012/09/14/negative-environment-will-not-feed-3rd-party-uprising/57778000/1

[181] The Center for Responsive Politics' website is a comprehensive source of current and historical data about money in US politics. http://www.opensecrets.org/bigpicture/

[182] *The Problem of the Media—U.S. Communication Politics in the 21st Century* Robert W. McChesney (2004 Monthly Review Press) 131

[183] http://www.sourcewatch.org/index.php?title=Swift_Boat_Veterans_for_Truth/Funding

[184] http://www.citizen.org/congress/campaign/articles.cfm?ID=5721

[185] http://fair.org/extra-online-articles/soundbites-23/
http://www.forbes.com/lists/2008/12/lead_bestbosses08_Leslie-Moonves_IDHK.html http://www.forbes.com/profile/leslie-moonves/

[186] See endnote 181

[187] *Blowing the Roof Off the Twenty-First Century—Media, Politics, and the Struggle for Post-Capitalist Democracy* Robert W. McChesney (2014 Monthly Review Press) 15

[188] Scroll down these pages:
http://www.sourcewatch.org/index.php?title=ALEC_Politicians#Legislators_with_ALEC_Ties and
http://www.sourcewatch.org/index.php?title=ALEC_Corporations

[189] http://www.thenation.com/article/161973/alec-exposed-koch-connection#
http://www.huffingtonpost.com/robert-greenwald-and-jesse-lava/time-for-kochs-to-resign_b_1431715.html

[190] For concise details, see an interview with The Nation's John Nichols and the Center for Media and Democracy's Lisa Graves at http://www.youtube.com/watch?v=BdENM29UQDU

[191] Center for Media and Democracy at http://www.prwatch.org/
Special ALEC web site at http://alecexposed.org/wiki/ALEC_Exposed

[192] http://www.thenation.com/article/161978/alec-exposed

[193] http://www.inthesetimes.com/article/11603/publicopoly_exposed/

[194] *Loser Take All—Election Fraud and the Subversion of Democracy, 2000-2008* Mark Crispin Miller, Ed. (2008 Ig Publishing)
The Best Democracy Money Can Buy—The Truth About Corporate Cons, Globalization, and High-Finance Fraudsters Greg Palast (2004 (Expanded Election Edition) Plume Books) Chapter 9 "Oil-slick Jim, the third ring and one million missing ballots"
Was the 2004 Presidential Election Stolen?—Exit Polls, Election Fraud, and the Official Count Steven F. Freeman & Joel Bleifuss (2006 Seven Stories Press)
What Happened in Ohio?—A Documentary Record of Theft and Fraud in the 2004 Election Robert J. Fitrakis, Steven Rosenfeld, and Harvey Wasserman (2006 New Press)

"The Sale of Electoral Politics" *Censored 2005—The Top Censored Stories* Peter Phillips & Project Censored (2004 Seven Stories Press) 57-60
"No Paper Trail Left Behind: The Theft of the 2004 Presidential Election" *Censored 2006—The Top Censored Stories* Peter Phillips & Project Censored (2005 Seven Stories Press) 185-201

[195] *Black Box Voting—Ballot Tampering in the 21st Century* Bev Harris with David Allen (2003 Plan Nine Publishing) 34-39

[196] "Legislating Under the Influence—Money, Power, and the American Legislative Exchange Council" http://www.commoncause.org/atf/cf/%7Bfb3c17e2-cdd1-4df6-92be-bd4429893665%7D/MONEYPOWERANDALEC.PDF

[197] *The American Prospect* July/August 2011 27

[198] "Publicopoly Exposed—How ALEC, the Koch brothers and their corporate allies plan to privatize government" *In These Times* August 2011 16-17

[199] https://www.cia.gov/library/publications/the-world-factbook/rankorder/2102rank.html
https://www.cia.gov/library/publications/the-world-factbook/rankorder/2091rank.html
http://articles.cnn.com/2006-05-08/health/mothers.index_1_mortality-rate-death-rate-world-s-mothers?_s=PM:HEALTH

[200] http://articles.latimes.com/2010/feb/11/business/la-fi-health-profits12-2010feb12

[201] "AMA Study Shows Competition Disappearing in the Health Insurance Industry" http://www.ama-assn.org/ama/pub/news/news/health-insurance-competition.page
http://en.wikipedia.org/wiki/Health_insurance_in_the_United_States

[202] *Deadly Spin—An Insurance Company Insider Speaks Out on How Corporate PR is Killing Health Care and Deceiving Americans* Wendell Potter (2010 Bloomsbury Press) 125-130, 134

[203] Potter concluded a June 2009 testimony before the US Senate Committee on Commerce, Science and Transportation:
"Americans need and overwhelmingly support the option of obtaining coverage from a public plan. The industry and its backers are using fear tactics, as they did in 1994 [during the Clinton's reform initiative], to tar a transparent, publicly-accountable health care option as a 'government-run system.' But what we have today, Mr. Chairman, is a Wall Street-run system that has proven itself an untrustworthy partner to its customers, to the doctors and hospitals who deliver care, and to the state and federal governments that attempt to regulate it."
Deadly Spin—An Insurance Company Insider Speaks Out on How Corporate PR is Killing Health Care and Deceiving Americans Wendell Potter (2010 Bloomsbury Press) 6
See Bill Moyers' interview of Potter and link to his congressional testimony of June 2009 at http://www.pbs.org/moyers/journal/07102009/profile.html

[204] Ibid. (Potter) at 203
[205] http://voices.washingtonpost.com/44/2009/08/22/tea_party_protest_organizers_t.html
[206] http://www.msnbc.msn.com/id/32386235/ns/msnbc_tv-rachel_maddow_show/t/rachel-maddow-show-tuesday-august/
[207] FreedomWorks stands opposed to: industrial and environmental regulation; progressive taxation; social safety-net programs; universal civil rights; estate taxes; and tort liability. Its favored causes are: government-to-business subsidies; privatizing Social Security; lower investment and capital gains taxes; and expanded school voucher programs.
http://www.freedomworks.org/ http://en.wikipedia.org/wiki/FreedomWorks
[208] *The Rise of the Tea Party—Political Discontent and Corporate Media in the Age of Obama* Anthony DiMaggio 2011 Monthly Review Press) 211
[209] "The troubling history of Tea Party leader Dick Armey" Beau Hodai *In These Times*, March 21, 2010
[210] http://www.sourcewatch.org/index.php?title=FreedomWorks#cite_note-10
[211] http://www.washingtonpost.com/wp-dyn/content/article/2006/07/22/AR2006072200683.html
[212] http://en.wikipedia.org/wiki/Colony_collapse_disorder
[213] A Bulletin of Insectology report concludes, "the results from this study show a profound and devastating effect of low levels of [neonics] on honey bee colonies." Bulletin of Insectology 65 (1) 99-106 2012 www.bulletinofinsectology.org/pdfarticles/vol65-2012-099-106lu.pdf European Food Safety Authority Journal January 16, 2013 http://www.guardian.co.uk/environment/2013/jan/16/insecticide-unacceptable-danger-bees
[214] A concise summary of the CCD saga can be found in "A Deadly Disorder at the EPA" Joel Bleifuss *In These Times* March 2013 20-21 http://inthesetimes.com/article/14598/a_deadly_disorder_at_the_epa/
[215] These six corporations control 74 percent of the global pesticide market and 49 percent of the proprietary seed market. Ibid. at 21
[216] http://www.croplifeamerica.org/pesticide-issues/protecting-our-pollinators
[217] An internet search for these corporations or people can verify their current earnings. The information here was found in February 2013. Listed by corporation, CEO, earnings, and year cited: Monsanto, Hugh Grant, $10 million, 2009; DuPont, Ellen Kullman, $11.3 million, 2010; Bayer, Marijn Dekkers, $8.61 million, 2008; Dow, Andrew Liveris, $21 million, 2011; BASF, Kurt Bock, $6.8 million (€5.25 million) 2011; Syngenta, Michael Mack, $5.4 million, 2010
[218] http://www.cnn.com/2012/11/27/health/tobacco-court-order
[219] *All Governments Lie!—The Life and Times of Rebel Journalist I. F. Stone* Myra MacPherson (2006 Scribner) 381
[220] *Nemesis: The last days of the American Republic* Chalmers Johnson (2006 Metropolitan Books) 93

[221] *Gentleman Spy—The Life of Allen Dulles*
Peter Gross (1994 Houghton Mifflin) 293
[222] *Mayday—Eisenhower, Khrushchev and the U-2 Affair*
Michael R. Beschloss (1986 Harper & Row) 129
[223] *The Secret Team—The CIA and Its Allies In Control of the United States and the World* L. Fletcher Prouty (1973 Prentice-Hall);
JFK and the Unspeakable: Why he Died and Why it Matters
James W. Douglass (2008 Orbis Books) 197
[224] A 1976 congressional inquiry estimated the number at 50, but Carl Bernstein of the *Washington Post* estimated the number closer to 400.
The Mighty Wurlitzer—How the CIA Played America Hugh Wilford (2008 Harvard University Press) 225-229
[225] Ibid. See also http://en.wikipedia.org/wiki/Operation_Mockingbird
[226] *Brothers—The Hidden History of the Kennedy Years*
David Talbot (2007 Free Press) 7
[227] *The Secret Team—The CIA and Its Allies In Control of the United States and the World* L. Fletcher Prouty (1973 Prentice-Hall) 117
[228] *Killing Hope—U.S. Military and C.I.A. Interventions Since World War II*
William Blum (2004 Common Courage Press) 84, 159, 414n26, 414n26,
[229] There are now 16 agencies in the US intelligence apparatus, with covert surveillance and operations often unknown even to Congress. It seems likely that the CIA's sprinkling of covert agents into various government sectors and media outlets has continued since its inception in the 1950s.
[230] *Strictly Personal—A Memoir*
John S. D. Eisenhower (1974 Doubleday & Company) 270;
Mayday—Eisenhower, Khrushchev and the U-2 Affair
Michael R. Beschloss (1986 Harper & Row) 65
[231] At 21 years of age, Dwight David Eisenhower enrolled at the West Point Naval Academy in 1911, commencing a military career that would span both world wars and culminate in his promotion to Supreme Allied Commander in December 1943. Following WWII, Eisenhower served as military governor of the US occupation zone before moving to Washington to become Army Chief of Staff in November 1945.

Once in Washington, powerful business leaders courted the WWII hero, providing him with rare opportunities for social and economic advancement. They invited him to join their clubs and helped him select new clothes and financial investments. Eisenhower's new Ivy League associates included Allen Dulles; the two were members of a study group at the Council on Foreign Relations in 1949. "Ike" was also invited into the Bohemian Club, famous for their Bohemian Grove gatherings of some of the world's richest, most powerful men.

But for a man driven to serve his country and all humanity, Eisenhower found the chief of staff position unfulfilling. When offered the presidency of Columbia University by IBM chair and Columbia Trustee Thomas

Watson, Eisenhower accepted in June 1947, hoping that Columbia would provide a new forum in which he might influence public opinion.

At President Truman's request, Eisenhower took leave from Columbia in 1950 to become Supreme Commander of the new North Atlantic Treaty Organization (NATO), but returned to the US when drafted as the Republican Party's presidential nominee in 1952.

The Declassified Eisenhower—A Divided Legacy of Peace and Political Warfare Blanche Wiesen Cook (1984 Penguin) 60-62

[232] *Killing Hope—U.S. Military and C.I.A. Interventions Since World War II* William Blum (2004 Common Courage Press);
Waging Peace 1956-1961 Dwight D. Eisenhower (1965 Doubleday) 265-266

[233] *A Thousand Days—John F. Kennedy in the White House* Arthur M. Schlesinger, Jr. (1965 Houghton Mifflin) 499, 910-911

[234] Khrushchev states in his second volume of memoirs: "I know there are now quite a few loudmouths who go around throwing dust in people's eyes, clouding up the issue, trying to extort money from the government to build aircraft carriers. 'Look how many carriers the US has!' they say. 'Look how many England has! And France! We're a great country, aren't we? Therefore we should have aircraft carriers, too.' Well, my answer to that is: nonsense."
Khrushchev Remembers—The Last Testament Strobe Talbott, editor (1974 Little, Brown and Company) 34, 519-520

[235] *Waging Peace 1956-1961* Dwight D. Eisenhower (1965 Doubleday) 544

[236] *Mayday—Eisenhower, Khrushchev and the U-2 Affair* Michael R. Beschloss (1986 Harper & Row) 132

[237] *Body of Secrets—The Anatomy of the Ultra-Secret National Security Agency* James Bamford (2002 Anchor Books) 54;
Mayday—Eisenhower, Khrushchev and the U-2 Affair Michael R. Beschloss (1986 Harper & Row) 133

[238] Ibid. (Beschloss) at 150-151

[239] *Body of Secrets—The Anatomy of the Ultra-Secret National Security Agency* James Bamford (2002 Anchor Books) 47

[240] Rather than bringing Powers' plane over from Incirlik Air Base in Turkey, to the CIA's airstrip at Peshawar, Pakistan, until the flight took place, "we were trying something new. Chiefly for security, to reduce plane exposure, we were ferrying it to Peshawar the night prior to flight, then, should the flight not take place as scheduled, for weather or some other reason, we would ferry it back to Incirlik."

This "security" and "exposure" rationale defies reason. How could daily round-trip flights offer less exposure than leaving the airplane sheltered at the Peshawar airstrip, ready for takeoff? This routine also contradicts another of Powers' remarks: "Taking off from one base and landing at another required two ground crews, doubling personnel, preparation, and *risk of exposure*." (emphasis added)

At any rate, repeated ferrying of the best plane (due to several flight postponements) resulted in enough air time to ground the "best plane we had" for routine maintenance.

Operation Overflight—The U-2 spy pilot tells his story for the first time Francis Gary Powers with Curt Gentry (1970 Tower) 75-77)

[241] Ibid. at 78 Indeed, 360 had achieved world headlines the prior September, when a test pilot had run out of fuel over Japan and made an emergency landing before a camera-toting audience on a glider club's airstrip.

[242] "It was an abort situation, and I had to make a decision. . . At maximum altitude, the fastest the plane could go was very close to the slowest it could go. This narrow range was known as the 'coffin corner.' . . . the exact speed required a great deal of attention."

Additionally, without the auto-pilot, high-altitude speed fluctuations could cause an engine flameout, and a restart would require a descent into thicker air—the haunt of Soviet MiG fighter jets. Ibid. at 83-84 & 34

[243] Ibid. at 83-84

[244] This is not surprising. The U-2's design traded off structural stability for ultra-high altitude capability. For example, its tail assembly was attached to the fuselage by only three bolts. In 1956, pilot Howard Carey was killed when his U-2 broke up merely from the turbulence of nearby Canadian Saber Jets. See *Bridge of Spies—A true Story of the Cold War* Giles Whittell (2010 Broadway) 119

[245] *Waging Peace 1956-1961* Dwight D. Eisenhower (1965 Doubleday) 543

[246] *Body of Secrets—The Anatomy of the Ultra-Secret National Security Agency* James Bamford (2002 Anchor Books) 48

[247] *Mayday—Eisenhower, Khrushchev and the U-2 Affair* Michael R. Beschloss (1986 Harper & Row) 37

[248] The diary of *New York Times* foreign correspondent C. L. Sulzberger is revealing: "Dulles is sure Gary Powers was not shot down at normal altitude (about 70,000 feet). The U-2, when it reaches rarefied altitudes, tends to get a flameout. We think Powers glided down to try and restart his motor. He was then shot down around 30,000-40,000 feet. Present Soviet defenses don't go above 60,000 feet. We think Powers parachuted."
Mayday—Eisenhower, Khrushchev and the U-2 Affair Michael R. Beschloss (1986 Harper & Row) 356;
JFK: The CIA, Vietnam, and the plot to assassinate John F. Kennedy L. Fletcher Prouty (1996 Kensington Publishing) 100

[249] *Waging Peace 1956-1961* Dwight D. Eisenhower (1965 Doubleday) 548

[250] *Strictly Personal—A Memoir*
John S. D. Eisenhower (1974 Doubleday & Company) 270;
Body of Secrets—The Anatomy of the Ultra-Secret National Security Agency James Bamford (2002 Anchor Books) 52

[251] Ibid. (Bamford) at 58-59

[252] These efforts required the act of perjury on the part of some Cabinet members and, had it been discovered, a subordination of perjury investigation of the President himself. CIA agent Richard Helms, who witnessed the hearings, said in 1983 of these testimonies, "They were all sworn. Knowing what they knew and what actually went on, if it isn't perjury I don't understand the meaning of the word." Helms would know. In 1977, he had been convicted of perjury and sentenced to two years in prison for statements made to this same committee over the CIA's involvement in the 1973 Chilean coup d'état (chapter 1). Ibid. at 314

[253] It was also widely assumed that each U-2 was sanitized of all incriminating identification—another misunderstanding that had been allowed to persist. When the Soviets showed Powers the wreckage of 360 following his capture, he was astounded to discover that the aircraft was not sanitized at all. The engine was stamped "Pratt & Whitney," and the destruct unit was labeled "DESTRUCTOR UNIT, Beck and Whitley, Inc."
Operation Overflight—The U-2 spy pilot tells his story for the first time Francis Gary Powers with Curt Gentry (1970 Tower) 139

[254] See this chapter's epigraph. Also, some assumed that U-2 pilots' handsome salaries of $30,000 (over $200,000 in 2010 dollars) were in part justified by the extreme risk involved.

[255] In 1964, Eisenhower explored both these matters while compiling the second volume of his presidential memoirs, *Waging Peace*. The CIA recorded and transcribed Eisenhower's questioning of then-CIA Director John McCone. ". . . As I understood it, I mean, as was told me all those years by both Bissell and by Allen [Dulles], this thing that the plane could never be recovered—it had self-destruction built in it and also they were—they assured me there was really no fear of ever getting back a live pilot if it was knocked down by a hostile action in Russia. . . . And the whole cover story was built on the basis that the man would never survive." McCone replied, "I realize that and I realized it at the time, but it was absolutely wrong." Eisenhower then said, "I don't want to be accusing people of having fooled me. But I do know that they told me that the possibility of anyone surviving—matter of fact, that's the reason I argued against putting out the cover story, and they said, 'You just don't have to worry, General. It is perfectly all right because there's nobody there.' That's all."
Waging Peace 1956-1961 Dwight D. Eisenhower (1965 Doubleday) 546

[256] "Annex to the report of DCI Ad hoc Panel on Status of the Soviet ICBM Program," August 25, 1959, Dwight David Eisenhower Presidential Library, Office of Staff Secretary, Intelligence, Box 15, as cited in *Body of Secrets—The Anatomy of the Ultra-Secret National Security Agency* James Bamford (2002 Anchor Books) 46

[257] *Waging Peace 1956-1961* Dwight D. Eisenhower (1965 Doubleday) 546

[258] *The Sorrows of Empire—Militarism, Secrecy, and the End of the Republic*
Chalmers Johnson (2004 Metropolitan Books) 41-42
[259] *A Thousand Days—John F. Kennedy in the White House*
Arthur M. Schlesinger, Jr. (1965 Houghton Mifflin) 215-216;
The Bay of Pigs Howard Jones (2008 Oxford University Press) 9-10
[260] *The CIA in Guatemala—The Foreign Policy of Intervention*
Richard H. Immerman (1982 University of Texas Press) 195
[261] http://en.wikipedia.org/wiki/Cuba_%E2%80%93_United_States_relations
[262] *New York Times* October 23, 1959
[263] *New York Times* February 20, 1960
[264] *Killing Hope—U.S. Military and C.I.A. Interventions Since World War II*
William Blum (2004 Common Courage Press) 192
[265] Bissell wrote in his memoirs, "My philosophy during my last two or three years in the agency was very definitely that the end justified the means." Accordingly, Bissell obtained various poisons and delivery systems from the CIA's Sidney Gottlieb (a.k.a. Dr. Death) and contracted Mafia figures Johnny Roselli (protégé of Al Capone), Sam Giancana (godfather of the Chicago Outfit), and Santo Trafficante (godfather of the Mafia's southern branch) to orchestrate the assassination. When the combined efforts of the Mafiosi produced no results, more creative measures were proposed in the spring of 1962.

The head of the CIA's Special Affairs Staff, Desmond Fitzgerald, suggested giving Castro a botulism-infected scuba-diving suit and other ideas such as planting an attractively noticeable seashell rigged with explosives in the waters where Castro enjoyed skin diving. There were more conventional attempts as well. An exile-piloted B-26 attempted to bomb a baseball stadium where Castro was speaking on November 20, 1964, but was diverted by Cuban anti-aircraft fire. Despite these and other failed efforts, Castro's assassination remained an integral part of the CIA's overall Cuban plan.
Reflections of a Cold Warrior: From Yalta to the Bay of Pigs
Richard M. Bissell (1996 Yale University Press) 157-158
The Bay of Pigs Declassified—The Secret CIA Report on the Invasion of Cuba Peter Kornbluh, Ed. (1998 New Press) 267-268
The Bay of Pigs Howard Jones (2008 Oxford University Press) 13, 22-29
Killing Hope—U.S. Military and C.I.A. Interventions Since World War II
William Blum (2004 Common Courage Press) 189
Bay of Pigs—The Untold Story
Peter Wyden (1979 Simon and Schuster) 109-110
See also Fabian Escalante's *Executive Action: 638 Ways to Kill Castro* (2006 Ocean Press), which became a British Channel 4 documentary.
[266] *Miami Herald* August 11, 2005, as cited in *Brothers—The Hidden History of the Kennedy Years* David Talbot (2007 Free Press) 47, and

http://havanajournal.com/politics/entry/bay_of_pigs_us_invades_cuba_failure_on_many_levels/

[267] *Body of Secrets—The Anatomy of the Ultra-Secret National Security Agency* James Bamford (2002 Anchor Books) 73

[268] *A Thousand Days—John F. Kennedy in the White House* Arthur M. Schlesinger, Jr. (1965 Houghton Mifflin) 247
Bay of Pigs—The Untold Story Peter Wyden (1979 Simon and Schuster) 139

[269] *A Thousand Days—John F. Kennedy in the White House* Arthur M. Schlesinger, Jr. (1965 Houghton Mifflin) 93, 291

[270] See the report at http://www.anusha.com/pigs-all.htm

[271] http://www.thenation.com/blog/nation-and-ny-times-bay-pigs-deja-vu

[272] *Bay of Pigs—The Untold Story* Peter Wyden (1979 Simon and Schuster) 155

[273] Among the implausible aspects of the defection story were these:

Zuñiga's status as a Captain in Castro's air force was immediately suspect when he jumped out of his plane in a white T-shirt, khaki pants, and a baseball cap.

Reporters converging on the plane discovered that, contrary to Zuñiga's tale of his attacks on Castro military assets, the plane's machine guns carried full rounds and had not been fired in flight.

US officials stated that the pilot's identity would not be revealed for fear of reprisal against his family still in Cuba. And just how long would it take Castro to determine which one of his air force captains was missing, along with his plane?

Zuñiga's B-26 bore a fresh coat of paint, shiny new Cuban insignia, and had a solid metal nose cone. All Castro's B-26s showed their age and had Plexiglas nose cones.

The CIA had implemented a back-up plan: in case the Miami deception failed or needed further endorsement, a second B-26 piloted by two more Cuban exiles had landed in Key West the same morning. The unrevealed identities of all three defectors in addition to rumors that they had quickly departed the US (where they were supposedly seeking asylum) gave credence to Castro's claim that they were, in fact, rebels who had flown from US training camps in Latin America.

The lie of the Miami and Key West performances was amplified by a landing the prior day in Jacksonville—a real defection! Castro's personal pilot and the pilot's brother had touched down in a tattered plane with Plexiglas nose cone that bore strikingly little resemblance to the freshly painted, metal-nosed counterfeits in Miami and Key West.
The Bay of Pigs Howard Jones (2008 Oxford University Press) 76-82;
Bay of Pigs—The Untold Story Peter Wyden (1979 Simon and Schuster) 174-176

[274] *Decision for Disaster—The Battle of the Bay of Pigs*

Grayston L. Lynch (2003 Pocket Books)
[275] See the report at http://www.anusha.com/pigs-all.htm
[276] *The Bay of Pigs Declassified—The Secret CIA Report on the Invasion of Cuba* Peter Kornbluh, Ed. (1998 New Press) 15
[277] *Robert Kennedy and His Times* Arthur M. Schlesinger, Jr. (1978 Ballantine Books) 486, as cited in *JFK and the Unspeakable—Why He Died and Why It Matters* James W. Douglass (2008 Orbis Books) 15
[278] Merton was a Trappist monk, Catholic priest, and the author of over 70 books on spirituality, social justice, and pacifism.
Letters from Tom: A Selection of Letters from Father Thomas Merton, Monk of Gethsemani, to W. H. Ferry, 1961-1968 W. H. Ferry, ed. (1983 Fort Hill Press) 15, as cited in *JFK and the Unspeakable—Why He Died and Why It Matters* James W. Douglass (2008 Orbis Books) 11
[279] Ibid. (Douglass) at 235
[280] *New York Times* March 24, 1961
[281] *JFK and the Unspeakable—Why He Died and Why It Matters* James W. Douglass (2008 Orbis Books) xxiii
The militarists did not give up; see *Killing Hope—U.S. Military and C.I.A. Interventions Since World War II* William Blum (2004 Common Courage Press) Chapter 21 "Laos 1957-1973—L'Armée Clandestine"
[282] *A Thousand Days—John F. Kennedy in the White House* Arthur M. Schlesinger, Jr. (1965 Houghton Mifflin) 428
[283] http://www.druckversion.studien-von-zeitfragen.net/NSAM%2055.HTM
[284] *New York Times* April 25, 1966
[285] Khrushchev's memoir states that he believed Eisenhower to be a "good man," but that he was "much too dependent on his advisors." At the 1955 Geneva conference, Khrushchev watched JF Dulles "making notes with a pencil, . . . sliding them under President Eisenhower's hand. Eisenhower would . . . read them before making a decision on any matter that came up." At this same conference, Khrushchev had hopes that Eisenhower and the Soviet minister of defense "would have a chance to talk alone together and that they would exchange views about the need for peaceful coexistence. But that vicious cur Dulles was always prowling around Eisenhower, snapping at him if he got out of line. Dulles could not tolerate the idea of peaceful coexistence with the Soviet Union." *Khrushchev Remembers* Strobe Talbott, editor (1970 Little, Brown and Company) 397-398
[286] http://en.wikipedia.org/wiki/Berlin_Crisis_of_1961
[287] In September 1961, General Lucius Clay (the President's personal representative in Berlin) ordered the secret construction of a barricade that duplicated the design and strength of the Berlin Wall. Located in an isolated German forest, US tanks fitted with bulldozer blades conducted experimental assaults on the demonstration wall. These rehearsals ended when discovered by the commander of US forces in Europe, but not before the Soviet KGB had discovered and filmed the exercises.

While the Kremlin feared that the Western powers were preparing to bulldoze their border installations, it appears that President Kennedy was never informed of these events.
Khrushchev Remembers Strobe Talbott, editor (1970 Little, Brown and Company) 459; *JFK and the Unspeakable—Why He Died and Why It Matters* James W. Douglass (2008 Orbis Books) 110

[288] *Khrushchev Remembers* Strobe Talbott, editor
(1970 Little, Brown and Company) Chapter 17 "The Berlin Crisis" 452-460

[289] *A Thousand Days—John F. Kennedy in the White House*
Arthur M. Schlesinger, Jr. (1965 Houghton Mifflin) Chapter 15;
JFK and the Unspeakable—Why He Died and Why It Matters
James W. Douglass (2008 Orbis Books) 109-113

[290] "Steel: A 72-Hour Drama With an All-Star Cast"
New York Times April 23, 1962

[291] Ibid.

[292] James Douglass writes: "John and Robert Kennedy had become notorious in the ranks of big business. JFK's strategy of withdrawing defense contracts and [the Robert Kennedy Justice Department's] aggressive investigating tactics toward men of power were seen as unforgivable sins by the corporate world. . . . a bitter gap opened up between Kennedy and big business, whose most powerful elements coincided with the military-industrial complex."
JFK and the Unspeakable—Why He Died and Why It Matters
James W. Douglass (2008 Orbis Books) 140;
A Thousand Days—John F. Kennedy in the White House
Arthur M. Schlesinger, Jr. (1965 Houghton Mifflin) 635

[293] Khrushchev further observed—true enough—that "The United States had already surrounded the Soviet Union with its own bomber bases and missiles." So with the Cuban installations, the US "would learn just what it feels like to have enemy missiles pointing at you." *Khrushchev Remembers* Strobe Talbott, editor (1970 Little, Brown and Company) 488-505

[294] *JFK and the Unspeakable—Why He Died and Why It Matters*
James W. Douglass (2008 Orbis Books) 21

[295] *New York Times*, October 23, 1962

[296] The Air Force launched an intercontinental ballistic missile from California's Vandenberg Air Base on Friday, October 26, 1962. The ICBM was an unarmed test missile destined for the Marshall Islands; however, its launch during the Cuban crisis was an unmistakable provocation. Had the Soviets launched a response to the ICBM, it is unlikely that Kennedy would have been able to prevent the release of missiles in the US arsenal.

Also during the crisis, US airborne-alert bombers flew past their customary turnaround points and entered Soviet airspace. This was an unambiguous threat that Soviet radar operators would certainly have recognized and reported. During this same critical period, a U-2 on a

routine mission from Alaska to the North Pole wandered out over the Soviet Union, attracting the attention of Soviet MiGs.
The Limits of Safety Scott D. Sagan (1993 Princeton University Press) 79, and *The New Yorker* June 19, 1995, both as cited in
JFK and the Unspeakable—Why He Died and Why It Matters James W. Douglass (2008 Orbis Books) 27-28, 396 n103 & n104;
A Thousand Days—John F. Kennedy in the White House Arthur M. Schlesinger, Jr. (1965 Houghton Mifflin) 828

[297] *Body of Secrets—The Anatomy of the Ultra-Secret National Security Agency* James Bamford (2002 Anchor Books) 117-118

[298] Arthur Schlesinger recalled, "We had no choice, it was argued, but a military response, and our tactical analysis had already shown that strikes at the bases would be little use without strikes at the airfields . . . it could hardly stop short of invasion." *A Thousand Days—John F. Kennedy in the White House* Arthur M. Schlesinger, Jr. (1965 Houghton Mifflin) 827

[299] *Khrushchev Remembers* Strobe Talbott, editor (1970 Little, Brown and Company) 497-498

[300] Undersecretary of State Averell Harriman told Arthur Schlesinger on Thursday, October 25, "Khrushchev is sending us desperate signals to get us to help take him off the hook. He is sending messages exactly as he did to Eisenhower directly after the U-2 Affair. In view of these signals from Khrushchev, the worst mistake we can possibly make is to get tougher and to escalate. . . . Incidents—stopping of ships, etc.—will begin the process of escalation, engage Soviet prestige, and reduce the chances of a peaceful resolution." Harriman refers here to Khrushchev's public statements suggesting that the CIA was responsible for the Soviet overflights and that Eisenhower was probably unaware of the incursions.
"U.S. Mission to the UN, Confidential/Limited Distribution memorandum, Schlesinger to Stevenson," as cited in *Body of Secrets—The Anatomy of the Ultra-Secret National Security Agency* James Bamford (2002 Anchor Books) 116-117, 497, 677n116

[301] *"One Hell of a Gamble"—Khrushchev, Castro, and Kennedy 1958-1964* Aleksandr Fursenko and Timothy Naftali (1997 W. W. Norton & Company) 240-315; *JFK and the Unspeakable—Why He Died and Why It Matters* James W. Douglass (2008 Orbis Books) 30

[302] Ibid. (Douglass) at 57-58

[303] *New York Times* April 6, 1963

[304] A *New York Times* front-page headline on April 17, 1963 announced, CUBAN EXILE CHIEF ACCUSES THE U.S. OF DEFAMING HIM. The following day's headline read, CUBAN EXILE CHIEF QUITS WITH ATTACK ON KENNEDY.

[305] *Body of Secrets—The Anatomy of the Ultra-Secret National Security Agency* James Bamford (2002 Anchor Books) 82-83

[306] Ibid. at 84-86
See also http://en.wikipedia.org/wiki/Operation_Northwoods#Content

[307] *Foreign Relations of the United States 1961-1963* Volume X (1994 US Government Printing Office) 21, as cited in
JFK and the Unspeakable—Why He Died and Why It Matters
James W. Douglass (2008 Orbis Books) 98, 410n15

[308] *Body of Secrets—The Anatomy of the Ultra-Secret National Security Agency*
James Bamford (2002 Anchor Books) 87

[309] *A Thousand Days—John F. Kennedy in the White House*
Arthur M. Schlesinger, Jr. (1965 Houghton Mifflin) 893, 895

[310] http://www.jfklibrary.org/AssetViewer/BWC7I4C9QUmLG9J6I8oy8w.aspx

[311] *A Thousand Days—John F. Kennedy in the White House*
Arthur M. Schlesinger, Jr. (1965 Houghton Mifflin) 904

[312] *President Kennedy: Profile of Power* Richard Reeves (1994 Simon & Schuster) 550, as cited in *JFK and the Unspeakable—Why He Died and Why It Matters* James W. Douglass (2008 Orbis Books) 51, 401 n208

[313] *The Best and the Brightest* David Halberstam (1972 Random House) 295-296, as cited in *JFK and the Unspeakable—Why He Died and Why It Matters* James W. Douglass (2008 Orbis Books) 220, 434n5

[314] *A Thousand Days—John F. Kennedy in the White House*
Arthur M. Schlesinger, Jr. (1965 Houghton Mifflin) 912

[315] *Small Is Beautiful: Economics As If People Mattered* E. F. Schumacher (1973)http://thinkexist.com/search/searchquotation.asp?search=Any+intelligent+fool&q=

[316] *People's History of the United States*
Howard Zinn (1980 Harper & Row) 460-462

[317] *Killing Hope—U.S. Military and C.I.A. Interventions Since World War II*
William Blum (2004 Common Courage Press) 122-123

[318] *People's History of the United States*
Howard Zinn (1980 Harper & Row) 462

[319] *New York Times* April 11, 1954

[320] Khrushchev's memoir states, "All would have been well if everyone had adhered to the commitments of the Geneva Accords. . . . But the that sinister man [JF] Dulles and the United States stepped in and imposed a long, bloody war on the Vietnamese people . . ." *Khrushchev Remembers* Strobe Talbott, editor (1970 Little, Brown and Company)

[321] *The Pentagon Papers* V2 22, as cited in *JFK and the Unspeakable—Why He Died and Why It Matters*
James W. Douglass (2008 Orbis Books) 105, 411n59

[322] Lansdale had just stage-managed the "election" of Philippine dictator Ramon Magsaysay, whose merciless rule would control the Philippine masses while US industries mined the region's lumber and mineral resources. Lansdale's CIA adventures supplied raw material for the novels/films The Ugly American and The Quiet American.
Killing Hope—U.S. Military and C.I.A. Interventions Since World War II
William Blum (2004 Common Courage Press) 39-44

[323] Northern Catholics were targeted with pamphlets proclaiming, "Christ has gone to the South" and "The Virgin Mary has departed from the North." Pamphlets and an almanac of bogus astrological predictions were widely disseminated to generate fear of communist rule in the north and favorably portray life in the south.
The Two Vietnams Bernard Fall (1967 Frederick A. Praeger) 153-154, and *The Pentagon Papers* New York Times edition (1971 Bantam Books), both as cited in *Killing Hope—U.S. Military and C.I.A. Interventions Since World War II* William Blum (2004 Common Courage Press) 125, 409n25, 409n26
Text and photos of this event in *JFK: The CIA, Vietnam, and the plot to assassinate John F. Kennedy* L. Fletcher Prouty (1996 Kensington Publishing) Chapter 6

[324] Before a House Subcommittee on Government Operations in 1971, CIA officer William Colby was asked, "Are you certain that we know a member of the [Vietcong] from a loyal member of the South Vietnam citizenry?" Colby replied, "No Mr. Congressman, I am not." (Colby ran the CIA's Phoenix Program under which at least 25,000 Vietnamese citizens were rounded up and slaughtered over seven years ending in 1972. Colby was promoted to CIA director in 1973.)
The Two Vietnams Bernard Fall (Frederick A. Praeger, 1967);
U.S Assistance Program in Vietnam Hearings before a Subcommittee of the House Committee on Government Operations July 19 1971 189, both as cited in *Killing Hope—U.S. Military and C.I.A. Interventions Since World War II* William Blum (2004 Common Courage Press) 131, 410n53
http://en.wikipedia.org/wiki/Phoenix_Program

[325] *A Thousand Days—John F. Kennedy in the White House*
Arthur M. Schlesinger, Jr. (1965 Houghton Mifflin) 538

[326] *The Pentagon Papers* V2 70, as cited in *JFK and the Unspeakable—Why He Died and Why It Matters* James W. Douglass (2008 Orbis Books) 105

[327] *People's History of the United States*
Howard Zinn (1980 Harper & Row) 468

[328] Ibid. at 469;
Killing Hope—U.S. Military and C.I.A. Interventions Since World War II William Blum (2004 Common Courage Press) 132-133

[329] *Secrets: A Memoir of Vietnam and the Pentagon Papers* Daniel Ellsberg 2002 Viking) 193, as cited in *JFK and the Unspeakable—Why He Died and Why It Matters* James W. Douglass (2008 Orbis Books) 108

[330] *The Pentagon Papers* V2 67, as cited in *JFK and the Unspeakable—Why He Died and Why It Matters* James W. Douglass (2008 Orbis Books) 106

[331] Ibid. (Douglass) at 129-131

[332] http://en.wikipedia.org/wiki/Madame_Nhu "Buddhist crisis"

[333] NSAM 263 is at http://www.jfklancer.com/NSAM263.html

[334] NSAM 273 is at http://www.jfklancer.com/NSAM273.html

[335] *Body of Secrets—The Anatomy of the Ultra-Secret National Security Agency* James Bamford (2002 Anchor Books) 295-297

[336] Ibid. at 295-298

[337] *The Uncensored War—The Media and Vietnam* Daniel C. Hallin (1989 University of California Press) 16-17

[338] *The Politics of Lying—Government Deception, Secrecy, and Power* David Wise (1973 Random House) 29

[339] http://www.sfgate.com/health/article/U-S-wars-and-post-traumatic-stress-disorder-2627010.php http://www.suicidewall.com/

[340] See any internet search for "JFK polls."

[341] *Breach of Trust—How the Warren Commission Failed the Nation and Why* Gerald D. McKnight (2005 University Press of Kansas) 182

[342] A United Press International report stated, "Dr. Malcolm Perry, 34 years old, said 'there was an entrance wound below his Adam's apple.'" *New York Times* November 23, 1963, 2

[343] House Select Committee interviewer Bob Kelley's notes on June 6, 1975, as cited in *JFK and the Unspeakable—Why He Died and Why It Matters* James W. Douglass (2008 Orbis Books) 308-310, 465n555-556

[344] Warren Commission Hearings, V6 p42, V3 p362, 273, V6 p25-26

[345] *JFK: Conspiracy of Silence* (1992 Signet) was revised, expanded, and republished as *Trauma Room One—The JFK Medical Coverup Exposed* Charles A. Crenshaw (2001 Paraview Press) Chapter 2 and the Appendix "Photographs, Illustrations, and Tables" (265-286)

[346] Navy medical corpsman Paul O'Connor assisted the doctors with the autopsy. Regarding the neck wound, O'Connor later stated, "[Admiral Galloway] stopped anybody from going further. Drs. Humes and Boswell, [and] Dr. Finck, were told to leave it alone, let's go to other things." *In the Eye of History* William Matson Law with Allan Eaglesham (2005 JFK Lancer Productions and Publications) 39-45, as cited in *JFK and the Unspeakable—Why He Died and Why It Matters* James W. Douglass (2008 Orbis Books) 311-321, 465n575-576

[347] *JFK and the Unspeakable—Why He Died and Why It Matters* James W. Douglass (2008 Orbis Books); *Legacy of Secrecy—The Long Shadow of the JFK Assassination* Lamar Waldron with Thom Hartmann (Counterpoint 2008); *Brothers—The Hidden History of the Kennedy Years* David Talbot (2007 Free Press)

[348] In addition to Dallas, there was an assassination trap in Chicago, where an emotionally unstable ex-Marine with a CIA background—exactly the mold of Oswald—had been provided a job in a warehouse overlooking a presidential motorcade route. The plan was thwarted when Kennedy cancelled his November 2 Chicago campaign stop in response to Secret Service intelligence of the plot. (For the media, the trip cancellation was attributed to the news of Diem's assassination the same day.)

  Similarly, an assassin was discovered in Tampa, just prior to the President's November 18 Florida campaign sweep—a person sharing no less than 18 career and personal parallels with Oswald, including a CIA background and employment along the scheduled route of a Kennedy motorcade.
Ibid. (Douglass) at 202-207, 213-217
Ibid (Waldron and Hartmann) at Chapter 5

[349] *Breach of Trust—How the Warren Commission Failed the Nation and Why* Gerald D. McKnight (2005 University Press of Kansas) 355

[350] In *The Dark Side of Camelot* (1997 Little, Brown and Company), Seymour Hersh explains other personal and political priorities of Bobby Kennedy during this time.

[351] *The Political Economy of Media—Enduring Issues, Emerging Dilemmas* Robert W. McChesney (2008 Monthly Review Press) 98

[352] Much information in this section is from
U.S. Television News and Cold War Propaganda, 1947-1960
Nancy E. Bernhard (2003 Cambridge University Press)

[353] Fulbright joined the Senate Foreign Relations Committee in 1949, and became its longest-serving chair (1959–1974). Rhodes Scholar, and former University of Arkansas president, Fulbright was the only senator to vote against the congressional appropriation supporting McCarthy's anti-communism committee. Fulbright was also the lone voice denouncing the CIA's Bay of Pigs plan at Kennedy's pivotal meeting of top advisors two weeks before the invasion. *A Thousand Days—John F. Kennedy in the White House* Arthur M. Schlesinger, Jr. (1965 Houghton Mifflin) 251

[354] The Pentagon's share of this munificence had funded efforts that included a bureau of high-ranking military speakers, a literary agency promoting militaristic perspectives to media outlets, and a special projects division providing parachute jumpers and military bands for public events.
The Pentagon Propaganda Machine
J. W. Fulbright (1970 Liveright) 25, 27, 33-34

[355] Robert Parry, Consortium News founder and author of *Neck Deep: The Disastrous Presidency of George W. Bush* (2007 Media Consortium), chronicles the continuation of this divide from the Carter era forward at http://consortiumnews.com/2012/04/23/mitt-romney-professional-liar/

[356] *Killing Hope—U.S. Military and C.I.A. Interventions Since World War II* William Blum (2004 Common Courage Press) 290

[357] Ibid. at 292

[358] *20 Years of Censored News* Carl Jensen and Project Censored (1997 Seven Stories Press) "The Top Ten Stories of 1987" 203-205

[359] Webb's awards included a 1990 Pulitzer Prize and a 1996 Journalist of the Year recognition from the Bay Area Society of Professional Journalists. Webb's exposés were credited with crooked politicians' removal from

office, fines levied against corrupt corporations, and the exposure of organized crime in the Kentucky coal industry.

[360] http://www.fair.org/index.php?page=1366

[361] The Oakland and Los Angeles City Councils and both California senators joined the chorus, as well as the Congressional Black Caucus, Jesse Jackson, and the National Association for Advancement of Colored People (NAACP). *Into the Buzzsaw—Leading Journalists Expose the Myth of a Free Press* Kristina Borjesson, editor (2002 Prometheus Books) 301-305

[362] On September 24, 1996, Christopher Matthews interviewed Webb on his CNBC show, attempting to discover errors in the *Dark Alliance* story. Matthews challenged Webb on various details, but Webb bested the television host at every turn. Webb later reported that Matthews stormed off the set following the interview, berating his staff, "This is outrageous. I've been sabotaged." *Whiteout—The CIA, Drugs and the Press* Alexander Cockburn and Jeffrey St. Clair 1999 Verso) 29, 32-33

[363] Ibid. at 33-37

[364] Ibid. at 37-38

[365] *Into the Buzzsaw—Leading Journalists Expose the Myth of a Free Press* Kristina Borjesson, editor (2002 Prometheus Books) 305

[366] *Whiteout—The CIA, Drugs and the Press* Alexander Cockburn and Jeffrey St. Clair 1999 Verso) 45

[367] Britt stated, "Columnists, cabdrivers and corner philosophers say [Webb's] series proves what some African Americans have long believed: The government purposely planted killer drugs in the black community. That the CIA could so cruelly discount black citizens' lives to fight communism abroad is obscene." Thus, Britt's article disparaged Webb for a claim that he never made, namely that a purpose of the CIA-Contra drug operation was to destroy the lives of African Americans. (And on the side, Britt reminds readers that the CIA is fighting communism abroad.)

[368] Married to Federal Reserve Board Chair Alan Greenspan, Alexander Cockburn referred to Mitchell as "about as snugly ensconced a member of the Washington elite as you could hope to find." Ibid. at 31

[369] In one effort to dismiss the entire affair, the *Washington Post*'s Walter Pincus (a former CIA associate) asserted that a reported five tons of cocaine was not enough to make a difference in the South Central Los Angeles situation, because it wasn't nearly enough to go around. (CIA and Justice Department reports that disproved Pincus' assertions were classified beyond public reach at the time.)
Into the Buzzsaw—Leading Journalists Expose the Myth of a Free Press Kristina Borjesson, editor (2002 Prometheus Books) 305

[370] The day after press stories of this report were filed, the Justice Department announced that a public release of the report would damage current (but undisclosed) criminal investigations. This was an amazing feat. For 16 months, CIA and Justice Department assurances had defused calls for any

investigations other than their own. Then, the CIA's exoneration of itself made national headlines—without even a peek at the report that supposedly justified this pronouncement.

[371] *New York Times* December 19, 1997

[372] *Whiteout—The CIA, Drugs and the Press* Alexander Cockburn and Jeffrey St. Clair 1999 Verso) 42-43

[373] *Crossing the Rubicon—The Decline of the American Empire and the End of the Age of Oil* Michael C. Ruppert (2004 New Society Publishers) 17

[374] Ibid.

[375] http://en.wikipedia.org/wiki/Gary_Webb#Supporters_and_Corroboration

[376] A television interview with Robert Parry of Consortium News summarizes Webb's personal story at
https://www.youtube.com/watch?v=A0DAKBz2Sp0

[377] http://www.youtube.com/watch?v=oTldYbqlJc8

[378] http://www.youtube.com/watch?v=Fv28_q98Xe8

[379] Again, *I'm not making this up.*
See http://www.youtube.com/watch?v=Fv28_q98Xe8

[380] In another example of the revolving door, Nayirah's handler at Hill & Knowlton (Vice President Lauri Fitz-Pegad), went on to become assistant commerce secretary in the Clinton administration.

[381] See http://en.wikipedia.org/wiki/Nayirah_(testimony)#Investigations

[382] *Toxic Sludge is Good For You—Lies, Damn Lies and the Public Relations Industry* John Stauber & Sheldon Rampton (1995 Common Courage Press) Chapter 10 & p. 173

[383] MacArthur's Op-Ed is referenced on the *Times'* web site in a "News Summary" entry, however the actual Op-Ed is *not* accessible—the only search failure I have encountered in the *Times'* electronic archives. I found it on microfiche at the University of Washington's Suzzallo Library in 2009.

In 1992, MacArthur also published *Second Front: Censorship and Propaganda in the 1991 Gulf War* (Hill and Wang)
The *Times* was the first US outlet to mention the new truth. The CBS program *60 Minutes* was critical of the Nayirah story on January 19. *The Nation* carried the story on February 4, as did ABC *World News Tonight* on March 15.
http://fair.org/extra-online-articles/20-stories-that-made-a-difference/

[384] http://www.inthesetimes.com/article/428/war_with_no_winners/

[385] *The Nation* June 15, 2009

[386] *Why We Did It* Rachel Maddow (2014 MSNBC)
Maddow discusses the documentary with Jon Stewart at
http://www.towleroad.com/2014/03/maddowiraq.html

[387] *Nemesis—The Last Days of the American Republic* Chalmers Johnson (2006 Metropolitan Books) 98-99;
The Road to 9/11—Wealth, Empire, and the Future of America

Peter Dale Scott (2007 University of California Press) 192-3
[388] http://www.guardian.co.uk/world/2003/jul/17/iraq.usa
[389] http://motherjones.com/politics/2004/01/lie-factory
[390] http://dir.salon.com/story/opinion/feature/2004/03/10/osp_moveon/index.html
[391] http://www.newyorker.com/archive/2003/05/12/030512fa_fact?currentPage=4
[392] http://www.thenation.com/article/more-missing-intelligence
[393] *The Political Economy of Media—enduring issues, emerging dilemmas*, Robert W. McChesney (2008 Monthly Review Press) 111
[394] Dixie Chicks singer Natalie Maines told a London audience, "we're ashamed the President of the United States is from Texas."
[395] http://www.wnd.com/2012/04/rocker-takes-swipe-at-evil-obama/
http://en.wikipedia.org/wiki/Clear_Channel_Communications#Censorship
[396] *The New Media Monopoly* Ben H Bagdikian (2004 Beacon Press) 1;
The Political Economy of Media—Enduring Issues, Emerging Dilemmas Robert W. McChesney (2008 Monthly Review Press) 178, 419
[397] *The New Media Monopoly* Ben H Bagdikian (2004 Beacon Press) Chapter 2
[398] "Americans spend 34 hours a week watching TV, according to Nielsen numbers" *New York Daily News* September 19, 2012;
In the Absence of the Sacred—The Failure of Technology and the Survival of the Indian Nations Jerry Mander (1991 Sierra Club Books) Chapter 5, "Television (I): Audiovisual Training for the Modern World" 76
[399] CBS News anchor Walter Cronkite was known for his nightly signoff, "And *that's* the way it is . . . ," a catchphrase that lent an air of authority not only to this highly trusted man, but to the television medium itself. Other positioning, such as the *New York Times'* self-anointed "Newspaper of Record" moniker, lends a silent authority to the corporate mass media's news and information.
[400] "Brazilian Leader Hears Boos From Unusual Direction, the Left" *New York Times* January 28, 2005
[401] "Tea Party vs. U.S. Social Forum" Julie Hollar
Extra!—The Magazine of FAIR, The Media Watch Group September 2010
[402] Ibid.
[403] *New York Times* February 25, 2010
[404] *The Rise of the Tea Party—Political Discontent and Corporate Media in the Age of Obama* Anthony DiMaggio (2011 Monthly Review Press) 47-48
[405] Ibid. at 114
[406] "National Equality vs. Tea Party" Julie Hollar
Extra!—The Magazine of FAIR, The Media Watch Group December 2009
"They Are the 1 Percent" Jim Naureckas Ibid., November 2011
[407] When mentioning ALEC in other contexts, the *Times* described it as a little known, business-backed, or conservative group. "Battle Lines Drawn Over Medicaid in Texas" *New York Times* November 11, 2010
"Conservative Group Drafts, Promotes Anti-EPA Bills in State Legislatures" *New York Times* April 4, 2011

The independents' coverage is at
http://www.inthesetimes.com/article/11603/
http://www.democracynow.org/2011/7/15/alec_exposed_state_legislative_b
ills_drafted

[408] Following Martin's murder on February 26, 2012, news of ALEC's promotion of Florida's Stand Your Ground law (used to defend Martin's killer) took several weeks to appear in the *Times* (April 21, 2012).

[409] *Give Me Liberty—A Handbook for American Revolutionaries*
Naomi Wolf (2008 Simon & Schuster) 173-187;
"The Progressive Interview: Bill Moyers"
Peter Dreier *The Progressive* March 2014 23

[410] *Deliberation Day*
Bruce Ackerman and James S. Fishkin (2004 Yale University Press) 9

[411] *The Atlantic* January 17, 2013

[412] "McCaskill gets security boost after threat" CBS News, May 9, 2012;
"Claire McCaskill Foe, A Tea Party Activist, Says, 'We Have To Kill The Claire Bear'" *Huffington Post* May 8, 2012

[413] "Surprised by Solidarity in Wisconsin—Media erred in assuming public shared their distaste for unions" and
"Millionaire Pundit: Public Sector Pensions Are the Real Threat"
Peter Hart Fairness and Accuracy in Reporting April 1, 2011, June 15, 2012

[414] The underfunding of US public media resulted from a battle waged during the advent of radio, between 1927 and 1935. Corporate interests won this battle, and the regulatory and business practices that were established for radio (enshrined in the Communications Act of 1934) were later extended to television in the 1940s and 1950s. These US developments were not somehow preordained; many nations chose other alternatives. For example, the domination of US commercial media interests aroused alarm in the Canadian House of Commons, provoking Canadians to establish a nonprofit, noncommercial, government-subsidized broadcasting system in 1932.
Rich Media, Poor Democracy—Communication Politics in Dubious Times
Robert W. McChesney (1999 New Press) Chapter 4, "Educators and the Battle for Control of U.S. Broadcasting, 1928-35," Chapter 5, "Public Broadcasting: Past, Present, . . . and Future?"

[415] *Rich Media, Poor Democracy—Communication Politics in Dubious Times*
Robert W. McChesney (1999 New Press) 248

[416] Although certain economies of scale could enable the US system to operate at a lower per capita cost than a smaller nation, these economies would not erase the need for local news and programming spanning the entire breadth of US broadcast localities.
Changing Media: Public Interest Policies for the Digital Age (2009 Free Press) 267, as cited in *The Death and Life of American Journalism—The*

Media Revolution That Will Begin the World Again Robert W. McChesney and John Nichols (2010 Nation Books) 192, Chart 1, Chapter 4

[417] *Rich Media, Poor Democracy—Communication Politics in Dubious Times* Robert W. McChesney (1999 New Press) 248

[418] "In Public TV We Trust" *Electronic Media* July 22, 2002 10, as cited in *The Problem of the Media—U.S. Communication Politics in the 21st Century* Robert W. McChesney (2004 Monthly Review Press) 243, 342n98

[419] See Moyers defend *NOW* against Tomlinson's attacks in a speech to the 2005 National Conference for Media Reform:
http://www.youtube.com/watch?v=bb45JxG2q2A
http://en.wikipedia.org/wiki/Media_bias_in_the_United_States

[420] http://mediamatters.org/research/200506220009 and http://en.wikipedia.org/wiki/Kenneth_Tomlinson#CPB_tenure

[421] *The Machinery of Nature* Paul Ehrlich 1986 (Simon and Schuster) 17-18, as cited in *Wisdom of the Elders—Honoring Sacred Native Visions of Nature* David Suzuki and Peter Knudtson (1992 Bantam Books) 229, 267n9

[422] There are about three dozen third parties in the US, the largest of which are the Libertarian, Constitution, and Green Parties. The Green Party was used in this examination due to its comprehensive agenda and Values, as compared to the narrower interests typical of other third parties.
http://en.wikipedia.org/wiki/Third_party_(United_States)#Largest_.28voter_registration_over_75.2C000.29

[423] The link to this page no longer works. The original document appears at this endnote number on the website associated with this book.

[424] http://www.democrats.org/issues

[425] The Trans-Pacific Partnership (TPP) is an initiative that was launched during the GW Bush administration and has been enthusiastically carried forward under President Obama. The TPP has been billed as another free trade agreement; trade, however, will be one of the least significant aspects of the agreement. Public Citizen's Global Trade Watch Director Lori Wallach explains that the "TPP now threatens a slow-motion stealth attack against a century of progressive domestic policy." Among other objectives, the TPP aims to roll back domestic consumer-safety, financial, environmental, and other safeguards. The pact even includes incentives for exporting US jobs to other signatory nations.
"A Stealth Attack on Democratic Governance"
Lori Wallach *The American Prospect* April 2012 51-54
Two additional initiatives that the Obama administration is pursuing are the Transatlantic Trade and Investment Partnership (TTIP) and the Trade in Services Agreement. See "What Happens in Geneva…" Cole Strangler *In These Times* September 2014 25-28

[426] http://www.gp.org/tenkey.shtml

[427] Currently, there are 17,000 nuclear weapons on the planet; over 90 percent of these are in US and Russian arsenals. The US has 2,150 active nuclear

warheads, with some 180 tactical nuclear weapons in five European countries, and has never had a "no first use" nuclear weapons policy. See "Indefensible—David Krieger on the Continuing Threat of Nuclear Weapons" *The Sun* January 2013
See also http://en.wikipedia.org/wiki/List_of_states_with_nuclear_weapons

[428] Republican-corporate ties are a generally understood political reality. However, as Juliet Schor has observed, "The Democratic Leadership Council, which has dominated the Democratic Party since the beginning of the Clinton administration, is as tied to corporate cash and influence as the Republican Party." *The Insecure American—How We Got Here and What We Should Do About It* Hugh Gusterson and Catherine Besteman, eds. (2010 University of California Press) 200

[429] The Republicans offer not one word on this issue. The Democrats want to end "tax loopholes that let corporations hide profits overseas," and on their fair elections page, they state that they "have fought to limit the influence of special interests and have proposed tough disclosure rules that would bring these shadow groups into the light . . ." But as corporate donations continue to flow into Democratic Party coffers, these aspirations have not been realized.

[430] "Here Comes the Sun" *Mother Jones* September-October 2014 8

[431] "The Progressive Interview—Bill Moyers"
Peter Dreier *The Progressive* (March 2014) 22

[432] "TPP—'The Largest Corporate Power Grab You've Never Heard Of'" Steve Randall *Extra!—The Magazine of FAIR, The Media Watch Group* March 2014 6

[433] Bill Moyers states, "He even jeopardized his pledge to preserve women's rights under *Roe v. Wade* in order to get a health care bill written by the corporate lapdog Max Baucus and the gang of revolving door mercenaries he hired to write a bill friendly to industry." "The Progressive Interview—Bill Moyers" Peter Dreier *The Progressive* (March 2014) 23

[434] See endnote 425

[435] http://www.motherjones.com/mojo/2008/11/obama-taps-larry-summers-recalling-summers-days-regulation-foe
http://www.motherjones.com/politics/2013/07/lawrence-summers-federal-reserve-chair-financial-regulation

[436] http://www.huffingtonpost.com/2009/11/24/land-mine-treaty-wont-be_n_369658.html

[437] Regarding the Keystone XL pipeline proposal, actor and ecological activist Robert Redford recently stated that the project would "move some of the dirtiest oil on our planet through America's heartland, exposing our precious farmlands to toxic tar sands oil spills." *The Progressive* April 2014 20-21.

Indeed, the pipeline industry has a record of ecologically damaging pipeline ruptures and failures. Shortly after going on line in 2011, for example, the Keystone 1 pipeline between Alberta and Oklahoma had a failure that spilled 21,000 gallons; during its first two years of operation, 13 more spills occurred. Obama's signing of the Pipeline Safety, Regulator Certainty, and Job Creation Act of 2011 has put an industry beset with faulty construction, defective parts, and ineffective safety management in charge of itself. "Keystone Whistleblower: Catastrophe Ahead" Julie Dermansky *The Progressive* October 2013 23-26

[438] This program is US-sponsored terrorism. Even some US officials have acknowledged drone attacks and killings are fomenting anti-US sentiment and encouraging terrorist actions in reply.
The Progressive October 2013 34

[439] Congressional insider Mike Lofgren offers a scathing review of the two parties similarities in *The Party is Over—How Republicans Went Crazy, Democrats Became Useless, and the Middle Class Got Shafted* (2012 Viking). See Chapter 11, "Are the Democrats Any Better?"

[440] http://en.wikipedia.org/wiki/Third_party_(United_States)#Debate_rules

[441] As an exceptional case, the Bush/Gore contest in 2000 *was* pivotal, and Ralph Nader's run as the Green's candidate remains a classic case of the "spoiler" effect. The Nader campaign's conviction that (ultimately) there was no difference between Bush and Gore kept Nader in the contest and tipped the election to Bush. In this instance, the numerous PNAC neoconservatives that were then appointed to high government positions immediately pursued the Wolfowitz Doctrine (ahead in chapter 14) and pushed domestic policy to the right (chapter 11)—maneuvers that probably would not have transpired under a Gore administration.

[442] *Why We Fight* (Eugene Jarecki 2005)

[443] http://www.americanrhetoric.com/speeches/dwightdeisenhowerfarewell.html

[444] http://investing.businessweek.com/businessweek/research/stocks/people/relationship.asp?personId=161604&ticker=HON:US

[445] http://www.northropgrumman.com/leadership/board/index.html

[446] *Blackwater—The Rise of the World's Most Powerful Mercenary Army* Jeremy Scahill (2007 Nation Books) xv-xvii

[447] http://en.wikipedia.org/wiki/List_of_United_States_defense_contractors

[448] This progression is detailed in Matt Ehling's documentary *Urban Warrior—The Militarization of American Law Enforcement*. (2004 ETS Pictures) Trailer at: https://www.youtube.com/watch?v=NQLK6AaH9g4
The Sorrows of Empire—Militarism, Secrecy, and the End of the Republic Chalmers Johnson (2004 Metropolitan Books) 120-122;
The End of America—Letter of Warning to a Young Patriot Naomi Wolf (2007 Chelsea Green);
It Can Happen Here—Authoritarian Peril in the Age of Bush Joe Conason (2007 St. Martin's Press)

[449] "Rise of the Stealth Oligarchy"
Jim Hightower *The Progressive* February 2015 50

"The Warrior Cops Suit Up"
Shane Bauer *Mother Jones* November-December 2014 19-23
[450] *Nemesis: The last days of the American Republic*
Chalmers Johnson (2006 Metropolitan Books) 248-252
[451] http://en.wikipedia.org/wiki/Military_Commissions_Act_of_2006
http://www.aclu.org/national-security/military-commissions-act-2006
[452] Watch Oliver North evade Congressman Jack Brooks' attempt to question North's involvement in COG planning at http://www.youtube.com/watch?v=lNhFiWF3qlw
"Cheney, The Federal Emergency Management Agency, and Continuity of Government" in *The Road to 9/11—Wealth, Empire, and the Future of America* Peter Dale Scott (2007 University of California Press) Chapter 14
[453] "Taking on TransCanada"
Dave Saldana *The Progressive* April 2014 15-18
[454] Ibid. (Scott)
Constitutional law and civil rights attorney Glenn Greenwald details how US law is being used to destroy equality and enhance Elite power in *With Liberty and Justice for SOME* (2011 Metropolitan Books) Greenwald states, "The criminal justice system is now reserved almost exclusively for ordinary Americans, who are routinely subjected to harsh punishments even for the pettiest of offenses." In contrast, numerous Elite crimes have been shielded from any legal consequence: "the creation of a global torture regime; the systematic plundering by Wall Street, leading to the 2008 economic crisis; the serial obstruction of justice by high-ranking political officials; the fraudulent home foreclosures by the nation's largest banks."
[455] http://prospect.org/article/outmatched
[456] George Lakoff describes this effort in *Don't Think of an Elephant—Know your values and frame the debate* (2004 Chelsea Green) 15-16, and in *Thinking Points—Communicating our American Values and Vision* (2006 Farrar, Straus and Giroux) 28, and on video: *How Democrats and Progressives Can Win: Solutions from George Lakoff* (2004 Educate the Base)
[457] http://www.iraqwatch.org/perspectives/rumsfeld-openletter.htm
[458] Dick Cheney was a founding member of PNAC, although not a signatory of the Clinton letter. The signatories were:
Donald Rumsfeld—Secretary of Defense
Paul Wolfowitz—Deputy Secretary of Defense
Richard Perle—Chair of the Defense Policy Board Advisory Committee
Elliott Abrams—Special Assistant to the President and a Senior Director on the National Security Council
Richard Armitage—Deputy Secretary of State
John R. Bolton—Undersecretary of State for Arms Control and International Security
Paula Dobriansky—Undersecretary of State for Democracy and Global Affairs

William J. Bennett—National Security Advisory Council member from the Center for Security Policy think tank
Zalmay Khalilzad—Ambassador to Afghanistan (2003-2005), Ambassador to Iraq (2005-2007)
Peter W. Rodman—Assistant Secretary of Defense
William Schneider, Jr.—Defense Science Board in the Rumsfeld Pentagon
James Woolsey—Defense Policy Board Advisory Committee, & the Pentagon's Deterrence Concepts Advisory Panel
Robert Zoellick—Deputy Secretary of State
The Sorrows of Empire—Militarism, Secrecy, and the End of the Republic Chalmers Johnson (2004 Metropolitan Books) 227-229

[459] In *Leo Strauss and the Politics of American Empire* (2004 Yale University Press), Anne Norton recounts Wolfowitz's tutelage under "Straussian" Allan Bloom, author of the 1987 bestseller *Closing the American Mind*, in which Norton says Bloom "longs for a lost world of hierarchy and exclusion." (65) Elite rule is a central Straussian theme. Leo Strauss' enduring influence on the neoconservative movement is detailed in the BBC documentary *The Power of Nightmares* at http://news.bbc.co.uk/2/hi/programmes/3755686.stm

[460] See http://en.wikipedia.org/wiki/Wolfowitz_Doctrine

[461] http://georgewbush-whitehouse.archives.gov/news/releases/2002/06/20020601-3.html

[462] *Hijacking Catastrophe* (2004 Media Education Foundation) As stated by its producers, the film "places the Bush Administration's original justifications for war in Iraq within the larger context of a two-decade struggle by neoconservatives to dramatically increase military spending while projecting American power and influence globally by means of force." See http://www.mediaed.org/cgi-bin/commerce.cgi?preadd=action&key=126

[463] http://www.defense.gov/ucc/
http://en.wikipedia.org/wiki/Energy_usage_of_the_United_States_military

[464] Estimates of total foreign bases range to over a thousand. Pentagon reports omit US espionage and other bases that could be embarrassing to the US, and do not list many Middle East bases, although several colossal base structures were established in that region following 9/11.
Dismantling the Empire—America's Last Best Hope Chalmers Johnson (2010 Metropolitan Books) Chapter 8: America's Empire of Bases 109-119;
The Capitalism Papers—Fatal Flaws of an Obsolete System Jerry Mander (2012 Counterpoint) Part VIII, Propensity Toward War 167-171

[465] PNAC *Rebuilding America's Defenses*
http://en.wikipedia.org/wiki/Project_for_the_New_American_Century#Rebuilding_America.27s_Defenses

[466] http://www.youtube.com/watch?v=6K5M0xtxQVQ

[467] "FBI says, 'No Hard Evidence Connecting Bin Laden to 9/11'"

Ed Haas *Muckraker Report* June 6 2006, as cited by David Ray Griffin at http://www.globalresearch.ca/index.php?context=va&aid=15892 Claire Brown of the International News Network also confirmed Rex Tomb's statements. See *9/11 Contradictions—An Open Letter to Congress and the Press* David Ray Griffin (2008 Olive Branch Press) 191-194

[468] "The 9/11 Commission Controversy" Robert Windrem and Victor Limjoco *Deep Background: NBC News Investigations* January 30, 2008 http://911research.wtc7.net/cache/post911/commission/msnbc_commission_torture.html

[469] *Without Precedent: The Inside Story of the 9/11 Commission* Thomas H. Kean and Lee H. Hamilton (2006 Alfred A. Knopf) 119-120

[470] http://www.youtube.com/watch?v=Atbrn4k55lA

[471] *Waking Up From Our Nightmare—The 9/11/01 Crimes in New York City* Don Paul and Jim Hoffman (2004 Irresistible/Revolutionary) 3 See television commentator Bill Alford's show examining the WTC tower collapses at http://seattlecommunitymedia.org/node/24530

[472] *New York Times* November 29, 2001

[473] FEMA *World Trade Center Building Performance Study* Chapter 5 6.2, "Probable Collapse Sequence," as cited in *The 9/11 Commission Report: Omissions and Distortions* David Ray Griffin (2005 Olive Branch Press) 26, 300n10

[474] NIST Final Report, as cited in *The Mysterious Collapse of World Trade Center 7—Why the Final Official Report about 9/11 is Unscientific and False* David Ray Griffin (2010 Olive Branch Press) XIX

[475] http://911research.wtc7.net/wtc/analysis/compare/windsor.html http://www.ae911truth.org/news/41-articles/315-explosive-evidence-at-wtc-cited-by-former-cdi-employee.html

[476] Collapse information in *The Mysterious Collapse of World Trade Center 7—Why the Final Official Report about 9/11 is Unscientific and False* David Ray Griffin (2010 Olive Branch Press) XIV

[477] Ibid. at XIX

[478] "Theories of 9/11" *Hartford Advocate* January 29 2008, as cited in *Cognitive Infiltration—An Obama Appointee's Plan to Undermine the 9/11 Conspiracy Theory* David Ray Griffin (2011 Olive Branch Press) 49

[479] "Active Thermitic Material Discovered in Dust from the 9/11 World Trade Center Catastrophe" Ibid. at 70 http://www.webcitation.org/5tmFOBanU

[480] http://www.ae911truth.org/news/41-articles/343-1000-architects-a-engineers-challenge-official-report-of-wtc-destruction.html

[481] http://patriotsquestion911.com/professors.html

[482] Incidentally, Securacom, the WTC's security contractor in 2001, was run by GW Bush's cousin Writ Walker III, and Bush's brother Marvin was another principal in the company.

[483] *The 9/11 Commission Report—Final Report of the National Commission on Terrorist Attacks Upon the United States* (No publication date given, W.W. Norton & Company) 20, 458n116

[484] A press release stated that President Bush had "asked Vice President Cheney to oversee the development of a national effort so that we may do the very best possible job of protecting our people from catastrophic harm." http://www.gpo.gov/fdsys/pkg/WCPD-2001-05-14/pdf/WCPD-2001-05-14-Pg718.pdf

[485] *The Road to 9/11—Wealth, Empire, and the Future of America* Peter Dale Scott (2007 University of California Press) 216-218; *Crossing the Rubicon—The Decline of the American Empire and the End of the Age of Oil* Michael C. Ruppert (2004 New Society Publishers) 333-356

[486] Ibid. and *Aviation Week and Space Technology* June 3, 2002; *9/11 Synthetic Terror—Made in the USA* Webster Griffin Tarpley (2006 Progressive Press) 207-212

[487] *Aviation Week* September 9, 2002, Ibid. at 212

[488] Ibid. at 212

[489] http://en.wikipedia.org/wiki/September_11_attacks_opinion_polls

[490] http://nz911truth.org/news/poll-in-germany-89-5-doubt-official-version-of-911/ Poll information also in *The 9/11 Commission Report: Omissions and Distortions* David Ray Griffin (2005 Olive Branch Press) 2-4

[491] *The Rise and Fall of the Third Reich—A History of Nazi Germany* William L. Shirer (1990 (first pub. in 1959) Simon and Schuster) 191-196

[492] *Dreaming War—Blood for Oil and the Cheney-Bush Junta* Gore Vidal (2002 Nation Books) Barrie Zwicker describes similarities between 9/11 and the Reichstag fire in *Towers of Deception—The Media Cover-Up of 9/11* (2006 New Society Publishers) 234-239

[493] All polls cited at http://en.wikipedia.org/wiki/September_11_attacks_opinion_polls

[494] "Sense Making Under 'Holographic' Conditions: Framing SCAD Research" *American Behavioral Scientist* V53 N6 February 2010 (Sage Publications) SCADs defined by Lance deHaven-Smith at 796

[495] Florida State University professor Lance deHaven-Smith explains that Senator Robert Kennedy's assassination occurred after he had denounced the Vietnam War and become the Democratic frontrunner in the 1968 presidential election. Among other possible motives, Robert Kennedy's assassination was a pre-emptive elimination of an anti-war president. Evidence contradicting the official Sirhan Sirhan story (another lone assassin legend) includes medical evidence of Robert's physical wounds, indicating that fatal shots were fired at point-blank range, an impossible feat for Sirhan Sirhan, who remained several feet away from Kennedy.

American Conspiracies—Lies, Lies, and More Dirty Lies that the Government Tells Us Jesse Ventura with Dick Russell (2010 Skyhorse Publishing) Chapter 6: The Assassination of Robert Kennedy
Brothers—The Hidden History of the Kennedy Years
David Talbot (2007 Free Press) Chapter 8;
JFK and the Unspeakable—Why He Died and Why It Matters
James W. Douglass (2008 Orbis Books) 371-374;
Legacy of Secrecy—The Long Shadow of the JFK Assassination
Lamar Waldron with Thom Hartmann (Counterpoint 2008) Chapters 56-59

[496] *Washington Post* April 12, 2002

[497] For the history and current implications of the conspiracy theory label and concept see *Conspiracy Theory in America*
Lance deHaven-Smith (2013 University of Texas Press)

[498] *World as Lover, World as Self* Joanna Macy (1991 Parallax Press) 4

[499] Peck also states, "Since power confers status, nothing can be more enhancing of self-esteem," and "Since power in all its varieties can be so alluring, it is no wonder that most people cling to it for all it is worth and as long as they can—usually until it is finally wrested away from them . . ."
In Search of Stones—A Pilgrimage of Faith, Reason, and Discovery
M. Scott Peck, M.D. (1995 Hyperion) 45-46, 409-410

As legendary economist John Kenneth Galbraith put it, "People of privilege will always risk their complete destruction rather than surrender any material part of their advantage."
The Age of Uncertainty, a 1977 book and television series.

[500] See epigraphs of chapters 6 and 7

[501] Charles and David Koch (Koch Industries) have funneled over $67 million into climate-denial front groups. These efforts have amplified the voices of a few industry-funded skeptics in an attempt to counteract the scientific consensus that global warming is underway and that fossil fuel-driven industrial civilization is causing it.
http://www.greenpeace.org/usa/en/campaigns/global-warming-and-energy/polluterwatch/koch-industries/
The Heat is On: The high stakes battle over the Earth's threatened climate
Ross Gelbspan (1997 Addison-Wesley) "The Battle for Control of Reality"

[502] See endnote 181

[503] "How ALEC Fronts for Fossil Fuels" Nick Surgey *The Progressive* July-August 2014 57-59;
"If Your House is On Fire" An interview with Kathleen Dean Moore *The Sun* December 2012;
http://www.heatisonline.org/contentserver/objecthandlers/index.cfm?ID=8361&Method=Full

[504] *People of the Lie—The Hope for Healing Human Evil*
M. Scott Peck, M.D. (1983 Simon & Schuster) 42 74-75

[505] http://www.nytimes.com/interactive/2014/12/09/world/cia-torture-report-key-points.html
http://en.wikipedia.org/wiki/Enhanced_interrogation_techniques

[506] Although GW Bush was unwavering in his support, a CIA chief was apparently worried enough to destroy videotapes of CIA torture sessions in the mid-2000s. The CIA's head of directorate of operations stated that he thought the tapes would be "devastating to the CIA," and that "the heat from destroying [them would be] nothing compared to what it would be if the tapes ever got into [the] public domain."
http://en.wikipedia.org/wiki/Enhanced_interrogation_techniques

[507] "41 men targeted but 1,147 people killed" *The Guardian* November 24, 2014

[508] "Turning a Wedding Into a Funeral" *Democracy Now!* February 21, 2014

[509] "The Unblinking Stare" *The New Yorker* Steve Cole November 24, 2014
https://www.aclu.org/blog/tag/targeted-killings
http://www.youtube.com/watch?v=LyfsmUXAsfM
http://www.huffingtonpost.com/peter-van-buren/this-memorial-day-remembe_b_3331650.html

[510] *Managing Without Growth—Slower by Design, Not Disaster*
Peter A. Victor (2008 Edward Elgar Publishing)

[511] "A Hell of a Time Up at the Palace" *Overthrow—America's Century of Regime Change From Hawaii to Iraq* Stephen Kinzer (2006 Times Books)

[512] When the Carter administration was renegotiating the US treaty with Panama, the *New York Times* commented that "We stole it, and removed the incriminating evidence from our history books." *A People's History of the United States* Howard Zinn (1980 Harper Colophon) 555

[513] *The Great Quotations*
George Seldes with J. Donald Adams (1966 Caesar-Stuart) 53

[514] *Give Me Liberty—A Handbook for American Revolutionaries*
Naomi Wolf (2008 Simon & Schuster) 7, 12

[515] *The Tipping Point—How Little Things Can Make a Big Difference*
Malcolm Gladwell (2002 Little, Brown, and Company) 12

[516] *Wisconsin Uprising—Labor Fights Back*
Michael D. Yates, ed. (2010 Monthly Review Press)

[517] *The Precariat: The New Dangerous Class*
Guy Standing (2011 Bloomsbury Publishing)
Twilight Of The Elites: America After Meritocracy
Christopher Hayes (2012 Crown Publishers)
Citation from a July 2012 *In These Times* essay adapted from Hayes' book.

[518] *New York Times*, September 17, 18, 19, 20, 21, 23, 2011

[519] http://www.huffingtonpost.com/colin-delany/by-the-numbers-how-social_b_1011049.html

[520] http://www.themediaconsortium.org/our-members/

[521] *The Great Quotations*
George Seldes with J. Donald Adams (1966 Caesar-Stuart) 592

[522] The NSA's intercepts were surveilling over a billion people worldwide when Edward Snowden revealed details of the Agency's secret programs in 2013. Snowden's evidence also proved that government officials, including the NSA chief, had been lying to Congress about the purpose and comprehensive nature of the NSA's citizen surveillance operations. But in the national discourse, outrage was directed *not* at the NSA and these corporate invasions of citizen privacy; it was directed at Snowden. Media pundits began calling Snowden a traitor and a criminal, while Obama's Justice Department talked of prosecuting him under the 1917 Espionage Act. The White House defended the NSA's information collection programs, calling them "a critical tool in protecting the nation from terrorist threats." Diane Feinstein, then chair of the Senate Intelligence Committee, also backed up the NSA stating, "people want the homeland kept safe."
No Place to Hide—Edward Snowden, the NSA, and the U.S. Surveillance State Glenn Greenwald (2014 Metropolitan Books) Chapters 2 & 3
"They'll be Watching You" Steven Renderos
Extra!—The Magazine of FAIR, The Media Watch Group May 2014 11-12

[523] The other nine characteristics Britt found were: disdain for the recognition of human rights; religion intertwined with government; cronyism and corruption; powerful and continuing nationalism; identification of enemies/scapegoats as a unifying cause; rampant sexism; obsession with national security; disdain for intellectuals and the arts; and obsession with crime and punishment. "Fascism Anyone?"
Laurence W. Britt *Free Inquiry* Spring, 2003, V23 N2

[524] Urban warrior, see chapter 14; corporate vote tampering, see chapter 7.

[525] *The End of America—Letter of Warning to a Young Patriot*
Naomi Wolf (2007 Chelsea Green)

[526] *It Can Happen Here—Authoritarian Peril in the Age of Bush*
Joe Conason (2007 St. Martin's Press) 141

[527] Millions were evicted from their homes following Elite machinations that brought on the 2008 financial crisis. Then, private equity firms went on a buying spree, turning the houses into rentals. The Blackstone Group, one of the largest private equity firms, bought 1,400 Atlanta houses in one day, and has acquired over 40,000 homes, most of them through foreclosures.
"The Wolf of Your Street" *Mother Jones* March-April 2014 12-16
Overall, home ownership is down and rent prices are rising.
See "Game of Homes" *In These Times* April 2014 18-23

[528] *The Great Thoughts* Compiled by George Seldes with David Laskin and Henry Steele Commager (1996 Ballantine Books) 215

[529] http://www.huffingtonpost.com/daniel-burrus/some-advice-for-occupiers_b_1143668.html

[530] Senator Russ Feingold (D-WI cast the only senate vote against the Patriot Act. In the House, only 15 percent voted against it.

"The USA PATRIOT Act Was Planned Before 9/11"
Jennifer Van Bergen Truthout May 20, 2002
http://www.ratical.org/ratville/CAH/PAplndbefore.html
See also "Conquering the American People" in *Crossing the Rubicon—The Decline of the American Empire and the End of the Age of Oil*
Michael C. Ruppert (2004 New Society Publishers) Chapter 28

[531] Not only did Wall Street operatives create the conditions that precipitated millions of home foreclosures, they are now buying these foreclosed properties and turning them into profitable rentals.
"Whose Recovery Is It, Anyway?" Sarah Jaffe
Extra!—The Magazine of FAIR, The Media Watch Group May 2014 9-10
See also *Inside Job*
Audrey Marrs and Charles H. Ferguson (2010 Sony Pictures Classics)

[532] For example, see http://sacramento.cbslocal.com/2011/08/12/bart-officials-blocked-cell-phones-during-transit-protest/

[533] Recall how the CIA hired gangs of thugs to stage battle against each other in order to generate chaos in Tehran (chapter 1). The proposed *solution* to this bedlam was the return of the Elite's friend the shah, the Iranian's dreaded dictator. The Joint Chiefs' Operation Northwoods plan followed this same logic: Pentagon-sponsored terrorism against US citizens was to be attributed to Castro; a military invasion of Cuba was to be the solution.

[534] An agent provocateur is an undercover agent who, for example, might incite violence at an otherwise peaceful protest rally, and thus enable the entire demonstration to be portrayed as an anarchist endeavor. There are now numerous incidents of covert infiltration of protest groups and public demonstrations. Police officers and FBI agents are known to have acted as agents provocateurs in the United States.
http://www.theguardian.com/politics/2009/may/10/g20-policing-agent-provocateurs
http://www.youtube.com/watch?v=TbLU9tdDwxo
http://en.wikipedia.org/wiki/Agent_provocateur

[535] *Thinking Points—Communicating our American Values and Vision* George Lakoff (2006 Farrar, Straus and Giroux) 102

[536] Millions protested the 2003 plan to invade Iraq; the invasion proceeded. The Occupy Wall Street movement drew attention to Wall Street corruption; there have been no noteworthy investigations, reprimands, or financial reforms. A majority of the electorate favors a public option for health care; the two dominant political parties won't even discuss it.

While not a single conviction has resulted from the corruption that led to the 2008 crash, some of those involved in the perpetration of this debacle have made off with fortunes. Hedge fund manager John Paulson made $3.7 billion in 2007; then approximately doubled his net worth in 2008.

Mother Jones lists the top ten winners at http://www.motherjones.com/politics/2009/03/10-people-who-are-profiting-global-economic-crisis

[537] Ackerman and Fishkin's Deliberation Day concept evolved from 15 years of experimental and scholarly research. Fishkin conducted Deliberative Polling experiments for over a decade, and collaborated with Ackerman to study Citizen Juries, National Issues Forums, Planning Cells, and other deliberative formats as well.
Deliberation Day
Bruce Ackerman and James S. Fishkin (2004 Yale University Press)

[538] Ibid., chapter 1: Imagine

[539] The four circumstances Surowiecki deems necessary for the wisdom of crowds to be expressed are:
Diversity: A wide assortment of group members yields differing perspectives and helps avoid what has been labeled groupthink.
Independence: Circumstances that allow group members to develop and maintain their own opinions can prevent particularly outspoken or charismatic members from influencing others toward a particular opinion.
Decentralization: A broad-based, non-hierarchical group organization puts the people who are closest to a problem in the best position to propose solutions to those problems.
Aggregation: Some mechanism is employed to turn private judgments into a collective decision.
The diversity, independence, and decentralized decision-making of Deliberation Day would be ensured through random selection of participants, transparency in compiling conclusions, and the skill of professional facilitators. *The Wisdom of Crowds—Why the many are smarter than the few and how collective wisdom shapes business, economies, societies, and nations* James Surowiecki (2004 Doubleday)

[540] The EU averages 77 percent voter turnout, compared to US presidential election-year turnouts of around 56 percent—curiously close to the average South and Central American voter turnout of 54 percent since 1945, when US interventions became common. Voter turnout in the 2014 midterm election was about 37 percent. http://en.wikipedia.org/wiki/Voter_turnout

[541] http://en.wikipedia.org/wiki/List_of_countries_by_military_expenditures and *Deliberation Day*
Bruce Ackerman and James S. Fishkin (2004 Yale University Press) 144

[542] Currently, the Cabinet is composed of 15 Departments: State, Treasury, Defense, Justice, Interior, Agriculture, Commerce, Labor, Health and Human Services, Housing and Urban Development, Transportation, Energy, Education, Veterans Affairs, and Homeland Security. Additionally, the senior officers of the federal executive branch include the president and vice president, the directors of the Office of Management and Budget and the EPA, the US Trade Representative and Ambassador to the UN, the chair of

the Council of Economic Advisors, and the administrator of the Small Business Administration.

[543] For example, Robert McNamara was the president of Ford Motor Company but knew virtually nothing about the inner workings of the Pentagon behemoth. Nevertheless, President Kennedy recruited McNamara as his secretary of defense, and McNamara then presided over the full expansion of the Vietnam War.

Five Cabinet members of the GW Bush administration possessed net financial wealth estimated between $10 million and $200 million, a roster headed by former Alcoa CEO Paul O'Neill. Obama's Commerce Secretary Penny Pritzker's net worth is estimated at $1.85 billion.
http://www.commondreams.org/headlines02/0918-06.htm

[544] *The Death and Life of American Journalism—The Media Revolution That Will Begin the World Again*
Robert W. McChesney and John Nichols (2010 Nation Books) 190

[545] Robert McChesney and John Nichols have proposed various mechanisms to give the electorate a voice in public media funding. Anchored in global research and analysis, their proposal includes mechanisms for citizen input and public accountability, and safeguards against special interest domination.
The Death and Life of American Journalism—The Media Revolution That Will Begin the World Again Robert W. McChesney and John Nichols (2010 Nation Books) Chapter 3 "Why the State," and Chapter 4 "Subsidizing Democracy" See also "How to Save Journalism" John Nichols and Robert W. McChesney *The Nation* January 25, 2010
http://www.thenation.com/article/how-save-journalism-0

[546] *Let me tell you what I've learned": Texas Wisewomen Speak*
Paula Pierce (2002 University of Texas Press) 21

[547] *Shattered Peace—The Origins of the Cold War and the National Security State* Daniel Yergin (1977 Houghton Mifflin) 11

[548] *Killing Hope—U.S. Military and C.I.A. Interventions Since World War II* William Blum (2004 Common Courage Press) 7-8

[549] *A People's History of the United States*
Howard Zinn (1980 Harper Colophon) 399-400

[550] *The Second World War* Winston Churchill (1951 London) V4 p428, as cited in *Killing Hope—U.S. Military and C.I.A. Interventions Since World War II* William Blum (2004 Common Courage Press) 7

[551] *Shattered Peace—The Origins of the Cold War and the National Security State* Daniel Yergin (1977 Houghton Mifflin) 12-13

[552] *Killing Hope—U.S. Military and C.I.A. Interventions Since World War II* William Blum (2004 Common Courage Press) Chapter 2 "Italy 1947-1948—Free elections, Hollywood style" 32

[553] Zelikow's résumé at that time included service with Condoleezza Rice on the GHW Bush National Security Council, co-authorship of a book with Rice

during the Clinton years, and directorship of the Aspen Strategy Group, a foreign policy think tank whose membership included Rice, Dick Cheney, and Paul Wolfowitz. Then, as a member of the National Security Council's transition team (ushering in the GW Bush administration), Zelikow again worked closely with Rice. Bush then appointed Zelikow to the President's Foreign Intelligence Advisory Board.

The same year Zelikow became the 9/11 Commission's executive director, Rice (as National Security Advisor) enlisted him to develop her National Security Strategy. So at the same time Zelikow's longtime associate Condoleezza Rice was denying that "anybody could have predicted that these people would . . . use an airplane as a missile," the 9/11 Commission completely ignored all of these conflicts of interest, save one. "As the Executive Director of the Commission, Zelikow has recused himself *from our work on the Clinton-Bush transition at the National Security Council.*" (emphasis added) (The 9/11 Commission's Final Report, p509n165, as cited in *The 9/11 Commission Report: Omissions and Distortions* David Ray Griffin (2005 Olive Branch Press) 8-9)

[554] *The Commission: The Uncensored History of the 9/11 Investigation* Philip Shenon (2008 Twelve) 388

[555] *Without Precedent: The Inside Story of the 9/11 Commission* Thomas H. Kean and Lee H. Hamilton (2006 Alfred A. Knopf) 116

[556] *The Commission: The Uncensored History of the 9/11 Investigation* Philip Shenon (2008 Twelve) 389

[557] Ibid. at 84-86

[558] *Crossing the Rubicon—The Decline of the American Empire and the End of the Age of Oil* Michael C. Ruppert (2004 New Society Publishers) 50-68

[559] Ibid.

[560] The Land of Desire concept is borrowed from
Land of Desire—Merchants, Power, and the Rise of a New American Culture William Leach (1993 Vintage Books)

[561] The full quote is "We talk about the American Dream, and want to tell the world about the American Dream, but what is that dream, in most cases, but the dream of material things? I sometimes think that the United States for this reason, is the greatest failure the world has ever seen." From an unpublished play entitled "Give Me Liberty and—" *The Great Quotations* George Seldes with J. Donald Adams (1966 Caesar-Stuart) 535

[562] *Land of Desire—Merchants, Power, and the Rise of a New American Culture* William Leach (1993 Vintage Books) 359-367

[563] Ibid. at 7, 8

[564] Ibid. at 305, 339, 341, 377

[565] Ibid. at 298, 299

[566] *Shoveling Fuel for a Runaway Train—Errant Economists, Shameful Spenders, and a Plan to Stop Them All* Brian Czech (2000 University of California Press) 22-24

[567] Economist and General Systems Theory cofounder Kenneth Boulding once stated, "Anyone who believes exponential growth can go on forever in a finite world is either a madman or an economist."
The Great Delusion—A Mad Inventor, Death in the Tropics, and the Utopian Origins of Economic Growth Steven Stoll (2008 Hill and Wang) 153

[568] See Appendix I, Current Ecological Trends, Item 5.
Actually, nearly *all* gains from Keynesian efficiencies derive from petroleum. As Steven Stoll observes, "Oil is not simply implicated in everything we call growth—there has never been growth without it."
The Great Delusion—A Mad Inventor, Death in the Tropics, and the Utopian Origins of Economic Growth Steven Stoll (2008 Hill and Wang) 158

[569] *In the Absence of the Sacred—The Failure of Technology and the Survival of the Indian Nations* Jerry Mander (1991 Sierra Club Books) 23

[570] *New York Times* February 4, 1899

[571] http://www.footprintnetwork.org/en/index.php/GFN/

INDEX

Page numbers with an *n* denote an endnote; *t* refers to a table.

A

Abel, Jennifer, 156
Academi, Blackwater as, 148
Acheson, Dean
    on Communist threat, 41, 231n100
    instructions on Greek profiteering, 233n123
    on Marshall Plan, 37
    "rotten apple" depiction, 47, 103–4
Ackerman, Bruce, 183–84, 271n537
Adams, John Quincy, 25
addiction, 165–66
Adler, Julius, 18
advertising
    broadcast network profits from, 130
    campaign expenditures for, 66–67
    by Clear Channel Communications, 129
    prosperity from, 218
    public involvement as replacing, 184
    underwriting as, 134
Affordable Care Act
    insurance stranglehold on, 139, 143
    women's reproductive rights and, 261n433
Afghanistan
    invasion of, 153
    opium poppy production, 167, 215–16
agents provocateurs, 181, 270n533-534

agrarian reform in Guatemala, 14, 15–16, 17, 20
air defense paralysis, 9/11, 157–59
air space violations, missile crisis and, 250n296
aircraft carriers, Khrushchev on, 244n234
aircraft industry
    after World War II, 36–37, 229n77
    military budgets as boost for, 40–41
airlines, deregulation of, 59
Akron Beacon-Journal, 29
Alar scare, 58, 235–36n147-148
ALEC (American Legislative Exchange Council). *See* American Legislative Exchange Council (ALEC)
alien species, relocation, 199
Allende, Salvador, 6–8
Alliance for Progress, 8, 222n14
Allied merchant vessels, sinking of, 226n54
Alonso, José, 208, 209
Alpha 66, 100
al-Qaeda
    as information source, 125, 154, 214
    skepticism of 9/11 role, 159, 213
AlterNet, 173
Altgeld, John Peter, 171
American Behavioral Scientist, 161
American Exceptionalism, 138
American Legislative Exchange Council (ALEC)
    about, 67–70

government privatization and, 68, 132, 175
media coverage of, 132, 258n407
renewable energy reversals, 167
Republican funding of, 138
on Stand Your Ground laws, 132, 259n408
Amnesty International, Iranian human rights, 3
Anderson, Rudolf, 99
Anglo-Iranian Oil Company, 2
Angola, conflicting US roles in, 77
Another World is Possible, 130–31
anti-communism
 defense industry and, 153
 in Greece, 47
 in Guatemala, 20
 McCarthyism, 17
 Truman's reelection victory, 53
 in US, 42–44
 in Vietnam, 104
anti-US demonstrations. *See* protest demonstrations
Arbenz Guzman, Jacobo
 CIA regime change, 4
 demonizing, 225n33
 presidency of, 16–19
Arévalo, Juan José, 15
armaments industry
 board interlocks with, 148
 government links to, 147–48
 Marshall Plan as boost for, 37
 Southeast Asia as cash cow, 104, 105, 109
 See also Defense Department
Armas, Carlos Castillo
 as CIA choice, 3–4, 225n35
 dictatorship of, 20
 rebellion, 19
 recruitment of, 18
Armey, Dick, 72
Ashcroft, John, 150
Asian markets, World War I economic concerns, 31

aspartame
 Hayes' approval of, 186
 Rumsfeld's finagling of, 62, 63, 237n165
 as toxic sweetener, 237n165
assassinations
 of Allende, 7
 Castro, attempts on, 6, 90, 247n265
 Church Committee revelations, 77
 of Diem, 107, 110
 of Kennedy (John). *See* Kennedy, John
 of Kennedy (Robert), 266n495
 of Lumumba, 5–6
 of Polk (George), 48–49, 51
 of Schneider, 7
Atlantic Charter, 103–4
Atomic Energy Commission, test ban treaty opposition, 102
attack advertising, 66
austerity budgets, xiv
autopsies
 Kennedy, John, 110–12, 254n342, 254n346
 Kennedy, Robert, 266n495

B

Bacevich, Andrew, 187
balance, definition, xi
ballot access laws, 144
ballot boxes, proprietary technology of, 69
Bamford, James, 100
Bank of America, 63, 148
Barrett, Edward, 41
BASF
 CEO compensation, 242n217
 lobbying, 73
 market share, 242n215
Batista, Fulgencio, 21, 87–88
Baucus, Max, 261n433
Bauerlein, Monika, 58
Bay of Pigs
 about, 89–92

battle of, 207–12
CIA covert activities exposure, 77
Fulbright's lone opposition, 255n353
Kennedy on, 87
Bayer
   CEO compensation, 242n217
   lobbying, 73
   market share, 242n215
   neonics toxicity, 73
Beck, Glenn, 131
Beneficent Uncle Sam Worldview
   about, 8
   as camouflage, 10–11, 167
   as shield from critical review, 169
Berlin crisis, 97
Berlin Wall, facade for demolition practice, 249n287
Bernabe, José, 20, 225n37
Bernays, Edward, 17, 18–19, 20
Bernstein, Carl, 243n224
BFDC (Bureau of Foreign and Domestic Commerce), 218
Big Steel, Kennedy vs., 97–98, 250n292
Bigart, Homer, 51, 52, 234n129
Bill and Melinda Gates Foundation, 186
bin Laden, Osama, 153–54, 160
biotechnology lawsuits against farmers, 62
Bissell, Richard
   as CIA deputy director, 81, 89
   in Cuban debacle, 91–92
   misleading information from, 85, 90, 246n255
   resignation of, 96
   U-2 intelligence instructions, 83
Blackstone Group, 269n527
Blackwater, 148
Bleifuss, Joel, 124–25
Bloom, Allan, 264n459
board interlocks
   about, 60–61
   with armaments industry, 148
   network programming and, 130
Boeing, 36, 148
Bohlen, Charles, 203
Boland Amendment, 117
Bolshevik Revolution, 203
Bomber Gap, 78
Bonsal, Philip, 88
Boston, Scott, 133
Boston Tea Party, 56
Boulding, Kenneth, 274n567
Bovine spongiform encephalopathy, 58
Boyer, Harold, 36
BP Deepwater Horizon drilling rig, 57–58
Braden, Spruille, 16
Bradley, Omar, 39
Brandeis, Louis
   about, 238n175
   on wealth concentration, 65, 66, 67
breast milk, chemicals in, 198
Breen, Joseph, 33, 228n71
Brennan, John, 168
Bright, Chris, 199
Britt, Donna, 119
Britt, Laurence, 175, 269n523
Broad, William, 125–26
Bryan, William Jennings, 226n54
Buddhist movement in Vietnam
   vs. Diem, 106
   US support for, 107
Bugliosi, Vincent, *Reclaiming History*, 112
Bureau of Foreign and Domestic Commerce (BFDC), 218
Burkley, George, 112
Burma, conflicting US roles in, 77
Bush, George H. W. (GHW), 120, 122–23
Bush, George W. (GW)
   appointments, 238n169, 262n441
   Dixie Chicks on, 129, 258n394

income of, 237n163
Iraq war, 124–27
landmines, 143
post-9/11 quote by, 153
on pre-emptive wars of aggression, 151
Supreme Court decision for, 160
on torture, 168, 268n506
Trans-Pacific Partnership, 260n425
WTC security, 265n482
Bush, Marvin, 265n482
Business Roundtable, 67
Butler, Smedley, 23
Byondananda, Swami, 170

C

Cabell, Charles, 92
Cabinet Secretaries, 186–87, 271–72n542-543
Cabot, John Moors, 16
Cabot, Thomas Dudley, 16
Calero, Adolfo, 118
Cambodia, French troops in, 104
Camp David,
  Eisenhower/Khrushchev at, 79, 80
campaign financing
  amounts of, xiv, 66–67
  Center for Responsive Politics, 240n181
  corporate ties for, 261n428
  expenditures, 167
  Green Party reforms, 141–42
  in state elections, 69–70
  wealth concentration and, 166
campaigns, network television, 239n179
Canadian Broadcasting Corporation, *To Sell a War*, 123
Capra, Frank, *Why We Fight*, 33
Caribbean nations. *See* Latin America/Caribbean nations
Carpenter, Liz, 192
Carreras, Enrique, 210

carrying capacity of Earth, 168
Carson, Rachel, *Silent Spring*, xiv, 198
Carter administration
  airline deregulation during, 59
  Hussein and, 122
  Panama Canal renegotiations, 268n506
Castro, Fidel
  about, 87–88
  air power/missiles, 209–11
  CIA assassination attempts, 6, 90, 247n265
  contrived incidents attributed to, 100–101
  Kennedy's relationship with, 100
  terrorism attributed to, 270n533
  unification behind, 88–89
  US opposition to, 89–90, 247n265
  See also Bay of Pigs
Cato Institute, 150
cattle industry lawsuit against Winfrey, 58
Cavero, Father, 210, 211
CBS, 130
CCD (colony collapse disorder), 73, 242n213
censorship
  Espionage Act (1917), 29, 42, 180, 269n522
  Sedition Act (1918), 29, 42, 180
  World War I, 29
  World War II, 33
  See also civil liberties attacks
Central Intelligence Agency (CIA)
  advent/history of, 75–77
  Alpha 66 sponsorship of, 100
  in Bay of Pigs debacle, 89–92
  conflicting roles of, 76–77
  Contra affair
    about, 117–120, 215
    crack cocaine epidemic,

117, 215
Reagan administration role in, 172
self-exoneration, 119, 256n370
See also *Dark Alliance* (Webb)
corruption in, 166
deadly detonations by, 106
induced migration, 105, 253n323-324
as Kennedy assassination architect, 112
Kennedy curbs on, 96
Kennedy on, 87
in Laos, 95
mass media infiltration, 76, 176, 182, 224n27
public awareness of, 77
regime changes, 2–8, *8t*
See also *specific countries*
scrutiny as threat to, 92
surveillance within government agencies, 75–76, 243n229
test ban treaty, opposition, 102
CEO compensation, 72–74
Ceppos, Jerry, 120
Chamber of Commerce lobbying, 58, 67, 236n151
Chamberlin, Stephen, 38–39
Chamoun, Camille, 4
character assassination, 133
Charles I (King of England), 56
chemical pollutants, 198
Cheney, Dick
as defense secretary, 148, 186
income of, 237n163
Office of National Preparedness, role in, 158, 266n484
as PNAC founding member, 263n458
revolving door career, 61–62, 147–48
as vice-presidential candidate, 61, 237n162

Chile, CIA regime change, 6–8, *8t*, 181
Chinese in Korean War, 42
Christian Science Monitor, Tea Party analysis, 131
Church Committee, CIA revelations by, 77
Churchill, Winston
on Greek Royalists' brutality, 46–47
on iron curtain, 45
on US in Bolshevik Revolution, 203
World War I memoir, 29
CIA (Central Intelligence Agency). See Central Intelligence Agency (CIA)
CIGNA, 71
Cirincione, Joseph, 147
Citigroup, 63, 143
Citizens for a Free Kuwait (front group), 123
Citizens United v. Federal Election Commission, 57, 235n141
civil liberties attacks
loyalty oaths, 42–43, 116
McCarthyism, 17, 42–44
under Patriot Act, 149–150, 160, 162, 180, 269n530
See also censorship
Clark, Tom, 42–43
classification of government records, 182
Clay, Lucius, 38–39, 249n287
Clean Air Act, WTO challenges to, 60
Clear Channel Communications, 129–130
Clifford, Clark, 38, 40, 48
climate change denial, 167, 267n501
Clinton, Bill
Democratic Leadership Council and, 261n428
PNAC advisory letter to, 150, 263n458

279

regressive legislation signed
  by, 143
COG ("continuity of government"),
  149–150
Colby, William, 253n324
Cold War
  overview
    about, 35
    post-WWII industrial
      slump, 36–37
    Soviet
      capabilities/intentions,
      exaggeration of, 38–44
    Truman reelection
      campaign, 37–38
  blueprint for, 41
  in Cuba, 87–93
  maintenance of
    about, 75–77
    CIA aggravation of US-
      Soviet relations, 85–86,
      92–93
      See also Bay of Pigs;
        U-2 Affair
    Eisenhower's peace
      efforts, 79–80
    military budgets, 78–79
    peace efforts, 79–80
    reconnaissance, 80–83
    U-2 aftermath, 83–84
  Rascal worldview in, 169
  television news advent, 115–16
  worldview of. *See under*
    worldviews
colonialism, US, 169
colony collapse disorder (CCD),
  73, 242n213
Comcast, 130
Commerce Department, 63, 98, 218
commercial media, public
  broadcasting vs., 134
Communications Act (1934),
  259n414
Communism
  as front for Polk's murder, 50,
    233n126

nationalization seen as, 37
trumped-up for justification
  for global expansion, 169
  in Guatemala, 17–18,
    224n29
  in Vietnam, 104
Conason, Joe, 175
Congo
  CIA regime change, 5–6, *8t*
  conflicting US roles in, 76–77
Connally, John, 110
conscription (draft), 29, 40
conspicuous consumption, 219–220
conspiracies and conspiracy theory
  CIA-Contra Affair as, 172
  Dark Alliance portrayed as,
    119, 256n368
  documented, 162
  GW Bush derision of, 153–54
  history of, 267n497
  Kennedy assassination and,
    161–62
conspiracy theory repository
  (CTR), 161, 162, 176
Constitution Party, 260n422
constitutional rights, policing and,
  149
consumerism, 217–220
"continuity of government" (COG),
  149–150
controlled demolition, 156–57
Corcoran, Thomas G., 16
corporate networking, 148
corporate personhood, 56–59
Corporate Social Responsibility,
  235n144
corporate television, 130
corporate-government merger,
  174–75, 181
Corporation for Public
  Broadcasting (CPB), 134, 188
corporations
  about, 53, 55
  corporate personhood, 56–59
  defense industry. *See*
    armaments industry

global synergism, 60–61
Hayes on, 55
Jackson on, 55
lobbying by, 67
regulation/deregulation, 59–60
revolving doors, 61–64, 147–48
Roosevelt on, 65
shareholders and stakeholders, 235n144
corruption, recognizing, 166–67
Costa Rica, Eisenhower's interference in, 78
country-of-origin meat labeling, WTO challenges to, 60
cover-up operations, 11
CPB (Corporation for Public Broadcasting), 134, 188
crack cocaine epidemic. *See under* Central Intelligence Agency (CIA)
creation, definition, xi
credit, consumer, 218–19
Crenshaw, Charles
   JFK: Conspiracy of Silence, 111
   as Kennedy attending physician, 112–13
Crespo, José, 210, 211
criminal justice system, Elite power and, 263n454
Cronkite, Walter, 258n399
CropLife America, 73
CTR (conspiracy theory repository), 161, 162, 176
Cuba
   CIA regime change, 6, *8t*
   Cold War era in, 87–88
   contrived incidents to justify invasion, 100–101
   defection, deception of, 91, 248n273
   Kennedy's relationship with, 100
   US
      Cuban exiles' invasion of, 87–92
      diplomatic ties, severance, 89
      interests in, 26–27
      overflights of, 99, 100
Cuban exiles
   at Bay of Pigs, 207–12
   CIA and, 100
Cuban Missile Crisis, 98–100, 250n293, 250n296
Cuban Revolutionary Council, 100
Cutler, Robert, 16
Cuyamel Fruit Company, 14
Czechoslovakia, 39–41, 230n89-90

D

Dallek, Robert, 230n91
Dark Alliance (Webb), 118–120, 172, 256n361-362
de Gasperi, Alcide, 204–5
Debs, Eugene V.
   arrest of, 29, 225n39
   quote by, 23
Decision for Disaster (Lynch), 91–92
Deepwater Horizon drilling rig, 57–58
Defense Department
   privatization of functions, 61–62
   public opinion shaping, 116, 255n353-354
   size of, 151
   in Southeast Asia, 104–5
   steel contracts, 98, 250n292
defense industry. *See* armaments industry
deforestation, 195
Deliberation Day, 141, 183–84, 271n537, 271n539
democracy as Green Party value, 141–42
Democracy Movement
   about, xiii
   definition, xi
   demands, focus on, 179–180

Elite response to, 175–76
goals of, 170
importance of, 191
launching, xiv, 171–77
public information role in, 192
Democracy Now! as independent news, 131, 132, 173
Democratic Party
   ALEC and, 68
   Democratic Leadership Council, 144, 261n428-429
   Republican Party similarities, 262n439
   in rigged system, 144–45
   shortcomings of, 139–140
   values, 138–39
democratic strategic initiatives. *See* Strategic Initiatives
demonstrations. *See* protest demonstrations
Diamond, Jared, 195
dictatorships
   in Cuba, 87
   in Guatemala, 13, 14, 20
   in Korea, 42
   military aid for, 222n14
Diem, Ngo Dinh
   about, 104–5
   assassination of, 107, 110
   Buddhist oppression, 106
Dien Bien Phu, French defeat at, 104
direct democracy options, 185–86
Disney, 130
Dixie Chicks, 129, 258n394
Dobrynin, Anatoly, 99
Dodge v. Ford Motor Company, 57, 64, 170
Dole, Sanford, 169
dolphin-safe tuna, WTO challenges to, 60
domestic policies, attacks on, 260n425
domino theory, 47, 103–4
Donovan, Bill, 51, 52
Donovan, James, 100

Dow
   CEO compensation, 242n217
   lobbying, 73
   market share, 242n215
draft (conscription), 29, 40
Dreyfus, Robert, 127
drone program
   Obama's expansion of, 144
   as terrorism trigger, 168, 169, 262n438
drug trafficking, CIA, 117–120, 215
   See under Central Intelligence Agency; *Dark Alliance* (Webb)
Dulles, Allen
   administrative skills of, 80
   as CIA Director, 10, 16
   in Cuban debacle, 92
   Eisenhower (John) on, 78
   misleading information from, 83, 85, 90, 246n255
   on pre-emptive action against Cuba, 95
   regime change in Guatemala, 18
   replacement of, 76
   resignation of, 96
   secret network of, 75
   Soviet overflights, 81
   on U-2 downing, 83, 245n248
   as UFCO attorney, 16
   Warren Commission role, 112–13
Dulles, John Foster
   on Guatemalan government changes, 10
   Khrushchev on, 249n285, 252n320
   on military intervention in Vietnam, 104
   regime change in Guatemala, 18
   as secretary of state, 16
   as UFCO attorney, 16
DuPont

CEO compensation, 242n217
government connections, 63
lobbying, 73
market share, 242n215

E

East India Company, 56
echo chamber for news, 173–74
ecological balance, Green Party
    values, 140, 142
ecological cliff, overindulgence
    and, 165, 191
ecological footprint, 202, 217, 220
ecological imperative
    about, xiii–xiv
    definition, xi
    fossil fuel industry and, 167
    healthy course toward, 165
    worldviews and, 168
ecological trends
    alien species, relocation of, 199
    fossil fuel depletion, 196
    fresh water depletion, 196–97
    genetic diversity, diminishing,
        194–95
    global warming, 200
    habitat disintegration, 193
    human environmental impact,
        201–2
    human overpopulation, 201
    photosynthetic ceiling, 197–98
    soil erosion, 195
    toxic chemicals, 198–99
    wild foods, diminishing, 194
economic growth, preoccupation
    with, 168
economic restructuring as Green
    Party value, 141
ecosystems, sustainability of, xiii
Egypt, Eisenhower's interference
    in, 78
Ehrlich, Paul, 201
Einstein, Albert, 43
Eisenhower, Dwight
    about, 243n231
    information withheld from, 83–
        84, 246n255, 251n297
    Khrushchev on, 249n285
    in Laos, 95
    on military-industrial
        influence, 147
    peace efforts, 79–80
    Soviet threats, postwar derision
        of, 38
    U-2, role in, 80–84, 246n252
    Waging Peace, 78, 83, 85,
        246n255
Eisenhower, John S. D., 78
Eisenhower Administration
    counter-revolution in Cuba,
        89–90
    on Guatemalan government
        changes, 10
    Lebanese election interference,
        4–5
    military budgets during, 78–79
    UFCO influence in, 16
ELAS (Greek People's Liberation
    Army), 45–46
elections
    reform, media opposition to,
        66–67
    rigged/canceled
        in Greece, 46
        in Italy, 204–5
        in Korea, 42
        in Vietnam, 105
    US
        about, 69–70
        campaign coverage,
            239n179
        fraud, 69
        voter turnout, 271n540
Elite power
    bipartisan support of, 139–140,
        144
    criminal justice for, 263n454
    definition, xi
    Democracy Movement,
        response to, 175
    as global emergency, xiii
    media and, 132, 133

as plutocracy, 67
status quo defense, 189–190
time use by, 182
"Elite rule," 264n459
Elizabeth I (Queen of England), 56
Ellsberg, Daniel, 106
embassy bombings, 154
Emnid Institute, 159
employment termination, loyalty oaths and, 42
The End of America (Wolf), 175
enemy combatant status, Ashcroft on, 150
energy policies, foreign policy intertwined with, xiv
Enron scandal, 59
environmental impact (human), 201–2
Environmental Protection Agency, 62–63, 73
environmental protections, WTO challenges to, 60
erosion, 195
Espionage Act (1917), 29, 42, 180, 269n522
European market access, Marshall Plan and, 37, 40
European Union, Kantor's pressure on, 62
evil, Terror War and, 167–68
evolution in reverse, 199
executive branch oversight, 186–87
explosives, evidence after 9/11, 156–57
extinctions
alien species as cause, 199
DDT role in, 198
genetic diversity decline from, 194
overpopulation and, 201

F

Fairness Doctrine, 189
farmers, biotechnology lawsuits against, 62
fascism, 174–75, 269n523

fast track authority, 143
FCC (Federal Communications Commission), 188–89
FDA (Food and Drug Administration). *See* Food and Drug Administration (FDA)
fear-mongering, healthcare, 71–72
Federal Communications Commission (FCC), 188–89
Federal Election Commission, Citizens United v., 57, 235n141
Federal Emergency Management Agency (FEMA), 155–57
Federal Employee Loyalty Program, 42–43
Federal Reserve, revolving doors, 63
Feingold, Russ, 269n530
Feinstein, Diane, 269n522
Feith, Doug, 126
FEMA (Federal Emergency Management Agency), 155–57
Ferrer, Eddie, 210, 211
fertilizers, petroleum-based, 196
Figueres, José, 76
financial crisis (2008), 143, 269n527, 270n536
Financial Services Modernization Act (1999), 143
financial-industrial sector, aircraft industry impact on, 36
Fireside Chats, FDR, 33
fish, decline in, 194
Fisher, Linda J., 62–63
Fishkin, James, 183–84, 271n537
Fleischer, Ari, 161–62
food
aid supplies unused, 46, 49, 103
chemical pollutants, 198
disparagement laws, 58, 235n147
energy for production, 196
malnutrition in Guatemala, 15
poisoning from war profiteering, 27

284

scarcity, landownership changes and, 14
shortages after World War II, 37
topsoil and, 195
Food and Drug Administration (FDA)
    aspartame release, 237n165
    Bush's appointments, 238n169
    revolving doors, 63
Ford, Gerald, 7–8
Ford Motor Company, Dodge v., 57, 64, 170
foreclosures, 172, 269n527, 270n531
foreign policy
    Beneficent Uncle Sam in, 169
    clandestine classification of, 76
    during Eisenhower Administration, 78–79
    electorate's opinions in, 22
    energy policies intertwined with, xiv
    international perspective on, 21
    media use in
        about, 115–16
        CIA-Contra affair, 117–121
        Iraq, 122–27
        as multiple failures, 127–28
    privatization in action, 150–52
    textbook misrepresentations of, 1–9
Forrestal, James, 37, 38, 39
fossil fuels
    depletion, 196
    ecological peril of, 167
    Green Revolution dependence on, 219
    sustaining through military action, xiv
Fourteenth Amendment, 56
Fox, Sam, 66
Fox News, Tea Party promotion, 131

France in Vietnam, 103–4
Free Press, 174
Free Speech TV, 173
free trade, hype vs. reality, 59–60
FreedomWorks, 72, 138, 242n207
fresh water depletion, 196–97
Froman, Michael, 63
Fulbright, J. William
    The Pentagon Propaganda Machine, 116
    Senate voting record, 255n353

G

G. D. Searle & Company, government connections, 62, 237n165
Galbraith, John Kenneth, 106
Galloway, Calvin, 111–12
García, Eduardo, 207, 210
General Agreement on Tariffs and Trade (GATT), 59
General Motors, 36, 148
genetic diversity, diminishing, 194–95
genetically engineered crops, 62
Geneva Accords, 104, 252n320
Geneva conference
    Eisenhower/Khrushchev at, 79, 249n285
    mandated elections, 105
    Vietnam's independence and, 104
Geneva Conventions, 149
genocide
    in Americas, 223n23
    in Vietnam, 253n324
Germany in Vietnam, 103
Gladwell, Malcolm, 171
Glanz, James, 155
global financial crisis (2008), 59, 181, 268n527, 270n536
Global Greens, 142
global warming, 167, 200, 267n501
Gochenaur, Jim, 111
Golden, Tim, 119
Goldman Sachs, 148

Good Neighbor Policy, 117
Goodman, Amy, 131
Goodpaster, Andrew, 83
Gore, Al, 262n441
government agencies
    appointments, 186
    CIA positions within, 75–76, 243n229
    corporate "capture" of, 63
    television news symbiosis, 115
government privatization
    ALEC and, 68, 132, 175
    Defense Department functions, 61–62, 186
    of elections, 69
    in foreign policy, 150–52
    of military forces, 148
    Republican Party and, 138
government subsidies, aircraft industry, 36–37, 229n77
Grandin, Greg, 21, 223n25
Grant, Ulysses S., 24
grassroots movements, media coverage of, 132
Great Depression, 219
Greece
    British rule, 45–46
    US aid, 51, 234n129
    US role in, 47–53, 233n120
Greek People's Liberation Army (ELAS), 45–46
Greek Royalists
    brutality, 46
    leadership corruption, 49
    Polk's assassin among, 51
    Truman backing of, 48
    US intervention on behalf of, 47
Greek-Turkish Aid Act, 47
Green Party
    about, 260n422
    Nader's candidacy, 262n441
    values, 140–42
Green Revolution, 196, 219
Greenglass, David, 43
greenhouse gasses, 200

Greenwald, Glenn, 263n454
Greider, William, 235n139
Griffin, David Ray, 213
Gross, Robert E., 229n77
Grumman Corporation, 228n74
The Guardian, 125
Guatemala
    CIA regime change, 3–4, *8t*, 18, 225n35
    Eisenhower's outlook on, 78
    history of
        colonial period, 13–15
        counterrevolution, 16–19
        coup, 19
        democratic revolution (1944), 15–16
        restoration of dictatorship, 20
    Rascal in, 166
    in textbooks, 3–4, *8t*, 21–22
Guevara, Ernesto (Che), 87
Gulf War, private contractors in, 148

H
habitat disintegration, 193
Hagel, Chuck, 69
Halliburton, 61–62, 147–48
Hamilton, Lee
    on 9/11 investigation, 213
    Without Precedent, 154
Hammarskjöld, Dag, 5
Harding, Warren G., 219
Harper's Magazine, 48, 123
Harriman, Averell, 102, 229n83, 251n297
Harris, Bev, 69
Hartford Advocate, 156
Hawkins, Jack, 92
Hay, John, 26
Hayes, Arthur, 186, 237n165
Hayes, Rutherford B., 55, 234n138
health implications of extinctions, 195
health insurance industry
    Affordable Care Act, 139, 143

FreedomWorks funding from, 72
public health vs. profits, 70–71
public option vs., 185, 270n536
women's reproductive rights, 261n433
healthcare, universal, 70, 71, 241n203
Hearst, William Randolph, 26–27
Hedges, Chris, 11, 223n23
Helms, Richard, 76, 246n252
Heritage Foundation, 150
Herman, Edward S., 222n11
Herrick, John, 108
Hersh, Seymour M., 126
Herter, Christian, 97
Hijacking Catastrophe, 151, 264n462
Hill & Knowlton public relations, 123
Hindenburg, Paul von, 159–160
Hiss, Alger, 44
historical distortions, persistence of, 11
Hitchcock, Ethan Allen, 225n43
Ho Chi Minh, 103–5
Hoffman, Clare, 231n106
Holdren, John, 201
Hollywood Blacklist, 44
holocaust in Americas, 11
home foreclosures, 172, 269n527, 270n531
Homeland Security, 149
Honduras, CIA airstrips in, 18
honey bees, neonics toxicity and, 73, 242n213
Hoover, Herbert, 219
House's Committee on Un-American Activities (HUAC), 43–44, 255n353
Hubbert, M. King, 196
Hugo, Victor, 13, 179, 191
human ecological impact, 201
human overpopulation, 201
human rights. See *specific countries*
Humana insurance, 71
Hunt, Howard, 18
Hussein, Saddam, 122
hydroelectric dams, 194

I

ICBM (intercontinental ballistic missiles), 80, 250n296
ideological boundaries, public broadcasting, 134
IMF (International Monetary Fund), founding of, 59
imprisonment without specified charges, 149
In Breach of Trust (McKnight), 110
In Fact (newsletter), closure of, 43, 52
In These Times as independent news, 117, 124, 132, 173
income gap
  in Greece, 232n112
  in Guatemala, 14–15
  Piketty on, 239n177
  See also wealth concentration
independence movements
  Greece, 45–47
  Vietnam, 103–4
Indigenous populations
  genocide of, 223n23
  medicinal knowledge of, 195
  rights of, 20
Indonesia, Eisenhower's interference in, 78
industrial expansion, consumerism and, 217–18
Industrial Revolution, ecological problems, xiv
industry front groups, healthcare, 71
industry-government integration, 147–48
industry-to-government career moves, 63
infant mortality, 15, 70
infinite growth paradigm, 219,

274n567
information sources, 9/11 investigation, 154–55
Inspire group, 192
installment buying, 218–19
Institute for Legal Reform, 58–59, 236n151
insurance profit, healthcare vs., 70–71
intercontinental ballistic missiles (ICBM), 80, 250n296
International Monetary Fund (IMF), founding of, 59
interrogation techniques, US, 154
Iran
    CIA regime change, 2–3, *8t*
    Eisenhower's outlook on, 78
Iranian Hostage Crisis, 10, 122
Iraq wars
    about, 122–27
    chemical weapons use, 122
    Clinton letter signatories, 263n458
    invasion justification, 151
    Republican views on, 139
    Rumsfeld's role in, 186
Italy, US-induced regime change, 204–5

J

Jackson, Andrew, 55, 166
Jackson, Wes, 195
Japanese attack predictions (1941), 31–32, 228n66
Jefferson, Thomas, 24
Jeffery, Clara, 58
JFK: Conspiracy of Silence (Crenshaw), 111
JFK Records Act (1992), 112
Johnson, Lyndon, 107–9, 112
Joint Chiefs of Staff
    for pre-emptive action against Cuba, 95, 98, 100–101
    test ban treaty, opposition, 102
Jordan, Eisenhower's interference in, 78

Justice Department, steel corporation investigations, 98

K

Kantor, Michael (Mickey), 62
Kasavubu, Joseph, 5
Katanga, 5, 76–77
Kean, Thomas
    on 9/11 investigation, 213
    Without Precedent, 154
Keith, Minor, 14
Kellis, James G. L., 51–53
Kellogg, Brown, & Root, Cheney's role with, 61
Kennan, George, 39, 75
Kennedy, John
    Alliance for Progress, 8, 222n14
    assassination of
        about, 109–13
        autopsy of, 110–12, 254n342, 254n346
        Chicago as alternative site, 254n348
        as CTR benchmark, 161–62
        ideological reasons for, 109–10, 161, 266n495
        Tampa as alternative site, 254n348
        See also Warren Commission investigation
    on CIA, 87
    CIA appointments, 76
    in Cuban debacle, 90–92
    inauguration, 89
    information withheld from, 90, 92–93, 249n287
    issues
        Berlin crisis, 97
        Big Steel confrontation, 97–98, 250n292
        CIA curbs, 96
        Cuban Missile Crisis, 98–100, 250n293, 250n296

Cuban relations, 100
Laotian independence, 95–96
Nuclear Test Ban Treaty, 101–2
Operation Northwoods, 100–101
peace efforts, 96–97
Vietnam withdrawal orders, 107
Kennedy, Robert
aggressive investigations of, 250n292
assassination/autopsy of, 266n495
Castro, outlook on, 100
CIA, knowledge of, 76
Ellsberg communication, 106
Warren Commission role, 112
Keynes, John Maynard, 219
Keynesian economic assumptions, 219–220, 274n568
Keystone XL pipeline, 149–150, 261n437
Khomeini, Ayatollah, 122
Khrushchev, Nikita
on aircraft carriers, 244n234
back-channel dialogue with Kennedy, 96
on bomber bases and missiles, 250n293, 250n296
Cuban Missile Crisis, 98–99, 251n297
on Eisenhower, 249n285
Eisenhower and, 79–80
on Iron Curtain, 45
Kennedy's relationship with, 100
Laotian Neutrality Declaration, 96
peace efforts of, 96
Soviet overflights and, 81
U-2 aftermath, 84
on Vietnam, 252n320
on world peace, 101–2
Kimmel, Husband, 31, 32

Kissinger, Henry, 6–7
Klein, Julius, 218
Koch, Charles, 68, 267n501
Koch, David, 68, 267n501
Korean War, 41–42
Korry, Edward, 7, 181
Korten, David, 57, 60
Kurtz, Howard, 118
Kuwait, in Persian Gulf War, 122–23
Kwiatkowski, Karen, 125

L

labor
in Guatemala, 14–15
steel price controls vs., 97–98
strikes/unrest after World War II, 37
Labor Department, steel corporation investigations, 98
Lakoff, George, 183, 221n2
Land of Desire, 168, 217–220
landmines, 143
Lansdale, Edward, 105, 252n322
Laos, French troops in, 104
Laotian Neutrality Declaration, 95–96
Latin America/Caribbean nations
protest demonstrations, 18–19, 21, 88
US military in, 13, 224n25
See also Cuba; Guatemala; Nicaragua
Lebanon
CIA regime change, 4–5, *8t*
Eisenhower's outlook on, 78
legislation, corporate sponsorship of, 68
legislative agendas, 184–85, 188
LeMay, Curtis, 98
Lemnitzer, Lyman, 101
liability of stockholders, 56
Libby, I. Lewis (Scooter), 151
libel, food disparagement laws and, 58, 235n147
Libertarian Party, 260n422

Liberty ships, 233n123
lies, persistence of, 10–11
life, definition, xi
life expectancy, 15, 70
Limbaugh, Rush, 133
Limited Test Ban Treaty, 102
Lincoln, Abraham, 25, 226n45
Linton, Ralph, 217
Lippmann, Walter, 51, 52
lobbying
    about, 67
    Chamber of Commerce, 59
    disproportionate influence of, 67
    expenditures, 167
    health insurance industry, 185
lobbyists, in regulatory agencies, 63
Lockheed, 36
Lodge, Henry Cabot, 107, 110
Loewen, James, 1–2, 20
Lofgren, Mike, 262n439
Lone Star State, 24
Los Angeles Times, 120
Louisiana Purchase, 24
loyalty oaths, 42–43, 116
Luce, Henry, 76
Lumumba, Patrice, 5–6
Lusitania, 28–29, 226n54
Lyman, Howard, 58
Lynch, Grayston
    Bay of Pigs, role in, 207–8, 209
    Decision for Disaster, 91–92
Lynn, William, 148

M

MacArthur, Douglas, 42
MacArthur, John R., 123, 257n383, n257n383
Macy, Joanna, 165
Macy's, 218
Mad Cow Disease, 58
Madame Nhu ("Dragon Lady"), 107
Maddow, Rachel, 72

Maddox, USS, 107–8
Mafia in Cuba, 87
Magsaysay, Ramon, 252n322
Maine, USS, 26
Maines, Natalie, 258n394
manifest destiny, 24, 225n41
Mansfield, Mike, 106
Marshall, George
    about, 229n79
    on Czechoslovakia, 39–40, 230n89
    on European Recovery Plan, 37
    Polk murder, PR for, 50
    Soviet Union, view of, 203–4
Marshall Plan, 37, 40
martial law, 50–51, 150
Martin, Trayvon, 132, 259n408
Marton, Kati, 48, 50
Marxism, nationalization seen as, 37
Masaryk, Jan, 40, 230n91
mass media
    about, 129–130
    air of authority in, 258n399
    campaign coverage, 239n179
    CIA infiltration of, 76, 176, 182, 224n27
    concentration and conglomeration, 130
    corporate television, 130
    editorial control of, 129
    in foreign policy shaping. *See under* foreign policy
    public broadcasting, 134–35
    rancor in national discourse, 133
    selective coverage, 130–32
Massachusetts Bay Company, 56
Massey Energy coal mine disaster, 57
materialism, 217–220
Matthews, Christopher, 256n362
McCarthy, Joseph, 43, 255n353
McCarthy Group, 69
McCarthyism, 17, 42–44

McCaskill, Claire, 133
McChesney, Robert W.
  on media complicity in war promotion, 127
  on public media, 134, 272n545
  quote by, 115, 188
McCloy, John, 16
McCollum, Arthur, 30–31
McCone, John, 76, 85, 246n255
McCormack, John, 17
McKinley, William, 26
McKinney, Cynthia, 161–62
McKnight, Gerald, *In Breach of Trust*, 110
McMahon Senate campaign, 66
McNamara, Robert, 78, 101, 272n543
media. *See* mass media
Media Consortium, 173–74
Media Matters for America, 174
medical care
  health insurance. *See* health insurance industry
  public option, 185, 270n536
  vital statistics, 15, 70
Medicare, Republican views on, 140
Mellett, Lowell, 32–33
Merton, Thomas, 95, 249n278
Mexican-American War, 24–25
Meyers, Richard B., 148
Mickelson, Sig, 76
middle class erosion, 181
Middle East oil, 151, 153, 162
military bases, foreign, 151, 264n462
military budgets
  during Eisenhower Administration, 78–79
  Eisenhower's resistance to, 78–79
  garnering support for, 41–42, 231n100
  neoconservative push for, 264n459
  squeezing the populace for, xiv
  testimony fabricated for, 38–39
  during Truman administration, 40
Military Commissions Act (2006), 149
military exercises (war games on 9/11), 158–59
military forces, privatization of, 148
military scripting and production, television news, 115
military support of CIA operations, 75
military-industrial complex
  about, 147–150
  foreign policy. *See* foreign policy
  globalization of, xiv, 151–52
  Kennedy vs., 250n292
  Southeast Asia as cash cow for, 109
  See also armaments industry
Missile Gap, as Pentagon deception, 78, 80–81
Mitchell, Andrea, 119, 256n368
Mobutu, Joseph, 5–6, 222n11
Mockingbird network, 76, 176, 182, 223n27
money as addiction, 165–66
monks, self-immolation, 107
Monopoly Investigation (1938), 174
Monroe Doctrine, 13
Monsanto
  CEO compensation, 242n217
  government connections, 62–63
  lobbying, 73
  market share, 242n215
  Searle purchase by, 237n165
Montalva, Eduardo Frei, 6
Monzón, Elfego, 225n35
Moore, Elmer, 111
Moore, Kathleen Dean, 1
moral supremacy, American Exceptionalism as, 8

291

Morgan, E. M., 52
Morgan, J. P., 28
Morse, Luís, 209
mosquitoes, avian extinction from, 199
Mossadegh, Mohammed, 2, 3, 10
Mother Jones
   on BP oil spill, 58
   as independent news, 173
   on OSP, 125
   on those profiting from global crisis, 270n536
Motion Picture Association of America, censorship guidelines, 33
Mouscoundis, Nicholas, 50, 51, 53
movements
   launching
      stories. *See* stories
      tipping points, 171–73
   sustaining, 179–182
MoveOn, 171
movie industry in public relations, 32–33
Moyers, Bill, 133, 134, 143, 196
Murphy, Robert, 18
Murrow, Edward R., 48, 230n91, 233n126

N

Nader, Ralph, 262n441
NAFTA (North American Free Trade Agreement), 62, 143
nano-thermite evidence after 9/11, 156–57
The Nation
   on ALEC, 132
   on CIA's Nicaraguan meddling, 117
   as independent news, 173
   on Iraq testimony, 124–25
   on OSP, 127
national emergency, proclamation of, 149
National Equality March (2009), 132

National Public Radio (NPR), 134, 179–180, 188
National Reconnaissance Office (NRO), 158
National Security Act (1947), 75
National Security Agency (NSA)
   about, 166
   Cold War, blueprint for, 41
   Snowden as whistleblower, 175
   surveillance by, 269n522
National Security Council directives, 75
nationalism
   in Guatemala, 18
   Republican Party, 138
   US, 8, 11
nationalization, as aircraft industry option, 36–37, 229n77
natural resource extraction, Rascal in, 168–170
Navigation Acts, 56
Nayirah's fabricated story, 122–23
Nebraska Senate race (1996), 69
neonics toxicity, honey bees, 73, 242n213
netroots groups, 171
network programming, 129, 130
networking, Democracy Movement, 192
New Deal, 183
New York Herald Tribune, 51
New York Times
   on ALEC, 258n407, 259n408
   during Cuban Missile Crisis, 251n304
   on Czechoslovakia, 40
   on *Dark Alliance*, 118–19
   on Eisenhower's views, 38
   on Guatemalan politics, 17, 18, 224n27
   on Iraq, 124
   McChesney on, 127
   on Nayirah's story, 123, n257n383
   on Occupy Wall Street, 172–73

on OSP, 125–26, 127
on Polk's murder, 53
selective coverage, 130–31, 132
on Tea Party, 131
on WTC7, 155
New Yorker magazine, 126
Newman, Michael, 156
news, 115–16, 173–74, 239n179
See also mass media
Newsweek, 19
Ngo Dinh Diem. *See* Diem, Ngo Dinh
NGOs (non-governmental organizations), 189
Nicaragua, 18, 117
Nicholas II, Czar, 203
Nichols, John, 188, 272n545
Nike-Hercules/Zeus missile projects, 78
9/11 terrorist attacks (2001)
about, 153–54
air defense paralysis, 157–59
alternative hypothesis (WTC7), 156–57
investigation/report, 154–55, 182, 213–14
Operation Northwoods, parallels with, 162
skepticism, 159–161
state crimes against democracy, 161–63
World Trade Center security, 157, 265n482
Nixon administration, Allende removal, 7
non-governmental organizations (NGOs), 189
North American Free Trade Agreement (NAFTA), 62, 143
North Vietnamese, migration south, 105, 253n323-324
Northrop Grumman, 148
Norton, Anne, 264n459
Norton, Charles Eliot, 26, 226n48
Nosavan, Phoumi, 95

NOW with Bill Moyers, 134
NPR (National Public Radio), 134, 179–180, 188
NRO (National Reconnaissance Office), 158
NSA (National Security Agency). *See* National Security Agency (NSA)
NSC-10/2, 75
Nuclear Test Ban Treaty, 80, 101–2
nuclear war, Kennedy's prevention of, 99
nuclear weapons, 260n427
Nugent, Ted, 129
Nuremberg Trials, 159–160

O

Obama, Barack
campaign spending, 66
Froman's incentives, 63
legislation shortcomings, 143–44, 261n437
Trans-Pacific Partnership, 139, 260n425
women's reproductive rights, 261n433
OBL&TT ("Osama bin Laden and the Terrorists"), 153
Occupy Wall Street (2011), 132, 171, 172–73, 179, 270n536
O'Connor, Paul, 254n346
Office of National Preparedness, 158, 266n484
Office of Special Plans (OSP), 125–27, 151, 187
oil industry
depletion, 196
Middle East, 151, 153, 162
military operations enabling expansion, xiv
pipeline deregulation, 144
US foreign policy and, 2
See also Iraq wars
Onassis, Aristotle, 233n123
O'Neill, Eugene, 217, 273n561
O'Neill, Paul, 272n543

293

one-percent group. *See* top one percent
Open Chemical Physics Journal, 156–57
Operation Ajax, 2
Operation Enduring Freedom, 167, 215–16
Operation Iraqi Freedom, 167
Operation Mockingbird, 76, 182, 243n224
Operation Northwoods, 100–101, 162, 270n533
Operation Success, 18
opium poppy production, US restoration of, 167, 215–16
O'Reilly, Bill, 133
Ortega y Gasset, José, 10
Orwell, George, 217
"Osama bin Laden and the Terrorists" (OBL&TT), 153
OSP (Office of Special Plans), 125–27, 151, 187
Oswald, Lee Harvey, 112
overpopulation, 201

P

Pahlavi, Mahammad Reza (Shah), 2–3
Paley, William, 76
Palin, Sarah, 131–32
Panama Canal, 169, 268n506
paradigm shifts, 1
Paris, Treaty of, 27
Paris Peace Summit
  collapse of, 80, 84, 85–86, 97
  U-2 flights and, 81
Parker, Theodore, 25
Pascrell, Bill, 71–72
Patchwork Nation, 131–32
Patriot Act, 149–150, 160, 162, 180, 269n530
Patriots Question 9/11, 157
Paulson, John, 270n536
PBS (Public Broadcasting Service), 134, 179–180, 188
peace

  as armaments industry threat, 104
  definition, xi
  Eisenhower's efforts, 79–80
  Kennedy's efforts, 96
Peace Corps, textbook coverage of, 8
Peace Summit. *See* Paris Peace Summit
Pearl Harbor, 31–32
Peck, Scott
  People of the Lie, 167
  The Road Less Traveled, 165–66
Pentagon
  CIA turf wars, 76
  OSP disinformation source, 125–27
  pre-emptive attacks, demands for, 98
  television news collaboration, 115–16
Pentagon Papers, 104–5, 106
The Pentagon Propaganda Machine (Fulbright), 116
people, definition, xi
People of the Lie (Peck), 167
Perot, Ross, 144
Perry, Diane, 126
Perry, Malcolm, 110–11, 113, 254n342
Persian Gulf oil, 151, 153, 162
Persian Gulf War resolution, 123
personality of corporate persons, 57
pesticides
  about, xiv
  colony collapse disorder and, 73, 242n213
  petroleum-based, 196
petroleum, Keynesian efficiencies derived from, 274n568
petroleum-based fertilizers/pesticides, 196
Peurifoy, John, 17–18, 224n29
Philippines, US interests in, 27,

169, 252n322
Phillips, David Atlee, 18, 19, 224n30
Phoenix Program, 253n324
photosynthetic ceiling, 197–98
Picasso, Pablo, 43
Pickens, T. Boone, 66
Piketty, Thomas, 239n177
pilot survival, U-2, 83, 84, 85, 246n254, 246n255
Pincus, Walter, 256n369
Pinochet, Augusto, 7
pipeline industry failures, 261n437
Pipeline Safety, Regulator Certainty, and Job Creation Act (2011), 261n437
planetary ecosystems, corporate priorities and, 72–74
Platt, Orville, 27
plausible deniability dilemma, 90–91
plutocracy, xiii, 67, 141–42
PNAC (Project for the New American Century), 150–51, 262n441, 263n458
polarization, media, 133
police state apparatus, 149
political parties
   about, 137
   advertising, 66
   campaigns, network television, 239n179
   candidates' campaign financing, 69
   Democratic Party. *See* Democratic Party
   Green Party. *See* Green Party
   Progressive Party, 36–37
   Republican Party. *See* Republican Party
   third parties. *See* third parties
   two-party system, revision of, 187
Polk, George, murder of
   investigative reporting of, 48–49, 233n123
   Lippmann's investigation of, 51–52
   murder of, 49–50
   US complicity in, 51
Polk, James K., 24–25
Pollan, Michael, 196
"pop-up" cruises, 31
Porter, Paul, 46
positive change, focus on, 191
Posse Comitatus Act (1878), 149
Post Office, anti-war confiscations by, 29
Potter, Wendell, 71, 241n203
Powell, Colin, 124–25
power as addiction, 165–66, 267n499
Powers, Gary
   release of, 100
   U-2 Affair
      about, 82–83
      aftermath of, 244–45n240-242, 245n244, 245n248, 246n253
PR (public relations). *See* public relations (PR)
precariat class, 171–72
presidential authority/powers, 149
presidential debates, limitations of, 144
Pritzker, Penny, 272n543
privatization. *See* government privatization
Production Code Administration, 33
profitability
   of Clear Channel Communications, 129
   of health insurance industry, 70–71, 139, 143
   legal environment for, 58
   maximization as legal requirement, 57, 64, 170
programming
   evenhanded, 189
   public media, 134, 259n416
   selective coverage, 130–32

See also mass media
progressive domestic policy, attacks on, 260n425
Progressive Party, 36–37
Project for the New American Century (PNAC), 150–51, 262n441, 263n458
propaganda films, 33
protest demonstrations
    Cuban, 88
    in Latin America, 18–19, 21
    limitations of, 183
    Soviet, 80, 81
    US
        agents provocateurs, 181, 270n534
        anti-war, 29, 124, 270n536
        Keystone XL, 149–150
        Occupy Wall Street, 132, 171, 172–73, 179, 270n536
        technological disruption of, 181
        WTO, 132
Prouty, L. Fletcher, 75
provocation, US
    Mexican-American War, 24–25
    for Pearl Harbor, 33
    in World War II, 31
pro-war campaigns. *See under* wars
psychopathy, corporations exhibiting, 58, 236n150
public broadcasting, 134–35, 188–89
Public Broadcasting Act (1996), 134
Public Broadcasting Service (PBS), 134, 179–180, 188
public education. *See* textbook shortcomings
public health, Guatemala, 15
public information
    corporate dominance of, 129–130
    as Democracy Movement key, 191
    FCC Fairness Doctrine, 189
    Tipping Points, 172–73
public media funding, 134, 188, 259n414, 259n416, 272n545
public opinion
    CIA influence on, 76
    Defense Department shaping, 116, 255n353-354
    stories in, 172–73
public opposition
    to Iraq wars, 124
    to Mexican-American War, 25
    to Spanish-American War, 27
    to World War I, 29
    to World War II, 30
    See also protest demonstrations
public option, medical care, 185, 270n536
public relations (PR)
    "Communist takeover" portrayal of Guatemala, 17, 18
    Hill & Knowlton, 123
    movie industry in, 32–33
Puerto Rico
    annexation of, 224n25
    US interests in, 27, 169
Pulitzer, Joseph, 26–27

Q
Quammen, David, 194

R
railroads, UFCO as financing for, 14
Rankin, Karl, 50–51, 53, 234n129
Rascal
    about, 165
    addiction as component of, 165–66
    agents of, 169–170
    corruption as component of, 166–67
    definition, xi
    health insurance industry

lobbying, 185
Terror War as work of, 167–68
violence as tool of, 181–82
watching, 180–81
worldviews and, 168–69
Raytheon, 148
Reagan, Ronald
   CIA-Contra affair, 117
   on communist threat, 232n107
   Hussein and, 122
Reagan administration
   continuity of government, 149–150
   crack cocaine epidemic during, 172
   deregulation during, 59
   Fairness Doctrine fate during, 189
Reclaiming History (Bugliosi), 112
reconnaissance, Cold War, 80–83
Redford, Robert, 261n437
Reed, John, 28
regulatory agencies, lobbyists hired by, 63
Reichstag fire, 159–160
Remington, Frederic, 27
renewable energy, 142, 167
rentals, foreclosed homes as, 269n527, 270n531
Rentschler, Fred, 229n77
Republican Party
   ALEC and, 68
   corporate ties, 261n428-429
   Democratic Party similarities, 262n439
   values, 137–38, 139–140
revolving doors, 61–64, 147–48, 257n380
Rhee, Syngman, 42
Rice, Condoleezza, 272n553
Richardson, James O., 31
rigged political system, 144–45
right-wing think tanks, 150
The Rise and Fall of the Third Reich (Shirer), 159
Roa, Raúl, 91

The Road Less Traveled (Peck), 165–66
Roaring Twenties, 219
robber baron era, wealth concentration as in, 66
Robertson, William "Rip," 209, 210
Rochefort, Joseph, 32
Rockefeller, Nelson, 102
Roe v. Wade, 261n433
Roman Catholic clergy in Guatemalan politics, 18
Romney campaign costs, 66
Roosevelt, Franklin Delano
   on Elite greed, 166
   on fascism, 174
   Good Neighbor Policy, 117
   New Deal, 183
   quote by, 30, 65
   Social Security, 138
   Stone on, 35
   World War II entry, 30–33
Roosevelt Corollary, 13
Rose, Earl, 111
Rosenberg, Ethel, 43
Rosenberg, Julius, 43
"rotten apple" depiction, 47
Rumsfeld, Donald
   aspartame, unscrupulous fight for, 237n165
   as Bush (GW) appointee, 150–51
   as defense secretary, 186
   as Reagan's envoy, 122
   revolving doors of, 62
   wealth of, 237n165
Rupert Murdock's News Corporation, 130
Rusk, Dean, 102
Russia, warplane sales to, 231n96
Russo, Sal, 72

S
Salinger, Pierre, 91, 96, 97
Salon.com, 125
SAM (surface-to-air missiles), 82,

85
San Jose Mercury News, 118–120
Sandinista government, Reagan sabotage of, 117
Santa Clara County v. Southern Pacific Railroad, 56
Sartre, Jean-Paul, 43
Savings & Loan Crisis, 59
SCAD (state crimes against democracy), xi, 161–63, 175
Schechter, Danny, 127
Schlesinger, Arthur, 250–51n296-297
Schmitt, Eric, 126
Schneider, René, 7
Schor, Juliet, 261n428
Schumacher, E.F., 103
sea battles, European investors behind, 56
Securacom, 265n482
Securities and Exchange Commission, revolving doors, 63
Sedition Act (1918), 29, 42, 180
Seldes, George, 43, 52, 231n106
self-determination, Atlantic Charter, 103–4
Selig, Stefan, 63
September 11th terrorist attacks (2001). *See* 9/11 terrorist attacks (2001)
shareholders and stakeholders, corporate, 235n144
Shenon, Philip, 213
Shirer, William, *The Rise and Fall of the Third Reich*, 159–160
Silent Spring (Carson), xiv, 198
Sirhan, Sirhan, 266n495
60 Minutes, 235–36n147-148
Smith, Howard K., 46–47, 232n116
Smith, Jean Edward, 38–39
Snowden, Edward, 175, 269n522
social fabric, disintegration in Vietnam, 105
Social Forums, 130–31
Social Security
 creation of, 138, 183

in Guatemala, 15
 privatization of, 139–140
 Republican views on, 140
socialism, nationalization seen as, 37
society collapses, soil erosion role in, 195
soil erosion, 195
Somoza, Anastasio, 117
South Vietnam as US creation, 104–5
Southern Pacific Railroad, Santa Clara County v., 56
Soviet KGB, filming of US exercises, 249n287
Soviet ships, Alpha 66 raids on, 100
Soviet threat, exaggeration of, 38–42, 89
Soviet Union
 Cold War worldviews of, 203–4
 Cuban alliance with, 88–89
 as non-threatening, 38, 41, 229n83
 US overflights of, 80–83
Spanish-American War, 26–27
special interest groups, media influence of, 133
Specter, Arlen, 111, 112
sperm count decline, 198
Sputnik (satellite), 80
Staktopoulos, Anna, 50
Staktopoulos, Gregory
 arrest/torture of, 50, 234n127
 confession evaluation, 52
 US focus on, 51
Stand Your Ground laws, 132, 259n408
standard of living, environmental impact of, 201–2, 220
Stanton, Frank, 49
state crimes against democracy (SCADs), xi, 161–63, 175
state elections, ALEC influence on, 69–70

Steel, Ronald, 234n133
steel price controls, 97–98
Steingraber, Sandra, 198
Stimson, Henry, 31, 228n65
Stinnett, Robert, 30
stockholders, liability of, 56
Stoll, Steven, 274n568
Stone, I. F., 35, 52, 75
stories
   announcing, 173–74
   with potential, 174–77
   in public opinion, 172–73
   See also Tipping Points
strategic corporate alliances, 61
Strategic Initiatives
   about, 183
   definition, xi
   Deliberation Day, 183–84
   direct democracy options, 185–86
   executive branch oversight, 186–87
   legislative agendas, 184–85, 188
   non-governmental organizations, 189
   public broadcasting, 188–89
   two-party system, revision of, 187
Strauss, Leo, 151, 264n459
suicide
   of Masaryk, as unlikely, 40, 230n91
   of Webb, 120–21
Sulzberger, Arthur Hays
   CIA involvement of, 76, 223n27
   Guatemalan politics portrayed by, 17
Sulzberger, C.L., 245n248
Summers, Larry, 143
Sunder, Shyam, 156
surface-to-air missiles (SAM), 82, 85
Surowiecki, James, *The Wisdom of Crowds*, 183–84, 271n539

sustainability
   ecological trends and, 193–202
   of ecosystems, xiii, xiv
   Green Party values, 140
Suzuki, David, 201
Swift Boat Veterans for Truth ads, 66
Symington, Stuart, 36, 229n77
Syngenta
   CEO compensation, 242n217
   lobbying, 73
   market share, 242n215
Syria, Eisenhower's interference in, 78

T

tax evasion, UFCO and, 14
taxpayer subsidies
   aircraft manufacturing, 36, 228n74
   for war/fossil fuel industry, xiv
   See also military budgets
Taylor, Maxwell, 101
Taylor, Michael R., 63
Taylor, Zachary, 24
Tea Party, 72, 131–33
Tea Party Patriots, 72
Telecommunications Act (1996), 129, 143
television
   air of authority in, 258n399
   average use of, 130, 258n398
   commercials, healthcare reform and, 71
   corporate domination of, 130
   news programs, 115–16, 239n179
Terror War
   about, xii
   anchorage in deceptions, 167–68, 182
   9/11 terrorist attacks (2001). *See* 9/11 terrorist attacks (2001)
Terror Worldview
   about, xii

terrorism
  Democratic/Republican
    Parties' support of, 140
  Green Party rejection of, 141
terrorism
  attribution to Castro, 270n533
  as drone response, 262n438
  Operation Northwoods as,
    100–101
  US acknowledgement of role
    in, 10
  US torture and drone programs
    as, 168
testimony falsification
  for military budgets, 38–39
  for Warren Commission, 113
textbook shortcomings
  error persistence in, 221n3,
    222n20
  foreign policy
    misrepresentations in, 1–9,
    21–22
The Theory of the Leisure Class
  (Veblen), 219–220
think tanks, 147, 150
third parties
  candidates, 144
  Green Party. *See* Green Party
  number of, 260n422
  Progressive Party, 36–37
  "spoiler" effects, 144, 262n441
Thomas, Clarence, 62
Thoreau, Henry David, 25
Time magazine, 19
Time Warner, 130
Times Square, 218
Tipping Points
  about, 171–72, 189–190
  creating, 179–180, 182
  definition, xii
  stories and, 172–73, 176–77
Tirado, Gus, 210
To Sell a War, 123
tobacco industry assertions, 73–74
Tomlinson, Kenneth, 134–35
Tonkin Gulf incident/resolution,
  108, 182

top one percent
  about, 65–66
  alignment against, 171
  dismantling power of, xiii
  income concealment, 239n177
torture
  in 9/11 investigation, 154–55,
    159
  authority to define, 149
  Beneficent Uncle Sam and, 10
  Bush's role in, 168
  CIA destruction of tapes,
    268n506
  as crime, 263n454
  Powell's WMD speech
    anchored in, 124–25
  as terrorism trigger, 168, 169
  US sponsorship in Iran and
    Chile, 2, 7
toxic chemicals, 198–99
  See also pesticides
TransCanada corporation, 149–150
transnational corporations
  interlocks, 61
  power of, 64
  trade regulations, dismantling,
    59–60
Trans-Pacific Partnership, 139,
  143, 260n425
Troy, Daniel, 238n169
Truman, Harry
  credibility problems, 231n96
  funding of Athens government,
    232n116
  on HUAC, 44
  Iranian regime changes under,
    2
  loyalty program, 42–43
  Minh's letters to, 103
  reelection campaign, 37–38
  Soviet threat, fabrication of,
    40–41
  Soviet Union, view of, 203–4
  Vietnam food issues, non-
    response, 103
Truman administration

Cold War Worldview, 38–44
Greek government support
   from, 46–47, 232n112
television news collaboration,
   115
Truman Doctrine, 47, 48, 52
Truth-Out, 173
Tsaldaris, Constantine, 49, 51,
   234n129
Tshombe, Moise, 5
turf wars, CIA-Pentagon, 76
Turner, Richmond K., 32
Twin Towers, 155, 157
two-party political system
   remedy for, 187
   as rigged system, 143–45

U
U-2 Affair
   about, 80–81, 244–45n240-
      242, 245n244, 245n248
   aftermath of, 84–86
   CIA exposure during, 77
   during Cuban Missile Crisis,
      99, 250n296
   downing of, 82–83, 99
   incriminating evidence, 85,
      246n253, 246n255
   overflights
      of Cuba, 99, 100
      of Soviet Union, 80–83
   pilot salaries, 246n254
Ubico, Jorge
   dictatorship of, 14, 15
   human rights violations under,
      225n37
UFCO (United Fruit Company), 14,
   16, 20, 166
Ulbricht, Walter, 97
"underwriting" agreements,
   PBS/NPR obligation to, 188
unemployment benefits,
   Republican views on, 140
unitary executive theory, 149
United Aircraft Corporation,
   229n77

United Fruit Company (UFCO), 14,
   16, 20, 166
United Nations, chemical weapons
   condemnation, 122
United States
   chemical weapons complicity,
      122
   foreign policy. *See* foreign
      policy
   Geneva Accords, 104
   nationalism, 8, 11
   overseas possessions, 169
   propaganda films, 33
universal healthcare, 70, 71,
   241n203
urban warrior initiative, 149
US Steel, 97–98
US Supreme Court
   corporate regulation by, 56
   presidential election decision,
      160

V
Vacant Sea order, 31–32
values
   about, 137
   definition, xii
   democracy and, 143–45
   Democratic Party, 138–140
   executive branch campaign
      slate, 186–87
   Green Party, 140–42
   Republican Party, 137–38,
      139–140
Van Buren, Martin, 25
Veblen, Thorstein, *The Theory of
   the Leisure Class*, 219–220
Viacom, 130
Vietnam
   17th parallel bisection, 104
   French occupation of, 103–4
   Johnson reversal of Kennedy's
      withdrawal, 107–9
   Kennedy withdrawal orders,
      107
   Khrushchev on, 252n320

McNamara's role in, 272n543
Pentagon news crews in, 115
US involvement in, 104–7
Vilanova, Maria Cristina, 16
violence
    Democracy Movement's avoidance of, 181–82
    incited by agents provocateurs, 181, 270n533-534
vital statistics, 15, 70
Voice of Freedom radio network, 18, 19
Voice of Liberation network, 224n30
voters
    issues, 69–70
    registration rolls, 185
    turnout, xiii, 271n540
voting machinery, 69

W

Waging Peace (Eisenhower), 78, 83, 85, 246n255
Walgreens, 148
Walker, Writ, III, 265n482
Wall Street bankers, 143, 172
Wallace, Henry, 36–37
war games on 9/11 (military exercises), 158–59
war industries
    Eisenhower's resistance to, 78–79
    World War I arms sales, 28
    World War II prosperity, 36, 228n74
    See also armaments industry
War on Terror, 160
    See also Terror War
Warner, Daniel M., 235n144
Warren, Elizabeth, 59
Warren Commission investigation, 110–13, 254n342, 254n346
wars
    Beneficent Uncle Sam as camouflage, 167
    garnering support for about, 23
    Iraq wars, 122–27, n257n383, 263n458
    Mexican-American War, 24–25, 225n43
    preemptive wars, 169
    Spanish-American War, 26–27
    World War I, 28–29
    World War II, 30–33
Washington Post
    on *Dark Alliance*, 118–19, 120, 256n369
    McChesney on, 127
water depletion, 196–97
waterboarding, 154
wealth concentration
    about, 166
    British Parliament and, 235n139
    campaign financing and, 66–67, 69–70
    CEO compensation and, 72–74
    electoral fraud, 69
    global financial crisis (2008), 59, 181, 268n527, 270n536
    government privatization, 68
    in Greece, 49, 232n112
    Green Party on, 141
    in Guatemala, 14–15
    healthcare, 70–72
    lobbying and, 67
    one-percent group, 65–66, 239n177
    planetary ecosystems and, 72–74
    state elections and, 69–70
weapons of mass destruction (WMD), 124–27, 172
Webb, Gary
    Dark Alliance, 118–120, 172, 256n361-362
    journalism awards, 255n359
Weiner, Tim, 119
Weyler, Rex, 11
Weyrich, Paul, 68

Whitman, Walt, 25
Why We Fight (Capra), 33
Wieland, William, 88
wild foods, diminishing, 194
Willkie, Wendell, 30
Wilson, Edward O., 200
Wilson, Woodrow, 28–29, 226n54
Winfrey, Oprah, 58
Wisconsin Uprising, 171
The Wisdom of Crowds (Surowiecki), 183–84
Without Precedent (Kean & Hamilton), 154
WMD (weapons of mass destruction), 124–27, 172
Wolf, Naomi
   The End of America, 175
   quote by, 171
Wolfowitz, Paul, 150–51, 264n459
Wolfowitz Doctrine, 151, 153, 262n441
worker safety, profits trumping, 57
Workers Independent News, 173
workforce discontent after World War II, 37
Works Progress Administration, 183
World Bank, founding of, 59
World Economic Forum, 131
world peace
   as Eisenhower's goal, 79–80
   as Green Party goal, 141
   Kennedy's efforts, 101–2, 109
   political obstacles to, 140
World Trade Center. *See* 9/11 terrorist attacks (2001)
World Trade Center Building Seven (WTC 7), 155–57
World Trade Center security, 157, 265n482
World Trade Organization (WTO)
   challenges to/enforcement of, 60
   founding of, 59
   Kantor's role in, 62
   Ministerial Conferences, 132

World War I, 28–29
World War II
   economic recovery from, 219
   garnering support for, 30–33
   prosperity from, 36, 228n74
WorldCom scandal, 59
worldviews
   overview
      about, xii, 1–2
      textbook role in, 2–9
      Uncle Sam beneficence view, 10–11
      See also textbook shortcomings
   of Cold War
      about, 203–5
      development and advocacy of, 169
      television promotion of, 115–16
   differences in, 223n23
   Ecological Imperative and, 168
   intergenerational resistance to change, 11, 222n20
   Lakoff on, 221n2
   of Rascal, 168–69
   of terror, xii
WTC 7 (World Trade Center Building Seven), 155–57
WTO (World Trade Organization). *See* World Trade Organization (WTO)

X
Xe Services, Blackwater as, 148

Y
Yergin, David, 39–40

Z
Zelikow, Philip, 213–14, 272n553
Zemurray, Sam, 14, 16–17, 166
Zervas, Napoleon, 49–50
Zogby International poll, 160–61
Zuñiga, Mario, 91, 248n273

About the Author

In 1990, a Seattle food-assistance charity gathered restaurant and winery operators to host a fundraising event in a downtown hotel ballroom. I attended this event with the chef of the landmark restaurant I was running at the time, and we served up our finest to a well-heeled crowd of philanthropic Seattleites. Loading out our wares at the close of the evening, I observed a man exploring the dumpsters in the hotel's back alley. "Wait right there," I said. The man smiled broadly when I returned with a platter piled high with gourmet leftovers from the ballroom's buffet. For this man, it was a lucky night. For me, it was an epiphany.

The personal journey that became this book dates back to that evening, when I resolved to discover a larger purpose for my life. I began shifting out of restaurant management in 1991 and earned a master's degree in social work administration in 1996. The MSW coursework and internships showed me that the roots of our social problems were much deeper than I had previously realized.

The following summer, I attended a demonstration project in sustainable living, founded by sustainability author and activist Jim Merkel. There I learned that our social issues, however worrisome, were being overshadowed by an ecological unraveling of potentially devastating magnitude. I became convinced that our expanding social and ecological troubles would continue to overwhelm our remedial efforts.

In business management, I had learned the importance of discovering and resolving the root causes of operational failings. My passion now became the discovery and resolution of the root causes of the social and ecological problems of our time. In 1999, I sold my Seattle home, acquired a parcel of forested land in northeastern Washington, and began building the straw bale home where this book was written.